PRAISE FOR *SUSTAINABLE INVESTING*:

'This splendid book provides up to date analyses of virtually the entire spectrum of socially related investment possibilities. The field is in a rapid state of change – Steve Viederman's lovely piece on the Fiduciary remains a constant guide – I recommend to everyone that you buy and read this book. Without it, you are playing yesterday's game.'
Robert A.G. Monks, shareholder activist and leading founder of the practice of Corporate Governance

'*Sustainable Investing* does two things brilliantly: it lays bare a financial system that is currently not fit for purpose, and then it draws a blueprint, with added operating instructions, for a transformational redesign.'
Andrew Simms, Policy Director, New Economics Foundation

'If you want to understand how finance can offer practical solutions for sustainable development – rather than being criticized for being an obstacle – read this very clear, comprehensive and persuasive book.'
Antoine de Salins, Fonds de Réserve pour les Retraites

'Krosinsky and Robins have assembled authors expert in their disciplines who collectively describe a dynamic force which is both effecting change and being affected by it. A generation of investors will look first to Robins and Krosinsky for answers about sustainable investing.'
Peter D. Kinder, President and Founder, KLD Research & Analytics, Inc.

'This book is packed with valuable insights into an area of growing importance.'
Akitsugu Era, Corporate Governance Manager, Equity Fund Management Dept, leading Japanese financial institution

'SRI is morphing into sustainable investing. Is this just "brand refreshment" or is it, as this rich collection of essays from the leading experts in the field argues, something more fundamental? So, whether you didn't like SRI first time round or whether you are worried about the SRI baby being lost with the bathwater, buy this book and read it!'
Raj Thamotheram, Director, Responsible Investment, Axa Investment Management

'This timely and thought-provoking collection of essays, written by some of the industry's leading experts, is essential reading for all those who want to understand how sustainability has influenced investment practice. It clearly demonstrates the potential for sustainable investment to become the new "mainstream".'
Emma Howard Boyd, Head of SRI, Jupiter Asset Management

'The thought leaders in this global framework on sustainable investment provide readers with a high-quality, topical mosaic of how to find capital appreciation in a sustainable manner.'
Mary Jane McQuillen, Director, Socially Aware Investment, ClearBridge Advisors, a unit of Legg Mason

'An excellent volume that puts sustainable investing front and centre in the debates about building a more equitable global economy and providing retirement security for working people.'
Michael Musuraca, Designated Trustee, NY City Employees Retirement System

'Krosinsky and Robins have captured an inflection point in the history of investment. We have truly moved from the socially responsible investment movement of the '60s to issues of sustainability. This is good for both society and the investor. Krosinsky and Robins have assembled a tremendous cast of authors to discuss the forefront of this movement. The result is a great book on the current and future state of sustainable investing.'
Donald H. Schepers, Associate Director, Robert Zicklin Center for Corporate Integrity, Baruch College, Zicklin School of Business

'*Sustainable Investing* succeeds in its goal of portraying the current generational shift in what has been a long-term effort to recast global capital markets and to achieve reliable risk-adjusted financial returns in the 21st century through the incorporation of environmental, social and corporate governance factors. The sweep of its view is comprehensive, from the effort of critical self-knowledge in Part I, through the well-reasoned advocacy and predictions in Part IV and the editors' concluding thoughts.

This is the book I now will recommend to quench the increasing thirst of my mainstream colleagues for an understanding of this important phenomenon. I will recommend it as well to the younger generation as a source providing both historical context and the emerging requirements for the practice of the subtle art and science of securities and investment analysis.'
Anthony Ginsberg, Ginsberg Consulting and Chair of Socially Responsible Investing Committee, NY Society of Security Analysts

Sustainable Investing

The Art of Long-Term Performance

Edited by Cary Krosinsky and Nick Robins

publishing for a sustainable future

London • Sterling, VA

First published by Earthscan in the UK and USA in 2008

ISBN: 978-1-84407-548-5

Typeset by MapSet Ltd, Gateshead, UK
Printed and bound in the UK by MPG Books, Bodmin
Cover design by Matt Hadfield

For a full list of publications please contact:

Earthscan
Dunstan House
14a St Cross St
London, EC1N 8XA, UK
Tel: +44 (0)20 7841 1930
Fax: +44 (0)20 7242 1474
Email: earthinfo@earthscan.co.uk
Web: **www.earthscan.co.uk**

22883 Quicksilver Drive, Sterling, VA 20166-2012, USA

Earthscan publishes in association with the International Institute for Environment and
Development

A catalogue record for this book is available from the British Library

Library of Congress Cataloging-in-Publication Data has been applied for

The paper used for this book is FSC-certified.
FSC (the Forest Stewardship Council) is an
international network to promote responsible
management of the world's forests.

Mixed Sources
Product group from well-managed
forests and other controlled sources
www.fsc.org Cert no. SA-COC-1565
© 1996 Forest Stewardship Council

Contents

PART I — THE RISE OF SUSTAINABLE INVESTING

PART II — CONFRONTING NEW RISKS AND OPPORTUNITIES

PART III — SUSTAINABILITY ACROSS THE OTHER ASSET CLASSES

PART IV — FUTURE DIRECTIONS AND TRENDS

List of Figures, Tables and Boxes

FIGURES

TABLES

BOXES

List of Contributors

EDITORS/AUTHORS

Cary Krosinsky is vice president for Trucost Plc. Trucost has built the world's most extensive database regarding over 700 emissions and pollutants of over 4200 public companies around the world, and uses this data to assist portfolio managers in understanding their carbon footprints, helping to lower them while maintaining and enhancing performance. Cary was a member of the 70-person Expert Group in 2005 that created the United Nations Principles for Responsible Investment (PRI), which have since been committed to by over US$14 trillion worth of asset managers and owners. He continues to participate in the United Nations Environment Programme's Finance Initiative (UNEP FI) and worked in collaboration with Trucost on their award-winning *2006 UK Trust Carbon Footprint* study, and the International Finance Corporation (IFC)-sponsored *Carbon Counts Asia 2007* report, the latter having been issued at the December 2007 UN meetings in Bali. Cary also works with the *Los Angeles Times*, and has written and spoken publicly over time as a leading interpreter of ownership on CNBC, in the *Wall Street Journal* and elsewhere.

Nick Robins is head of the HSBC Climate Change Centre of Excellence. Nick has 20 years' experience in promoting sustainable development and corporate responsibility in financial markets, business and public policy research. At the Economist Intelligence Unit, he published *Managing the Environment: The Greening of European Business* (1990) before joining the Business Council for Sustainable Development, where he contributed chapters and case studies to *Changing Course*. He worked as a special adviser to the Environment Directorate of the European Commission on the Earth Summit before returning to the UK, where he worked at the International Institute for Environment and Development, managing first its European and then its sustainable markets programmes. In 2000, he joined Henderson Global Investors as head of sustainable and responsible investing (SRI) research and subsequently became head of SRI funds, shaping the Industries of the Future investment strategy and launching the world's first carbon audit of an investment fund in 2005. He has written for a wide range of publications and is the author of *The Corporation that Changed the World: How the East India Company Shaped the Modern Multinational* (Pluto, 2006).

AUTHORS

Ray Cheung is responsible for overseeing the World Resources Institute's New Ventures programme in China, which seeks to promote sustainable growth in emerging markets by supporting and accelerating the transfer of capital to businesses that deliver social and environmental benefits. Ray has over ten years' experience in Chinese environmental and business issues. While based in China, he was a writer for the Economist Intelligence Unit's *Business China* report, in which he probed investment opportunities in China's environmental industries. He was also a China reporter for Hong Kong's *South China Morning Post* and a programme manager at the University of Hong Kong's Journalism and Media Studies Centre. Before journalism, Ray worked with the Chinese environmental organization Global Village of Beijing. Ray has a BS in conservation and resource studies from the University of California at Berkeley and an MBA from Georgetown University. In Washington, DC, he consulted for a major financial institution on a cleantech private equity investment strategy for China.

Julie Fox Gorte is the senior vice president for sustainable investing at Pax World Management Corporation. She oversees environmental, social and governance-related research on prospective and current investments, as well as Pax's shareholder advocacy, and work on public policy advocacy. Prior to joining Pax, Dr Gorte served as vice president and chief social investment strategist at Calvert. Her experience before she joined the investment world in 1999 includes nearly 14 years as senior associate and project director at the Congressional Office of Technology Assessment, vice president for economic and environmental research at the Wilderness Society, programme manager for technology programmes in the US Environmental Protection Agency's policy office, and senior associate at the Northeast–Midwest Institute. Dr Gorte received her BSc in forest management at Northern Arizona University, and an MSc and PhD from Michigan State in resource economics. Dr Gorte serves on the boards of the Coalition for Environmentally Responsible Economies (CERES), the Center for a New American Dream, the Endangered Species Coalition and the Pinchot Institute. She has served as the co-chair of UNEP FI's Asset Management Working Group and is on the steering committee for UNEP's work stream on biodiversity.

Sean Gilbert is responsible for overseeing the development of the Global Reporting Initiative (GRI) Reporting Framework and the accompanying resource material. He facilitates international working group processes and engages with external stakeholders about their relationship to the GRI. Sean has an extensive background in working on business environmental issues and regional experience in Asia. From 1995 to 2000 he worked as a consultant in Taiwan. His work included assessing business approaches to environmental management, analysing policy trends, and market research for environmental technologies and the chemicals sector. During this time, he also worked with the

American Chamber of Commerce Environmental Committee, including serving as chair of the committee.

Gordon Hagart is senior consultant at onValues Ltd, an investment consulting and research company based in Zurich, Switzerland. His experience encompasses both private and public sectors, having worked as a financial analyst for the United Nations. Prior to joining onValues, he was a programme manager with UNEP FI, a global partnership between UNEP and the financial sector. His principal responsibilities were the UN Principles for Responsible Investment and UNEP FI's Asset Management Working Group. He joined UNEP FI from the International Labour Organization, where he researched the reform and sustainability of public pension finance. Before entering the UN system, Gordon was a senior investment banking analyst with Greenhill & Co in London, working on mergers and acquisitions and debt restructuring mandates. His other professional experience includes time spent as a strategic consultant. Gordon has MA and MSc degrees in geophysics from the University of Cambridge, UK.

Emma Hunt works as an investment consultant in responsible investment at Mercer in London. She supports UK and European clients on issues relating to responsible investment (RI) and shareholder engagement. Emma joined Mercer in June 2005. Prior to this, she spent two years heading up the Centre for Sustainable Investment at Forum for the Future, a UK-based think tank. Previously, Emma spent four years as a senior analyst focused on governance and socially responsible investment with a UK-based global asset manager. Emma has authored numerous articles on RI; developed and delivered modules on sustainable investment for academic institutions, professional institutes and financial institutions; and sits on a number of advisory committees, including the UK Social Investment Forum's Sustainable Pensions Advisory Board. Emma holds the Investment Management Certificate, an MSc in environmental technology from Imperial College, London, a BSc in European business from Nottingham Trent University, Nottingham, and a Diploma in International Business from École Supèrieure de Commerce in France.

Abyd Karmali is managing director and global head of carbon emissions at Merrill Lynch, one of the world's leading wealth management, capital markets and advisory companies. Abyd has worked for 17 years on climate change and the carbon markets and serves as president of the Carbon Markets and Investors Association and member of Her Majesty's Treasury Carbon Market Expert Group. He is the point person for carbon business opportunities across Merrill Lynch's geographies and financial products and serves on the firm's Environmental Sustainability Working Group. Abyd has provided strategic advice on the commercial risks and opportunities posed by carbon emissions constraints to dozens of European, US and Asian companies in the Financial Times (FT) Global 500, as well as to several government agencies and regional development banks. Abyd holds an MSc in technology and policy from the Massachusetts Institute of Technology and was previously employed with ICF International in Washington, DC, Toronto and London where he served most recently as managing director, Europe. During 1996 to 1997 he was climate change officer at the UNEP's industry office in Paris and participated in the Kyoto Protocol negotiations.

Ivo Knoepfel is the founder and managing director of onValues Ltd, a Zurich-based investment strategy and research consulting company supporting a wide range of international clients in better integrating environmental, social and governance issues in their investment portfolios. Ivo is a certified international investment analyst and holds the degree of Swiss portfolio manager. He previously worked for Sustainable Asset Management (SAM), where he was responsible for research and the Dow Jones Sustainability Indices selection process, and for Swiss Reinsurance Co, where he was responsible for climate change and group-wide sustainability management. He received an MSc and a PhD from the Swiss Federal Institute of Technology (ETH), both with a focus on environmental technologies. He regularly publishes on issues relevant to long-term and sustainable investing, and is a member of several industry bodies and associations. He has been a founding member of the UNEP FI's Insurance Initiative and a co-chair of the Global Reporting Initiative's Measurement Working Group. He is a member of SustainAbility's faculty of international experts in the field of sustainability.

Matthias Kopp is project manager of the financial and energy sector of the World Wide Fund for Nature-Germany (WWF-Germany). Matthias joined WWF in 2005 to lead the work in WWF's climate and policy programme on the financial sector in Germany. He also served in this capacity for the WWF Climate Programme. He came from his previous position as management consultant with PwC's management consulting business in energy markets, energy trading and risk management, where he worked for four years on issues such as energy auctions, energy trading and risk management strategies. He holds a Diploma in Industrial Engineering and Management from the Technical University in Berlin where he graduated in 2001.

Ritu Kumar is a senior adviser on environmental, social and governance issues with Actis, UK, where she has advised on weaknesses and opportunities in health and safety, as well as environmental, social and business integrity since 2006. From 2000 to 2006 she was director, UK, with TERI-Europe, where she promoted collaboration between Europe and India on climate change, environmental technology, corporate social responsibility, sustainability reporting and SRI. While working with TERI-Europe, Ritu established and managed the European subsidiary of TERI-India, and was directly involved in promoting improved labour standards in South Asian companies. Ritu has also worked extensively with the Commonwealth Science Council, UK, as an environment consultant, as well as with the United Nations Industrial Development Organization, where her experience as an industrial development officer in Austria focused on developing and implementing cleaner production programmes for industry in developing countries. Ritu has a BA honours and an MA, both in economics, from the University of Delhi and the Delhi School of Economics, respectively, and an MSc in economics from the London School of Economics and Political Science, UK. Ritu holds a Diploma in Environmental Economics and Policy Analysis from Harvard University, US, and an SA 8000 Social Auditing Certificate.

Valery Lucas-Leclin is co-head of SRI research, Société Générale, and winner of the 2008 Extel Award for best SRI Analysis in Europe. Valery joined Société Générale in February 2006. The team was ranked first in the 2008 Thomson Extel Survey for the SRI category. Valery holds an MA in contemporary history from Paris X and a degree in economics and finance from Sciences Po Paris. After starting his career as a junior auditor with GAN and having worked in communications for two years, in 1998, he joined Arèse, the first French SRI rating agency as director of research. In 2002, he went to Innovest Strategic Value Advisors as analyst and head of research, France. Most recently, he worked as head of SRI research for CM-CIC Securities. The team has also been recognized by the Enhanced Analytics Initiative (EAI) as providing the best analysis of extra-financial issues.

Steven D. Lydenberg is chief investment officer for Domini Social Investments LLC. He has been active in social investing for 30 years as director of corporate accountability research with the Council on Economic Priorities; investment associate with Franklin Research and Development Corporation (now Trillium Asset Management); and director of research with Kinder, Lydenberg, Domini & Co (now KLD Research & Analytics). Steve is the co-author of *Rating America's Corporate Conscience* (Addison-Wesley Publishing, 1986) and *Investing for Good* (Harper Collins, 1993), a guide for socially responsible investors, and co-editor of *The Social Investment Almanac* (Henry Holt & Co, 1992). His is also the author of *Corporations and the Public Interest: Guiding the Invisible Hand* (Berrett-Koehler, 2005). He holds degrees from Columbia College and Cornell University and is a chartered financial analyst (CFA).

Paul McNamara, PhD, is director, head of research, with PRUPIM. Paul joined Prudential in 1987 and is responsible for the overall direction of property research within PRUPIM. An influential figure in the property industry, Paul has senior involvement in a number of industry-related and academic bodies. Among others, he is a member of the management board of the Investment Property Forum, a visiting professor at Oxford Brookes University and honorary president and past chairman of the Society of Property Researchers. In 2003 Paul was awarded an OBE for services to the property industry.

Katherine Miles Hill is responsible for developing and managing sector supplement projects on behalf of the Global Reporting Initiative. Integral to this role is coordinating the international multi-stakeholder working groups that develop this guidance. Katherine began working at GRI in communications, where among other responsibilities she worked in partnership with BBC World News to organize a BBC World Debate at the Amsterdam Global Conference on Sustainability and Transparency. Prior to working at GRI, Katherine spent four years working in the field of government relations and business strategy, mainly with the international healthcare company BUPA in the UK, Thailand and India. Katherine read anthropology (BA honours) at Durham University in the UK and subsequently gained an MSc (*cum laude*) in international develop-ment studies at the University of Amsterdam, The Netherlands. She has written for a wide range of publications on the issue of sustainability reporting.

Sarbjit Nahal is co-head of SRI Research at Société Générale (SG). SG's SRI team was ranked first for sustainability/SRI research in the 2008 Thomson Reuters Extel Survey, and its extra-financial research has also been recognized by the Enhanced Analytics Initiative (EAI). Sarbjit joined SG in 2006 and has worked in the field of SRI for 12 years including at CM-CIC Securities, Vigeo, the ICHRP and PIRC. He is a Canadian lawyer by background and holds an LLM (London), LLB (Osgoode Hall) and BA (Toronto).

Gary Pivo, PhD, is a founder of the field of Sustainable and Responsible Property Investing. His work on the subject has recently appeared in *Real Estate Issues* and *International Real Estate Review* and was referred to as the 'latest movement in real estate' by the *Wall Street Journal*. He is adviser to the Property Working Group of UNEP FI and head of research for the Responsible Property Investment Project of the Institute for Responsible Investment at the Boston College Center for Corporate Citizenship. He holds full professorships in the Urban Planning Degree Program and the School of Natural Resources at the University of Arizona, US, and is a senior fellow with the Office of Economic Development and Policy Analysis.

Previously, Dr Pivo served as chair of the Department of Urban Design and Planning, director of the Center for Sustainable Cities and director of the Interdisciplinary Group for the PhD programme in Urban Design and Planning at the University of Washington. He has also been associate dean of the College of Architecture, Planning and Landscape Architecture, dean of the Graduate College, and director of graduate interdisciplinary programmes at the University of Arizona. Dr. Pivo's comments on urban planning have been carried by the *Economist*, *The New York Times*, the *Christian Science Monitor*, national public radio and dozens of other local and national publications. He has an extensive record of consulting and public service, including special assistant to the governor's Growth Strategy Commission (Washington) and co-founder and president of 1000 Friends of Washington. He has addressed meetings sponsored by the United

Nations, the Real Estate Roundtable, the US Green Building Council, the National Science Foundation, the National Building Museum, the Urban Land Institute, the National Trust for Historic Preservation and the Tokyo Institute of Technology.

Rod Schwartz began his career with PaineWebber, Lehman Brothers and Banque Paribas as a financial services research analyst, corporate financier and senior manager. He co-founded Catalyst Fund Management & Research in 1997, a venture capital and research firm (www.catfund.com), which exists to help social businesses succeed. Catalyst Fund 1, launched in January 2008, will invest in profitable UK-based businesses in 'ethical consumerism', health, education, alternative energy and the environment. Catalyst also researches these sectors (published through the recently launched website www.socialinvestments.com) and provides a wide variety of advisory services to social businesses and social enterprises. In addition, it hosts an annual autumn conference for social business CEOs and selected investors, and sponsors the 'Catalyst in' series of trips to study and learn from social enterprise businesses from around the world. Catalyst's professionals also maintain the widely read *Social Business Blog*. Rod regularly lectures and participates in third-party produced reports on social business and social enterprise, with a focus on the business and enterprise side. He currently sits on the board of the UK Social Investment Forum, AXA Investment Managers and the Ethical Property Company, is non-executive chairman of The Green Thing and a former chairman of Justgiving.com and Shelter.

Dan Siddy is director of Delsus Limited, an advisory firm specializing in sustainable investment in the emerging markets. He has over 15 years' experience in the environmental and social aspects of finance and investment in developing countries. Prior to forming Delsus in 2006, he spent eight years at the International Finance Corporation (IFC), the private-sector arm of the World Bank, where he created and led a US$15 million grant programme for developing sustainable finance markets in emerging economies. He has been instrumental in most emerging market developments in the sustainable investment field in recent years, including Brazil's Bovespa ISE Index; the Latin American Sustainable Finance Forum; the S&P ESG India Index; new research coverage by Trucost and CLSA on emerging Asia equities; new research by IFC and Mercer into the ESG capabilities of emerging market fund managers; and business planning for a new 'social' stock exchange. In addition to his responsibilities at Delsus Limited, Dan works closely with the World Federation of Exchanges and the World Resources Institute, and is an associate director of the not-for-profit organization TERI-Europe.

Tessa Tennant is executive chair of the ICE Organization, a personal carbon management and loyalty programme. Tessa co-founded the UK's first equity investment fund for sustainable development in 1988. She was chair and co-founder of the UK Social Investment Forum and of the Carbon Disclosure Project. In 2001 she co-founded and was first chair of Association for

Sustainable and Responsible Investment in Asia, and remains on the board. She is a board member of the Calvert Social Funds, Washington, DC, member of the jury panel for the FT-IFC Sustainable Banking Awards, and an Ambassador for WWF-UK. In 2003 she received the Sustainability Leadership Award by SAM/SPG of Switzerland and in 2004 was joint winner of the City of Goteborg International Environmental Leadership Prize. She is an Honorary Fellow of the Schumacher Society.

Björn Tore Urdal joined the Sustainable Asset Management (SAM) Group in December 2004, where he is head of energy research and a senior equity analyst. At SAM, Björn covers the energy sector, spanning oil- and gas-related equities to renewable energy, alternative fuels and clean/efficient energy technologies. He is also the responsible analyst for the SAM Smart Energy Fund. Prior to joining SAM Group, Björn worked for five years as an equity analyst in Handelsbanken Capital Markets, one of the largest Nordic investment banks, where he covered the oil and gas sector, including energy and petroleum, shipping and oil services companies. Björn holds an MSc in economics from University College London, where he specialized in environmental and resource economics.

Stephen Viederman is the former president of the Jessie Smith Noyes Foundation and a leader in shareholder advocacy.

Steve Waygood, PhD, is head of engagement for sustainable and responsible investment at Aviva Investors, and manages the SRI analyst team. Steve joined Morley's Sustainable and Responsible Investment Team in 2006 as its head of engagement. Previously, he worked for Insight Investment, where he was a director in the Investor Responsibility Team. Prior to that, he was a senior analyst in the Governance and SRI Team of Friends Ivory and Sime (now F&C). Steve started his career at WWF-UK, where he chaired its business and industry core group. Steve is a member of both the expert and advisory groups to the United Nations Principles for Responsible Investment. He now chairs the UK Social Investment Forum (UK SIF) and has been on its board since 2003. He holds a BSc honours in economics and a PhD in SRI from the University of Surrey, UK. He also holds the UK SIP Investment Management Certificate (IMC) and has published two books on SRI.

Rachel Whittaker works as an investment consultant at Mercer. The focus of her role is responsible investment manager research. Rachel joined Mercer in April 2007. Prior to this she worked for one year in Investor Relations at SABMiller plc on their Africa and Asia operations. Previously, Rachel spent five and a half years as an equity research analyst, covering European consumer and business services companies, at Morgan Stanley and Merrill Lynch. Rachel holds an MA in anthropology and management from Cambridge University, UK, and is a CFA charter holder.

Foreword

Steve Lydenberg

Sustainable investing has come a long way. It was 25 years ago when we were calling public affairs departments of corporations to enquire about their corporate social responsibility initiatives, and most replied that they'd never heard of the concept. Some said they would ask around and get back to us, but rarely did. It was 15 years ago that it did not appear that the nascent socially responsible investment movement in the US would survive the end of the South Africa divestment campaign, only to see the growth of the sustainability movement around the world begin to take hold among forward-looking corporate managers and groundbreaking members of the financial community.

Today, the concept of sustainable investing is taking root, not only in corporations and the public equities market, but across asset classes as well – from clean technology venture capital, to sustainable fixed income, to green real estate development. It is creating financial markets that didn't exist before, including carbon markets to address climate change and microfinance to help alleviate poverty. It is changing the way responsible investors act. Farewell to the old 'Wall Street Walk' rule – if you don't like management, sell your stock. Engagement and dialogue with management on sustainability are becoming the word of the day. Changed, as well, are the expectations of how corporations report on their activities to society. Financial statements alone are no longer the whole story. One is tempted to congratulate those of us who have worked so long and hard to promote these moves towards sustainable finance. But at times you have to wonder how real these changes are, how deep their roots go, and whether we are occupying a niche market that deserves a nice pat on the back, but no more.

But I no longer ask myself whether sustainable investing will become mainstream. In many senses, it is already becoming so. The key question is, rather, will the mainstream become sustainable? That will require more fundamental and difficult change. Our financial markets and corporate managers will need to wean themselves off the kind of short-termism that has come to dominate both worlds during the last decades of the 20th century and take a longer-term view of their fortunes.

There is an underlying tension between the fast-paced speculative nature of today's financial markets and the longer view of sustainability. To move from the former to the latter, we need to understand better the value of corporations, in the specific, and investments, in general, to society. We need to rein in our obsession with price-based returns and understand the long-term implications of today's financial decisions. We have become a world of short-term price-takers, rather than long-term value-makers. Sustainability requires reversing those roles.

By 'long-term', one does not mean simply buying long and holding long – although that is certainly one characteristic of sustainable finance – but also incorporating environmental, social and corporate governance (ESG) factors into investment considerations. This is not so simple a task. ESG factors are not always easily correlated with today's price because they often deal with the risks to society of externalized costs: ozone depletion, climate change, abusive labour practices, obesity. Conversely, they attempt to quantify positive intangibles: the promotion of new technologies; the benefits of energy and resource efficiency; the virtues of a highly trained workforce and balance between work and family; the underlying justice of access to capital; and diversity in the workplace. Clearly these avoided risks and these embedded values have a relationship to what investments return to society in the long run; but we are still feeling our way on how exactly to express that relationship.

Once we understand the evolving relationships between sustainability, ESG, price and value, we will be well on our way to creating a truly sustainable finance or, rather, finance will be well on its way to realizing the true value of sustainability.

Introduction

Cary Krosinsky and Nick Robins

This book was conceived in the early summer of 2007 before credit markets crunched and the world economy experienced perhaps the worst financial shock since the Great Depression. Its scope and purpose were also designed in advance of the Bali conference, which after years of obstruction and inertia, laid the groundwork for a global deal to confront climate change, which if left unchecked could cause disruption similar to 'the great wars and the economic depression of the first half of the 20th century' (Stern, 2006).

These two apparently unconnected developments symbolize the urgent need for patterns of finance and investment that are truly focused on long-term value creation, on sustaining natural as well as financial assets and on directing financial innovation on the priorities of those who need it most: the world's poor. Fortunately, a shift in this direction is already under way with the rapid growth in sustainable investing practice over the past two decades. Today's expression of sustainable investing covers all asset classes and all regions of the world. It has strong links to the pioneering ethical and socially responsible investment communities, but goes one step further by placing the pursuit of financial returns in the context of the world's economic, environmental and social challenges.

At this point, it's necessary to provide some guidance on the terminology used in this book. Over the past 30 years, a range of terms, notably 'social', 'ethical', 'green', 'responsible', 'socially responsible' and 'sustainable', have been used to describe the emerging practice of incorporating extra-financial factors within investment decision-making. One woman's 'ethical investing' is another man's 'socially responsible investing', and one firm's 'responsible investing' is another manager's 'sustainable investing'. On reflection, this embarrassment of semantic richness is perhaps understandable for a rapidly evolving approach, where the final form has yet to be settled. In such a fluid field, we are well aware of the dangers of false precision. Indeed, one of our contributors, Rod

Schwartz, when trying to pin down socially responsible investment, revived John Morley's dictum that 'if you want a platitude, there is nothing like a definition'.[1] In the face of this, we could ignore the problem and take an 'anything goes' approach. However, this, we feel, would perpetuate consumer and analytical confusion, glossing over major generational shifts that are taking place in the investment arena.

In our experience, sustainable investing combines two profound appreciations. The first is that the best way of generating superior risk-adjusted returns in the 21st century is to fully incorporate long-term environmental, social and economic trends within investment and ownership decision-making. The second is that achieving global sustainability requires the mobilization and recasting of the world's capital markets. If the first speaks the language of financial value at the micro-level, the second refers to the imperative of structural reform at the macro-dimension. Sustainable investing thus provides an agenda for action for purely financially motivated investors eager to mitigate risk and benefit from upside opportunities, as well as for civil society organizations aiming to achieve social and environmental progress. It encompasses the growing numbers of individual investors who wish to ensure that social and environmental factors are included in the ways that they allocate their savings. It also draws on the rising tide of institutional investors who appreciate the growing financial materiality of environmental, social and governance (ESG) factors. Added to this are clean tech investors who identify major potential for capital growth in companies providing solutions to mounting environmental constraints. And alongside these are investors explicitly seeking social as well as financial returns from new avenues such as microfinance. What unites these apparently disparate groups is an acknowledgement that value can now only be created on a long-term basis through fresh approaches to financial analysis, fiduciary duty and capital market regulation.

To guide the reader through this maze, we have provided some basic definitions in Box I.1 to distinguish the different strands.

Sustainable investing is also distinct from the investment mainstream, not least in its approach to time horizons. We would describe the mainstream as 'an approach to investing that applies conventional financial theories to the valuation and selection of assets and the exercise of ownership rights'. Clearly, as the importance of environmental and social factors becomes part of the conventional wisdom, so the investment mainstream will adopt aspects of the sustainable investing agenda. Indeed, as this book demonstrates, a growing share of the world's capital assets is already incorporating at least parts of the sustainability agenda. The McKinsey Global Institute has calculated that the value of public equities, as well as corporate and government bonds, amounted to some US$120 trillion in 2006 (McKinsey Global Institute, 2008). Our 'rule of thumb' estimate is that at most between one tenth and one quarter of this figure is now on a sustainable investing trajectory, but with the bulk of this limited to early stage shareholder engagement rather than active deployment of capital.[2]

Box I.1 By way of definition ...

Currently, we observe five distinctive investment styles:

1   *Ethical investing:* we will use the term ethical investing to describe 'an approach to investing driven by the value system of the key investment decision-maker' (Hudson, 2006). In many cases, this equates to traditional social investing in the US as well as to much of current socially responsible investing, and applies mostly to individual investors as well as to charities and foundations that have values as part of their mission.

2   *Responsible investing:* likewise, we will use the term responsible investing to describe 'an approach adopted by institutional investors to start taking ESG factors into account in pursuit of their fiduciary duties to clients and beneficiaries'.

3   *Clean tech investing:* this encompasses the surge in investment into environmental sectors such as energy efficiency, pollution control, renewable energy, sustainable transport, as well as waste and water management. Linked to this is the fast-growing practice of 'climate change investing', which may supplement clean tech with allocations to sustainable forestry, as well as (in some cases) to nuclear power.

4   *Social investing:* we will then use the term social investing to describe 'an approach to investing that seeks to generate social as well as financial returns'. While ethical investing tends to focus on the consistency of investments with the investor's value system, social investing examines outcomes in light of the impact upon others, often those most disadvantaged in society.

5   *Sustainable investing:* we will use the term sustainable investing to describe 'an approach to investing driven by the long-term economic, environmental and social risks and opportunities facing the global economy'. What distinguishes current practitioners of sustainable investing from the other approaches is the conviction of their commitment to systematically integrate environmental, social and economic factors within the valuation and choice of assets and the exercise of ownership rights and duties.[3]

Later in the book, we will use these distinctions to compare the financial performance of different types of funds.

One final clarification: SRI started out standing for 'socially responsible investment'. More recently, it has begun to stand for 'sustainable and responsible investment'. For us, the evolution of this acronym describes the generational shift that is now under way, and when we use SRI as a catch-all, we mean it to cover the five investment styles we have identified.

It is this dynamism that we and the other contributing authors in this book seek to present, outlining the emergence, growth and future prospects of what we consider to be one of the most exciting dimensions of contemporary financial markets. To do this, we have structured the book in four parts. Part I charts the rise of sustainable investing, with Nick Robins outlining its evolution and current status. Building on this, Cary Krosinsky turns to the thorny question of financial returns, comparing the performance of ethical, mainstream and sustainable investing approaches. Julie Fox Gorte then explores the factors contributing to the ongoing shift from socially responsible to sustainable investing strategies in the US. From an investment banking perspective, Valery

Lucas-Leclin and Sarbjit Nahal then examine what value SRI perspectives bring to the world of financial analysis.

Part II turns to the ways in which sustainability is impinging upon core investment risks and opportunities. Climate change is chief among these and Abyd Karmali looks in detail at the implications of global carbon markets for finance and investment. Matthias Kopp and Björn Tore Urdal investigate what the internalization of carbon costs means for the financial valuation of one of Europe's leading power generators. Emma Hunt and Rachel Whittaker present the emerging investment opportunities in the clean energy arena, followed by Katherine Miles Hill and Sean Gilbert, who examine one of the other major pillars of clean tech: investment in water security.

One of the positive features of sustainable investing is its growth beyond its equity roots to address all asset classes. Ivo Knoepfel and Gordon Hagart open Part III by examining the practice of sustainability among fixed-income investors, as well as pointing to new opportunities opening up in the realm of microfinance. Gary Pivo and Paul McNamara then turn to the rapidly expanding field of sustainable and responsible property investing. Ritu Kumar provides insight into the potential for private equity to bring sustainable value, while Rod Schwartz gives his perspective on the new trends in the field of social investing.

Investment is always about the future, and Part IV points to the potentialities and pitfalls that lie ahead. To date, sustainable investing has been dominated by the post-industrial economies. But among the world's fastest-growing countries such as Brazil, China and India, sustainability is perhaps an even more urgent priority. Ray Cheung leads off with an investigation into the way in which China's financial markets are responding to this burning challenge, followed by Dan Siddy offering a parallel portrait of India. Steve Waygood turns to that other emerging superpower – civil society – and examines the rise of capital market campaigning. Stephen Viederman then examines how the imperative of sustainability impinges upon the application of fiduciary duty in financial markets. Tessa Tennant presents her hopes and dreams for the sector. The book closes with a reflection from Nick Robins and Cary Krosinsky on how sustainable investing can realize its potential as the true art of long-term performance.

To date, sustainable investing has proved itself as a powerful addition to the investment landscape. The years ahead, however, are set to be increasingly dynamic as sustainability emerges from a niche to transform the rest of investment management, in the process becoming the new mainstream. We hope this book will help guide the reader through this transition.

NOTES

1 See www.catfund.com for the 'Social business blog' of 15 April 2008.
2 The upper band of this estimate is drawn from the 2008 assets under management supporting the Carbon Disclosure Project of US$67 trillion. To deal with the issue of double counting, we have simply halved this figure and then compared it with the overall total given by McKinsey. The lower band is derived from the assets under management supporting the United Nations Principles of Responsible Investment, which in May 2008 amounted to some US$13 trillion.
3 For example, Joe Keefe of Pax World defines sustainable investing as the 'full integration of environmental, social and governance factors into financial analysis and decision-making' (see Keefe, 2007).

REFERENCES

Hudson, J. (2006) *The Social Responsibility of the Investment Profession*, CFA Institute, Charlottesville

Keefe, J. (2007) 'From SRI to sustainable investing', *Green Money Journal*, summer, www.ens-newswire.com/ens/aug2007/2007-08-06-03.asp

McKinsey Global Institute (2008) *Mapping Global Capital Markets*, McKinsey Global Institute, San Francisco, CA

Stern, N. (2006) *The Economics of Climate Change*, HMSO, London

Acknowledgements

This book is the shared product of the more than 20 authors who contributed their time and words to communicate the burgeoning practice of sustainable investing. We would like to thank them for their frankness and insight, and state that all contributors have taken part in their personal capacity and not necessarily as representatives of their institutional affiliations which are given for information purposes only. We would also like to thank Valerie Brown, Mark Campanale, Matt Christiansen, Peter Kinder, My-Linh Ngo, Russell Sparkes and Rob West for their comments during the editing process.

Be part of the solution and not part of the problem. Your employees, your colleagues, your board, your investors, your customers are all soon going to place a much higher value – and the markets will soon place a much higher value – on an assessment of how much you are a part of the solution to these issues.

(Al Gore)

Part I

The Rise of
Sustainable Investing

The Emergence of Sustainable Investing

Nick Robins

THE ORIGIN OF THE SPECIES

It is said that it takes a generation for a potent idea to become common practice. In the case of sustainable development, it is now two decades since the Brundtland Commission first launched the concept onto the global stage, calling for a new pattern of growth that 'meets the needs of the present without compromising the ability of future generations to meet their own needs' (WCED, 1987). This poetically simple phrase contained within it three profound imperatives that challenged the prevailing models of economic performance: first, the identification of ecological constraints that human activity must respect (*ecology*); second, the concept of needs, particularly those of the poorest, to whom 'utmost priority must be given' in the commission's words (*equity*); and, third, the principle of intergenerational justice, adding a time dimension to the delivery of development so that long-term durability is not compromised by short-term speculation (*futurity*).

Looking back, the birth of sustainability was timely, coming as it did in the year that analysts believe that the global economy first entered a state of ecological debt – whereby resource extraction and pollution exceeds the carrying capacity of the planet, a deficit that has only deepened in succeeding years (WWF, 2007). Just as significant was its coincidence with the collapse of state communism, with the symbolic fall of the Berlin Wall, taking place just two years later. Critically, this meant that the realization of a sustainable economy would henceforth take place within the context of market-based capitalism. And if global capitalism is to become sustainable, then it makes sense to start with capital.

Yet, while some thought was given to the role that industry could play in the transition to sustainable patterns of development, the role of finance and investment was strangely absent, making investors the missing stakeholder in many subsequent negotiations to translate theory into practice. Indeed, when the then Business Council for Sustainable Development (BCSD) came to write its landmark report, *Changing Course*, for the 1992 Earth Summit, it acknowledged that 'little is known about the constraints, the possibilities, and the interrelationships between capital markets, the environment, and the needs of future generations' (BCSD, 1992; see also WBCSD, 1997). At the time, ethical investing was already practised by a growing number of individual and institutional investors in Europe and the US. But only a handful of the world's institutional investors had begun to include considerations of sustainability within their investment strategies. These included Bank Sarasin in Switzerland and Jupiter in the UK, both of which continue to be among the leading practitioners today. Nevertheless, a group of pioneers – led by Tessa Tennant and Mark Campanale in the UK, Peter Kinder in the US, Marc de Sousa Shields in Canada, and Robert Rosen in Australia – drafted the Rio Resolution, which sought to 'draw to the attention of investors worldwide the link between investment policy and sustainable development' (cited in Sparkes, 2002, p168).

Investment provides the bridge between an unsustainable present and a sustainable future – placing finance squarely at the heart of solutions to issues such as climate change and human rights. Across each of sustainability's three pillars of ecology, equity and futurity, the need for investment strategies that serve this transition is increasingly evident. Put simply, the world's capital markets fail to tell the ecological truth. According to Ernst von Weizsäcker: 'the system of bureaucratic socialism can be said to have collapsed because it did not allow prices to tell the economic truth' (von Weizsäcker, 1994). And despite the progress that has been made, he adds, 'market prices are a long way from telling the ecological truth'. Negative environmental externalities remain significant, accounting for almost half of the US GDP, according to Redefining Progress (Talberth et al, 2006). In many cases, these externalities continue to grow. This is particularly stark in the case of climate change, where less than 10 per cent of global emissions are covered by carbon pricing mechanisms. Even where pricing has been introduced, this still undervalues the cost of greenhouse gas emissions, estimated by the Stern Review at some US$85 per tonne of carbon dioxide (CO_2) equivalent (Stern, 2006). Carbon has still only been marginally integrated within asset valuations. Thus, the share prices of oil, coal and gas companies remain buoyed up by the expected future returns from their reserves of fossil fuels, ignoring the huge carbon liability that is attached to each barrel of oil equivalent. As a result, hundreds of billions, if not trillions, of dollars in capital are still being routinely misallocated. Yet, in spite of these market failures, a growing body of sustainable investors have anticipated the future direction of policy and allocated increasing amounts of capital to environmental solutions.

In terms of equity, the challenge is for the investment industry to be an engine of social cohesion rather than social division. Much of today's investment industry has its roots in the post-war welfare settlement that gave rise to the modern pension and mutual fund industry (see, for example, Bogle, 2005). More recently, however, in a process described as 'financialization', a growing share of global output is taken by the finance sector and its employees. In the US, for example, finance-sector profits rose from 14 per cent in 1981 to 39 per cent of the total in 2001; over a similar timeframe – between 1980 and 2000 – average compensation for a US securities analyst tripled; for the average US worker, it doubled (Blackburn, 2006). Former investment banker Philip Augar has calculated that, as a result, US\$120 billion was diverted from shareholders and customers to investment banking employees alone over the past two decades (Augar, 2006). Excessive remuneration and bonuses within the finance sector have attracted increasing public criticism not just for the social divisions that these create, but the perverse signals they often send for short-term profit-making. All of this has contributed to the wider rise in inequality, described as the emergence of a new Plutonomy by Ajay Kapur, until recently the chief global equity strategist at Citigroup (see Authers, 2007). In addition, the allocation of private capital for vital social infrastructure lags behind the surge in clean tech investing. As the unfolding sub-prime debacle in the US has demonstrated, conventional financial innovation has tended to progress without consideration of social impacts. The great challenge ahead is to harness the ingenuity of financial markets for social business, an issue addressed by Rod Schwartz in Chapter 12.

As for the core principle of futurity, the mainstream investment industry continues to foreshorten its time horizon when what is called for is the reverse. Technological innovation, financial deregulation and the rapid growth of hedge funds have served to make trading cheaper, easier and superficially more profitable – and so encourage short-term trading on the world's equity exchanges. In the UK, for example, the average holding period for shares on the London Stock Exchange has slumped from 9 years in 1986 to 11 months in 2006, suggesting that investors cannot wait between one annual report and the next before trading (Montier, 2005; see also Montier, 2007). Short-term performance measurement is a major profound driver of this behaviour, leading to extra costs and perverse results for the end investor. Indeed, there is a strong correlation between the time horizon of investment strategies and financial performance (see Chapter 2). Keynes's 70-year-old epitaph for the long-term investor still stands the test of time today. Writing in his groundbreaking *General Theory of Employment, Interest and Money* on the dynamics of investment practice, Keynes (1978) observed that 'it is the long-term investor, he who most promotes the public interest, who will in practice come in for the most criticism wherever investment funds are managed by committees or boards or banks'.

THE EVOLUTION OF THE SPECIES

Since the embryonic initiatives of the early 1990s, sustainable investing has become one of the most creative areas of investment practice developing new ways of thinking and shaping an agenda for others to follow. It has attracted rapidly growing flows of assets and created new models for assessing fund performance. Many different streams have contributed to its rise. One of these is the pioneering ethical and socially responsible investment community, who first attempted to bring social and environmental values to the world's stock markets. In practice, ethical investing represents a merger between age-old principles of stewardship inherent to many of the world's religions and the more modern trend of ethical consumerism, as active individuals integrate their personal beliefs within their shopping and investing decisions.

Over the past 35 years, sustainable and responsible investing (SRI) has generally been characterized by the application of positive and negative screens to investment selection – on issues such as alcohol, environmental protection, gambling, human rights, military involvement, nuclear power, pornography and tobacco – as well as shareholder activism and community investing (see Domini and Kinder, 1986; Sparkes, 1995; Domini, 2001; Sparkes, 2002; Hudson, 2006; Kinder, 2007).

Equally important has been a host of new entrants who have responded to the investment challenges created by growing environmental constraints, increased public expectations of business social performance, new value drivers and heightened understanding of impacts up and down extended supply chains. Practitioners of sustainable investing share an interest in many of the same issues as ethical investors. But there are also important differences. While the primary spur for ethical investing is the internal value system of the investor, the prompt for sustainable investing is the external realities of an economy out of balance: water stress is thus not a question of belief, but of fact.

In essence, sustainable investors recognize that physical, regulatory, competitive, reputational and social pressures are driving environmental and social issues into the heart of market practice and thus the ability of companies to generate value for investors over the long term. Sustainable investors therefore incorporate these factors both within their choices over the selection and retention of investment assets and within the exercise of their ownership rights and responsibilities. It is this alignment with the forces shaping the planet that gives sustainable investors a far better chance of delivering outperformance than traditional investors. Indeed, much of the secret of sustainable investing's recent growth has been in its ability to sniff out critical trends before the 'electronic herd' of conventional investors, to stay one step ahead of the pack and to do things that seem to be eccentric at first, but then become perfectly normal. It was sustainable investors who first raised climate change as a financial issue, building understanding and expertise in advance of an often dismissive mainstream, who are now

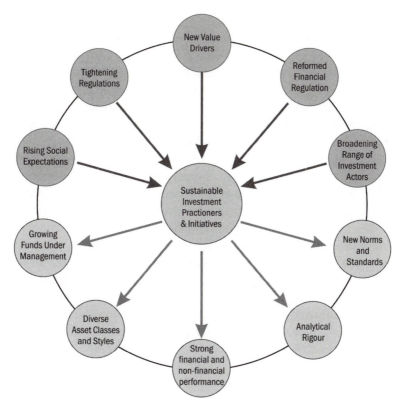

Source: Nick Robins

Figure 1.1 *The dynamics of sustainable investment*

hastily playing catch-up. Matching this is the downside potential of anticipating trends too far ahead of the market – of being right too early.

Five main forces are at work in this arena, fusing with the efforts of sustainable investing pioneers to create tangible outcomes in terms of scale, diversity, financial and non-financial performance, analytical rigour and market norms (see Figure 1.1).

Rising social expectations around environmental protection, health and safety, and equal opportunities at work have formed the basis for a significant tightening in policy frameworks across the world during the past two decades. These have combined to create new value drivers for business success, where intangible assets have assumed ever greater importance. Thus, in the pre-sustainability mid 1980s, financial statements were capable of capturing 75 to 80 per cent of the risks and value creation potential of corporations. By the early 21st century, this had collapsed to less than 20 per cent (cited in Kiernan, 2007). Factors such as human capital and resource efficiency, along with brand and reputation are now critical to business success. Yet, mainstream investors have long ignored these and other issues, leaving it to the more nimble far-sighted sustainability investors to start the quest to understand the extra-financial aspects of performance. The financial success of many sustainability-focused funds at the end of the 1990s – such as NPI's Global Care range in the UK – helped to create the basis of evidence for amending financial regulation to reflect these new realities. Thus, in 2000, the UK introduced new requirements for pension fund trustees to consider the extent to which social, ethical and environmental factors were part of their investment strategies, paving the way for similar reforms across Europe and internationally.

The end of the equities boom and the revelations of egregious corporate practices in companies such as Enron exposed the need for traditionally inactive institutional investors to behave as real owners of corporations and to take a longer-term approach to investing. As a result, the historically conservative community of pension funds became among the most innovative in the development of strategies to integrate environmental, social and governance (ESG) factors within investment and governance decision-making (UNEP FI and UK SIF, 2007). Rejecting the pure values-based focus of the original SRI fund managers, the entry of pension funds has been pivotal in creating 'responsible investment', essentially a brand of enlightened self-interest for the 21st century (for an overview of responsible investing, see Mackenzie and Sullivan, 2006). The rapid maturity of this movement was symbolized by the launch of the United Nations Principles for Responsible Investment in April 2006; by June 2008, these principles had attracted over 300 signatories with US$13 trillion of assets under management.

Brokering these dynamics have been a small but growing group of sustainable investing practitioners – notably, fund managers and rating agencies – along with a range of catalytic initiatives. One of the first research agencies established with the explicit aim of understanding the investment relevance of sustainability was Innovest Strategic Value Advisers, founded in 1995 with the mission of 'integrating sustainability and finance by identifying non-traditional sources of risk and value potential for investors' (see www.innovestgroup.com, accessed 12 May 2008). Others have joined the quest to unlock new sources of investment advantage – for example, Trucost in the UK and Vigeo in France. Importantly, the first generation of ethical research organizations, such as EIRIS and KLD, as well as corporate governance agencies, such as PIRC and RiskMetrics, have also expanded their services to incorporate the sustainability dimension. Trade associations and investor alliances have grown in stature and clout, notably the network of national and regional social investment forums (SIFs) across Europe, North America and Asia-Pacific, as well as specialist groups such as CERES and the Marathon Club. Internationally, the United Nations Environment Programme's Finance Initiative (UNEP FI) has been instrumental in building confidence and competence among leading banks, insurers and asset managers on issues such as fiduciary duty and investment performance. In emerging markets, the International Finance Corporation (IFC) has been an active exponent of underwriting sustainability investment research and backing innovative public and private equity funds.

All of this has produced tangible results. Over the past decade, the size and scope of the social, responsible and sustainable investment universe has grown consistently ahead of the wider investment market (see Figure 1.2). As this book demonstrates, sustainability investing is spreading out from the public equity arena to influence fixed income, private equity and property. Significant regional and national differences exist – and the world still lacks common standards similar to those governing organic agriculture to enable rigorous analysis. The terms 'social', 'ethical', 'responsible', 'socially responsible' and 'sustainable' are all used in a multitude of overlapping and competing ways to the frustration of practitioners and observers alike. As UNEP FI recently commented: 'This is not mere semantics, but a true reflection of the major shift in thinking associated with the huge environmental and social challenges our world is now facing, the corporate downfalls in recent memory, and the increasing belief that these changes have impacts on investment performance' (UNEP FI, 2007). Nevertheless, some broad observations can still be made.

The US remains the home of traditional social screening, with over US$2 trillion in assets applying one or more ethical factors in stock selection. In all, US$1 out of every US$9 under professional management was involved in SRI in 2007 (US SIF, 2008). Shareholder advocacy expressed in terms of stockowners filing and voting for SRI resolutions is on the rise, notably around climate change and human rights. The US is also home to a thriving, community investing market, whose assets under management rose by nearly one third between 2005 and 2007. Major state pension funds, such as CalPERS and CalSTRS in California, have not only set the standard for corporate governance, but have also launched new mandates for environmentally focused public and private equity, as well as property funds. In relative terms, however, the advances in Canada have been the most pronounced, with almost one fifth of the combined retail mutual fund and institutional investment market covered by SRI strategies in 2006 (SIO, 2007). This has largely been due to the adoption of responsible investment by some of Canada's leading pension funds.

It is in Europe, however, where most progress has been made in terms of sustainable and responsible investing. This is perhaps no surprise as it is in the European Union (EU) where the imperative of sustainable development has been most deeply integrated within broader economic policy from the early 1990s onwards.[1] In the investment world, the early pioneers in Switzerland and the UK were joined in September 1999 by the launch of the Dow Jones Sustainability Index (DJSI) series, underpinned by the work of Sustainable Asset Management. This provided the first independent benchmark of the financial and non-financial performance of companies with regard to sustainability. This was followed in July 2001 with the FTSE4Good Index, although this was more focused on corporate social responsibility than sustainability. By the middle of the decade, major European pension funds such as ABP and PGGM in The Netherlands, the FFR in France, Norway's Government Pension Fund, and USS and the Environment Agency in the UK had come to the forefront of individual and collaborative efforts to make ESG factors an increasingly normal part of mainstream investment practice. 2005 was also the year in which the EU's Emissions Trading Scheme (EU ETS) was introduced, the most forceful expression in the world of the global effort to implement the 1997 Kyoto Protocol. Far more effectively than repeated exhortation by government ministers or voluntary codes with business, the EU ETS symbolized a determination to progressively drive environmental costs into market prices. Alongside assertive renewable energy policies, notably in Denmark, Germany and now Spain, the EU's climate change convictions stimulated a sea change in clean tech, climate change and environmental investing. The previous wave of clean tech public equity investing at the turn of the century had been hit hard by the ending of the dot.com boom. Now, policies, markets and technologies were in alignment. According to New Energy Finance, public equity funds investing in climate solutions soared from US$1.4 billion in 2000 to US$24 billion in 2007, with Black Rock's New Energy and Impax's Environmental Market funds in the vanguard. By late 2007, the *Financial Times* reported that over 15 per cent of flows into European equity funds were targeted at ecological or environmental funds up from 2.6 per cent in 2006 and 0.6 per cent in 2005 (Johnson, 2007).

Japan's leadership in environmental technologies has been reflected in the investment world. Nikko launched the country's first Eco Fund in 1999, and over 50 SRI mutual funds were open to investors at the beginning of 2008. Elsewhere in Asia, South Korea has led the way in terms of integrating SRI within pension fund mandates, while Malaysia has over 80 Shari'ah-compliant funds. Australia has witnessed particularly rapid growth. The launch of AMP's Sustainable Future range in 2001 marked a new focus on sustainable investing strategies, and the market as a whole has grown strongly through this decade. Core SRI funds under management grew by 43 per cent in 2007 and represent around 1.8 per cent of the total market; alongside this, one quarter of all managed funds in Australia subscribe to the United Nations Principles for Responsible Investment (RIAA, 2007).

In the emerging world as a whole, South Africa and Brazil stand out as the two trailblazers. Since the struggle against apartheid, South Africa had always had a special place in SRI strategies. In 2002, the publication of the second King Report on corporate governance set a new benchmark for corporate standards globally – for example, requiring companies to report on the social, economic and environmental performance using the Global Reporting Initiative's disclosure framework. This was followed in May 2004 with the launch of the Johannesburg Stock Exchange's Socially Responsible Investment Index, the first in an emerging economy. The JSE SRI Index evaluates the environmental, social and economic sustainability practices and corporate governance of listed

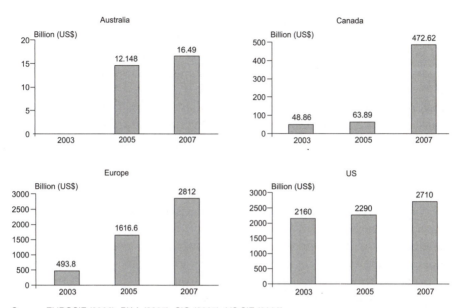

Source: EUROSIF (2006); RIAA (2007); SIO (2007); US SIF (2008)

Figure 1.2 *Key markets*

companies. Although the index has helped to raise the profile of SRI, the Johannesburg Stock Exchange remains disappointed at the slow uptake of sustainable investing practices (JSE, 2007). Among the fast-growing Brazil, Russia, India and China (BRIC), it is Brazil that is furthest advanced, symbolized by the launch of the Corporate Sustainability Index by the São Paulo stock exchange, Bovespa, in December 2005. Brazil's pension fund community has also been among the most committed to the United Nations Principles for Responsible Investment. The two Asian giants, China and India, are currently poised to enter the world of sustainable investing as Ray Cheung and Dan Siddy illustrate in Chapters 13 and 14.

The impacts of this surge in sustainable and responsible investing extend beyond the substantial growth in assets to real consequences for financial and non-financial performance. Conventional financial theory has generally been dismissive of, first, socially responsible and, now, sustainable investing strategies. The assumption is that the introduction of non-financial factors will harm diversification and thereby incur penalties in terms of risk and returns. The broad spread of extra-financial investing styles – as well as the diversity of academic approaches – makes it difficult to draw definitive conclusions. Yet, it is clear that conventional financial theory and practice do need to be updated in light of the sustainability imperative. In general, studies show that investments selected on the basis of identifiable ESG factors – such as eco-efficiency, employee engagement and corporate governance – do tend to outperform, confirming the validity of investors integrating extra-financial factors within the research process (see, for example, Bauer et al, 2006; Edmans, 2007; Association of British Insurers, 2008). The evidence in terms of fund performance is less clear cut. A 2007 review of the academic literature analysing the performance of funds adopting SRI screening suggests that out of 11 studies, 3 identified positive results, 2 were negative and 6 were generally neutral (UNEP FI, 2007). A 2008 paper from Sweden surveyed 16 studies between 1992 and 2007 and concluded that 2 showed a positive relationship, 1 identified a negative relationship, with the remainder concluding that SRI funds did not exhibit any significant difference in performance from regular funds; this same study then concluded that in the Swedish context, SRI funds did underperform (Stenstrom and Thorrell, 2007). At present, it appears that these performance evaluations are comparing very different investment strategies, requiring a more discriminating approach. New analysis conducted for this book for the first time disaggregates ethical from sustainable and responsible investment funds and suggests that ethical funds do underperform as a whole, while funds with a sustainability focus tend to outperform (see Chapter 2).

Part of the essence of contemporary sustainable investing is the realization that investors need to understand, measure and promote superior financial *and* non-financial performance. Climate change has been a focal point for recent investor activism, combining both a strategic awareness of the coming transition to a low-carbon economy as well as a more tactical engagement with companies to raise standards of disclosure, governance and performance. Central to this has been the Carbon Disclosure Project (CDP). Established in 2001, the investor-led CDP has won the support of 385 investment institutions with over US$57 trillion in assets under management to promote comprehensive and comparable corporate reporting of climate change risks and opportunities. The CDP has created the largest public register of climate change reporting, providing the basis for climate exposure to be integrated within regulated disclosures to the market. Alongside the CDP, regional initiatives such as the Institutional Investors Group on Climate Change (Europe), the Investor Network on Climate Risk (US) and the Investor Group on Climate Change (Australia) have mobilized investors to commit capital to climate solutions, frame policy frameworks and engage with corporate management.

Underpinning these outcomes is the growth in a compelling body of research showing when and how sustainability becomes a driver of investment returns. SRI research has moved a long way from the early days of screening through the 'best in class' era when sustainability performance was viewed as an indirect proxy for management quality to the current growth boom in sell-side investment analytics. As more and more funds adopt conviction sustainability strategies as well as pragmatic responsible investment overlays, so the market for high-quality analysis has grown. Much of this research is hidden from public view; but the Enhanced Analytics Initiative (EAI) has brought together leading asset owners and asset managers to reward investment research that takes account of the impact of extra-financial issues on long-term performance. In the six-month period between May and October 2007, the 30 EAI members recommended an impressive 158 reports for appraisal. London's claim to be recognized as the global capital of sustainable investment came to fruition with the London Accord: a unique collaboration between investment banks, research houses and academics to produce the first 'open source' resource for investors in climate change solutions. Released at the end of 2007, the result was a collection of 25 research papers with contributors including ABN AMRO, Barclays, Canaccord Adams, Chevreux, Credit Suisse, JPMorgan Chase, Merrill Lynch, Morgan Stanley, Société Générale and WestLB.

TAKING STOCK OF SUSTAINABLE INVESTING

Sustainable investing expresses a convergence of forces, bringing together those in the financial sector committed to the sustainability imperative, along with those simply happy to ride the investment opportunities that the ongoing shift in regulations and market practices are creating. Perhaps the best expression of the current model of change is contained in *The New Capitalists*, written by three leaders in corporate governance and responsible investment. Drawing out the consequences of the democratization of ownership represented by pension and mutual funds, the authors describe an emerging civil economy in which 'institutional owners accountable to their savers push corporations towards sustainable prosperity through responsible management' (Davis et al, 2006). In a similar fashion, the *Twenty-First Century Investment* report outlined the new realism of sustainable investing (see Figure 1.3).

This reversal of the traditional chain of value creation – where the planet has been seen purely as a source of materials or a sump for pollution – has profound consequences for the investment profession, many of which have still to be worked through. The case for sustainable investment has also been strengthened by the entry of respected mainstream investment professionals into the field. A case in point is Generation IM, a specialist fund manager established in 2004 by ex-Goldman Sachs executive David Blood and former US Vice-President Al Gore. For Generation, sustainable development will be a primary driver of industrial and economic change over the next 50 years. As a result, Al Gore believes that 'integrating issues such as climate change into investment research is simply common sense' (see www.generationim.com).

Yet, for all the sense of achievement that this progress brings, there is equally a need for a healthy sense of proportion. Initiatives such as the CDP are starting to attract majority attention among asset owners and asset managers. But the actual allocation of capital still lags far short of either the enlightened self-interest of responsible investment or the conviction commitments of sustainable investing. In addition, it is still fair to say that the SRI movement, as a

Successful investment
depends upon
identifying targets which can provide a good return
which depends upon
a vigorous population of enterprises
which depends upon
a healthy macro-economy
which depends upon
a healthy civil society
which depends upon
a sustainable planet

Source: Centre for Tomorrow's Company (2000)

Figure 1.3 *The constituents of 21st century investment*

whole, is not yet fully signed up to the goal of sustainability. While there are strong linkages between the ethical, responsible and sustainable styles of investing, it is important to recognize the issues that separate, as well as unite. Thus, the classic negative screens for ethical funds were designed during the 20th century and do not automatically make these portfolios well positioned for the sustainability issues of the 21st century. This creates the real threat of a 'first mover disadvantage' for traditional ethical funds as they are overtaken in the pursuit of higher-performing sustainable assets by more aggressive opportunity-driven investors. Equally, promoters of the new generation of clean tech and climate change funds – implicitly riding the sustainability wave – are often at pains to distance themselves from what went before in terms of socially responsible or ethical investing. Indeed, there are the first signs of a push-back against the perceived opportunism of this new surge of capital (see, for example, Novethic Etudes, 2007).

Others have called on the SRI community to avoid a slide into mere pragmatism. 'Best in class', for example, has proved useful as a technique to rate ESG performance within sectors. But it remains only a tool and needs to be complemented by a searching analysis of the sustainability of the 'class' itself. Unless this is done an Alice in Wonderland situation can emerge where 'everyone wins prizes', and relative benchmarking ensures there is always a sector leader, even if neither business model nor behaviour warrant such an outcome. Such an approach, of course, mirrors the benchmark hugging, tracking error-averse strategies of the investment mainstream. But here, the mainstream can be a false friend. On occasion, it seems that the understandable desire by advocates of SRI to be taken seriously by the mainstream has lead to a suspension of its critical edge. In a coruscating critique, Paul Hawken found that investment portfolios of SRI mutual funds were 'virtually no different' from conventional funds. Hawken also posed uncomfortable challenges for SRI, arguing that 'striving to attain the highest rate of financial return is a direct cause of social injustice and environmental degradation as it consistently leads to externalization of costs on the environment, the future, workers and others' (Hawken, 2004).

One source of the problem, according to Christoph Butz and Jean Laville, is what they call 'the materiality trap'. By this, they mean the tendency of SRI investors to address ESG issues only to the extent that they are financially material, adopting a narrow and formalistic interpretation of fiduciary duty. 'In view of this kind of reasoning', they write, 'we wonder whether the long struggle to put sustainable development on investors' agendas has not been futile', calling for the SRI community to 'go back to its roots' (Butz and Laville, 2007). Another weakness of many SRI funds has been an inability to evolve their strategies in light of changing circumstances. In a landmark review of climate change investing in the UK, leading financial advisers Holden & Partners found that many SRI funds are surprisingly badly positioned for climate change, arguing that 'investors in SRI funds who were hoping to be buying into the low carbon economy may find that they are largely exposing themselves to multinationals which are more part of the problem than part of the solution'. In a withering conclusion, the report stated that 'SRI and ethical funds perform just as well (if not slightly better) than their mainstream counterparts because in most cases they are, in fact, mainstream' (Holden & Partners, 2008).

Another perhaps surprising weakness has been in the area of transparency. The absence of objective standards, publicly reported upon, remains one of the great weaknesses of the SRI phenomenon. The introduction of transparency guidelines for retail SRI funds in Australia and Europe is a positive first step. In addition, the reporting requirements under the United Nations Principles for Responsible Investment (PRI) could, over time, produce the kind of comprehensive comparable information for savers that investors so often ask of companies. Yet, in spite of the massive mobilization of investor effort to press companies to report on climate change, it remains shocking that only a handful of SRI funds have voluntarily published their own 'carbon footprints'.[2] Without the discipline of external reporting, SRI funds have been able to avoid hard questions about the environmental and social outputs that they are generating along with financial returns.

To conclude, sustainable investing has arrived. It has proved itself to be in tune with investors' needs for attractive returns – and also to be acutely aligned with the reshaping of the investment landscape as a result of deepening ecological, social and economic shocks. If it is to avoid the fate of being just another interesting niche in the panoply of investment styles, sustainable investing will need to overcome the temptations of pragmatism and opportunism, and to reassert its strategic mission of structural change. Just as corporate social responsibility (CSR) is increasingly being seen as a phase en route to the more serious practice of sustainable enterprise, so today's focus on SRI looks set to become a staging post for the more profound task of ensuring sustainable patterns of global investment. And as the rest of this book amply demonstrates, there is already a wealth of experience in the sustainable investing arena – pointing to further transformations to come.

NOTES

1   By contrast, prior to the 2008 presidential elections, the high tide of sustainable development in US policy-making was achieved during the late 1990s in the Clinton
administration. See, President's Council on Sustainable Development (1999).
2   See, for example, the carbon audits of Henderson Global Investors' Global Care Income
and Industries of the Future funds (www.henderson.com/sri, accessed 12 May 2008).

REFERENCES

Association of British Insurers (2008) *Governance and Performance in Corporate Britain*, ABI,
London
Augar, P. (2006) *The Greed Merchants*, Penguin, London
Authers, J. (2007) 'Bankers are taking over where Marx left off', *Financial Times*, 17–18 March
Bauer, R., Derwall, J., Guenster, N. and Koedijk, K. (2006) *The Economic Value of Corporate
Eco-Efficiency*, http://papers.ssrn.com/sol3/papers.cfm?abstract_id=675628
BCSD (Business Council for Sustainable Development) (1992) *Changing Course*, MIT Press,
Cambridge, MA
Blackburn, R. (2006) *Age Shock: How Finance is Failing Us*, Verso, London
Bogle, J. (2005) *The Battle for the Soul of Capitalism*, Yale University Press, New Haven, CT
Butz, C. and Laville, J. (2007) *Socially Responsible Investment: Avoiding the Financial Materiality
Trap*, Ethos Fund, Geneva, Switzerland
Centre for Tomorrow's Company (2000) *Twenty-First Century Investment*, Centre for
Tomorrow's Company, London
Davis, S., Lukomnik, J. and Pitt-Watson, D. (2006) *The New Capitalists: How Citizen Investors are
Reshaping the Corporate Agenda*, Harvard Business School Press, Boston, MA
Domini, A. (2001) *Socially Responsible Investing: Making a Difference and Making Money*, Dearborn
Trade, Chicago, IL
Domini, A. L. and Kinder, P. D. (1986) *Ethical Investing*, Addison-Wesley, Reading, MA
Edmans, A. (2007) *Does Stock Market Misvalue Intangibles?* MIT, Cambridge, MA
EUROSIF (2006) *European SRI Study*, EUROSIF, Paris
Hawken, P. (2004) *Socially Responsible Investing: How the SRI Industry has Failed to Respond to People
Who Want to Invest with Conscience and What Can Be Done to Change It*, Natural Capital
Institute, Sausalito
Holden & Partners (2008) *Guide to Climate Change Investment*, Holden & Partners, London

Hudson, J. (2006) *The Social Responsibility of the Investment Profession*, CFA Institute, Charlottesville

Johnson, S. (2007) 'Fears over rush into green funds', *Financial Times*, 24 September

JSE (Johannesburg Stock Exchange) (2007) *The JSE's SRI Index Challenges Investors to Invest Responsibly*, Johannesburg, South Africa

Keynes, J. M. (1978) *The General Theory of Employment, Interest and Money*, Macmillan, London

Kiernan, M. (2007) 'Capturing next-generation alpha drivers', in *The Working Capital Report*, UNEP FI, Geneva, Switzerland

Kinder, P. (2007) *Socially Responsible Investing: An Evolving Concept in a Changing World*, KLD, Boston, MA

Mackenzie, C. and Sullivan, R. (eds) (2006) *Responsible Investment*, Greenleaf Publishing, London

Montier, J. (2005) *Seven Sins of Fund Management: A Behavioural Critique*, DrKW Macro Research, London

Montier, J. (2007) *Behavioural Investing*, John Wiley & Sons, Chichester, UK

Novethic Etudes (2007) *The New Frontiers of SRI: Green Investments Claiming to be SRI*, Novethic Etudes, Paris, France

President's Council on Sustainable Development (1999) *Towards a Sustainable America*, White House, Washington, DC

RIAA (Responsible Investment Association of Australasia) (2007) *Responsible Investment 2007*, RIAA, Sydney, Australia, October

SIO (Social Investment Organisation) (2007) *Canadian Socially Responsible Investment Review 2006*, SIO, Toronto, Canada, March

Sparkes, R. (1995) *The Ethical Investor*, Harper Collins, London

Sparkes, R. (2002) *Socially Responsible Investment: A Global Revolution*, John Wiley & Sons, Chichester, UK, p168

Stenstrom, C. and Thorrell, J. (2007) *Evaluating the Performance of Socially Responsible Investment Funds*, Stockholm School of Economics, Stockholm, Sweden

Stern, N. (2006) *The Economics of Climate Change*, HMSO, London

Talberth, J., Cobb, R. and Slattery, N. (2006) *The Genuine Progress Index 2006*, Redefining Progress, Oakland

UNEP FI (United Nations Environment Programme's Finance Initiative) (2007) *Demystifying Responsible Investment Performance*, UNEP FI, Geneva, Switzerland

UNEP FI and UK SIF (2007) *How Leading Pension Funds are Meeting the Challenge*, UNEP FI and UK SIF, Geneva and London

US SIF (Social Investment Forum) (2008) *2007 Report on Socially Responsible Investing Trends in the United States*, SIF, Washington, DC

von Weizsäcker, E. (1994) *Earth Politics*, Zed Books, Zed Books, London

WBCSD (World Business Council for Sustainable Development) (1997) *Financing Change*, MIT Press, Cambridge, MA

WCED (World Commission on Environment and Development) (1987) *Our Common Future*, Oxford University Press, Oxford, UK

WWF (World Wide Fund for Nature) (2007) *Living Planet Report*, WWF, Gland, Switzerland

Sustainable Equity Investing: The Market-Beating Strategy

Cary Krosinsky

Perhaps the most important battleground for advocates and opponents of social, ethical and sustainable investment strategies has been financial performance. Although scepticism remains, this chapter will show that sustainable investing funds have already outperformed consistently over the short, medium and long term, by disaggregating the returns of different strategies – distinguishing between mainstream, ethical and sustainable styles. The analysis will also highlight the fact that long-termism – another essential element of the sustainable investing philosophy – is also positively correlated with financial return.

CONFRONTING THE PERFORMANCE CHALLENGE

To date, conventional wisdom in investing circles has held that strategies that incorporate environmental or social factors must, by definition, underperform. This assumption is derived from traditional beliefs about the inapplicability of personal values and morals in a financial context. It is also based on experience with the first generation of ethical or socially responsible investment funds. Such funds typically invest against a mainstream index and screen out perceived worst actors in certain categories, or remove entire industries such as alcohol, tobacco and firearms. They also give preference to companies apparently displaying socially responsible business practices. These ethically screened funds continue to represent a majority of SRI assets to this day and typically do not outperform the mainstream. As a result, many investors with an overriding mandate of outperformance firmly believe that taking non-financial factors into account will cause them to fail, and so avoid the entire concept.

But what this obscures is that sustainable investing – a key, separate and distinct subcategory of SRI – has outperformed not only ethical funds, but mainstream indices as well over a one-, three- and five-year period. This outper-formance has far-reaching implications for the investment profession, suggesting that the early incorporation of factors such as climate change has already been paying off. With prospects suggesting that environmental and social threats may well intensify in the years ahead, this evidence suggests that sustainable investing arguably represents the best way forward to position one's equity for any investor.

What makes sustainable investing distinct is a dual approach, simultaneously pursuing the best opportunities that arise from the threats of climate change, water shortages and other factors, while at the same time seeking to avoid the risk in securities and industries that will most likely be affected negatively by environmental, social and governance (ESG) issues. There are numerous examples of this dual strategy having been deployed successfully over time, which we will highlight shortly. These sustainable investors stand in direct contrast to traditional ethical funds that do not look to highlight specific oppor-tunities, and the relative performance over time between these subcategories is quite dramatic.

Articles and papers continue to be published expressing scepticism as to whether one can invest according to one's personal convictions and not leave something on the table in the process. Just one such recent example would be Pepperdine University Business School's paper entitled *The Moral and Financial Conflict of Socially Responsible Investing* (Graziadio Business Report, 2007), and there are many other such examples. These deeply entrenched beliefs are held not only within the mainstream investor communities, but by many otherwise ethically minded individual investors as well.

Many other studies have been made attempting to discern whether and how socially responsible funds perform, and the results, to date, have been conflicting and confusing. For example, there are fully 17 studies listed at the Center for Responsible Business of the University of California at Berkeley's website (see www.sristudies.org, accessed 12 May 2008). The first one referenced, entitled *Doing Well While Doing Good? The Investment Performance of Socially Responsible Mutual Funds* (Hamilton et al, 1993), shows no statistical difference when invest-ing in a socially responsible manner. Furthermore, the study listed by Hong and Kacperczyk (2006), entitled *The Price of Sin: The Effects on Social Norms on Markets*, suggests that investors pay a price for not investing in so-called 'sin stocks'.

More recently, the United Nations Environment Programme's Finance Initiative (UNEP FI) published a study in October 2007 called *Demystifying Responsible Investment Performance*. Again, the report lists 20 separate studies, with results showing positive, neutral and negative returns. Other studies draw similarly inconclusive findings.

Table 2.1 *The 11 styles of SRI*

Style	Description
1 Ethical 'negative' screening	Avoiding companies on ethical, moral or religious grounds (e.g. alcohol, gambling and tobacco).
2 Environmental/ social 'negative' screening	Avoiding companies for involvement in environmentally or socially damaging sectors or practices (e.g. fossil fuels).
3 'Positive' screening	Active inclusion of companies because of environmental or social benefits.
4 Community and social investing	Allocation of capital directly to enterprises that explicitly provide social returns.
5 Extra-financial 'best in class'	Active inclusion of companies that lead their sectors in environmental or social performance.
6 Financially weighted 'best in class'	Active inclusion of companies that outperform sector peers on financially material environmental or social criteria.
7 Sustainability themes	Active selection of companies on the basis of investment opportunities driven by sustainability factors, such as renewable energy.
8 Constructive engagement	Dialogue between investors and company management to encourage improved management of ESG issues.
9 Shareholder activism	Use of shareholder rights to pressure companies to change environmental, social or governance practices.
10 Integrated analysis	Active inclusion of environmental and social factors within conventional fund management.
11 Norms-based screening	Avoiding companies for non-compliance with international standards such as those issued by the United Nations (UN), the Organisation for Economic Co-operation and Development (OECD) and the International Labour Organization (ILO).

Source: Eurosif (2006); Tyrrell and Brown (2007); US SIF (2008)

The consistent theme among these studies is that they analyse SRI funds as a whole as if they only undertake one approach to investment. But the fact of the matter is that SRI is a catch-all phrase, which represents numerous subcategories, each of which need to be considered separately and carefully in order to truly examine past and potential future performance. As we will demonstrate, there has been a great difference in performance between the more granular classifications.

Looking across the investment landscape, as many as 11 distinct styles within SRI emerge (see Table 2.1).

Often these styles are deployed in different blends by managers seeking to achieve different outcomes. In broad terms:

- Ethical and classical socially responsible strategies encompass styles 1, 2, 3, 4 and 11, as listed in Table 2.1.

- Sustainable investing generally involves styles 5, 6, 7 and 10, as listed in Table 2.1.

Styles 8 and 9 in Table 2.1 are not typically specific investment strategies. Rather, they are overlays, often deployed on top of either ethical or sustainability focused funds. Such overlay strategies have also been utilized against mainstream index-based portfolios without screening, such as has been the case with US state pension funds (e.g. CalPERS), and there are many similar such cases globally. Styles 8 and 9 are often a large part of what is meant by the term responsible investing.

For the purposes of comparing the performance of these very different styles, we have allocated public mutual funds across the world into the two groups: ethical funds and sustainable funds. Responsible investment, as mentioned above, is an overlay that can be performed on top of ethical, sustainable or mainstream investment deployment strategies. In addition, this overlay is often practised by pension funds and similar funds whose investments and performance are not often publicly available (as a result, they will not be considered in this chapter). We also further subdivided the sustainable fund class into 'clean growth' funds: those running sustainability themes focused on clean tech, climate change and other cross-cutting factors. Lastly, we also split out funds that deviated from their stated goals and call them 'style drift SRI' due to factors such as being significantly overweight in the oil and gas sector.

The study we performed, then, isolated all global publicly facing SRI portfolios, of which we found there to be 850 at present. We further isolated those with US$100 million or more in equity under management that have existed for five years or more as of the end of 2007 and assigned them one of these subcategories as appropriate to their specific approach. There are 135 such funds that met these criteria, and the relative subcategory return results seen in Table 2.2 are quite revealing indeed.

From this, we can see that ethical funds perform in line or underperform, suffering very poor returns over one year, slight underperformance over three years and minor outperformance against their benchmark indices apart from MSCI World over five years. Over longer time periods, other studies have shown that ethical investment broadly performs in line with the mainstream – this is certainly the experience of the KLD Social Index. Over a ten-year timeframe, a recent analysis of 90 ethical funds in the UK concluded that the annual return was just 0.1 per cent less than the FTSE All Share Index (Jewson, 2008).

More significant, however, is that sustainable investing funds have significantly outperformed their ethical peers and, even more so, their style drift compatriots. Even more impressive is that sustainable investing funds have significantly outperformed mainstream indices, returning +18.7 per cent, on average, over the last five years, versus the MSCI World, S&P 500 and FTSE 100's returns of +17.0 per cent, +13.2 per cent and +13.0 per cent, respectively.

Table 2.2 *Relative returns by SRI subcategory versus mainstream indices*

	One-year average percentage return (2007)	Three-year average percentage return (31 December 2004– 31 December 2007)	Five-year average percentage return (31 December 2002– 31 December 2007)
SRI subcategory			
Sustainable investing	14.0	19.3	18.7
Ethical	3.6	12.3	13.8
Style drift SRI	0.3	9.6	11.6
Mainstream Index			
MSCI World	9.0	12.7	17.0
S&P 500	5.5	8.7	13.2
FTSE 100	5.9	12.9	13.0

Source: Cary Krosinsky, using Yahoo! Finance and Bloomberg to verify mainstream Index returns, and Ivor Butcher's double-checking study as well, on the fund return portion, in combination with fund company websites and public disclosure websites such as www.sec.gov – compiled April and May 2008. See also Appendix B.

In effect, sustainable investing funds have already been providing the *alpha* that so many asset managers have been striving for. Similar outperformance was seen over one- and three-year periods, as well. (Note that the results of the returns in this study were independently and fully verified by investment banker Ivor Butcher. For more details on this returns study, see the Appendices at the end of this volume.)

Overall, the 135 SRI funds studied produced an average five-year return of +15.2 per cent. Compared with benchmark indices such as the S&P 500 and FTSE 100, this was quite competitive and arguably came with a much lower risk profile as these portfolios, unlike many mainstream ones, are more prepared for the potential of an environmentally changed future. Those funds that invest in a dual manner, both mitigating risk and seeking opportunity at the same time, have been outperforming most significantly of all.

A prime example of a successful fund that has been driving ahead on a sustainable investing approach for an extended period of time is the Winslow Green Growth Fund. The fund:

> ... *seeks to invest in small growth companies that have a positive or neutral impact on the environment. Portfolio companies are subjected to both financial and environmental analysis as part of the investment decision-making process. Many portfolio companies are in the business of developing environmental solutions; examples include companies in the organic food industry, or companies within the renewable energy sector.* (Winslow Management, www.winslowgreen.com/fund/default.aspx)

Managed out of Boston since 1994 primarily by Jack Robinson, the fund has maintained a consistent management style, and Winslow Green has frequently outperformed its industry peers and benchmarks. In 2007, Jack was voted second among all aggressive growth managers regardless of whether they invest in a sustainable manner or not by Barron's/Value Line. The fund recently had a five-star Morningstar rating and fully delivered 27.4 per cent average returns from 2003 to 2007. If US$10,000 had been invested at inception in 1994, it would have been worth almost US$100,000 at the end of 2007.

A similar European story to Winslow Green is the Jupiter Ecology Fund, which TrustNet recently found to be the top UK 'ethical' performer over the last three years. However, Jupiter Ecology was, in fact, established 20 years ago as the first UK SRI fund that went beyond ethical factors to invest with sustainability goals at its core. These investment objectives, combined with a stable approach, have paid off well. Initiated by Derek Childs and Tessa Tennant, whose thoughts are featured later in the book, and managed by Charlie Thomas since 2003, the fund's investments must meet both financial minimum thresholds, as well as fit six environmental themes. Jupiter Ecology has outperformed consistently over the course of the last five years to the end of 2007 to the benefit of both its retail and institutional clientele alike.

There are quite a few other examples of this successful dual approach globally, including those promoted and managed by Sarasin, the Orange SeNSe Fund and many others, and it cannot be argued that these results were unanticipated. In his industry standard *Socially Responsible Investment: A Global Revolution*, published right at the start of our study, Russell Sparkes contended that:

> *Traditionally, people working within financial markets have tended to be sceptical about the need to move towards sustainability. However, such people, even if they are personally dubious about the threat from global warning, should note that the combination of consumer pressure and government action implies major consequences for the operation of financial markets. There may be significant downside risks in some areas, but there are also likely to be great opportunities for financial practitioners who are able to exploit emerging new financial markets. Examples of potentially attractive new businesses include renewable energy, emissions trading, corporate environmental evaluation and pollution liability risk assessment.* (Sparkes, 2002)

Sparkes further went on to cite examples of leading public funds involved in renewable energy investing, including Merrill Lynch IIF New Energy and Impax Environmental Markets funds, launched earlier this decade. Over the last five years, these have been among the very strongest performers of all. Our study found that funds which focus solely on such 'clean growth' opportunities returned an average 22.9 per cent over the five-year period we studied.

Table 2.3 *The companies most owned by sustainable investing practitioners*

Company	Country	Sector	Description
Abengoa	Spain	Industrial	Abengoa applies innovative solutions for sustainable development in the infrastructure, environment and bioenergy sectors.
Aviva	UK	Insurance	Aviva is the world's fifth-largest insurance group, with a leading position in SRI funds and a group-wide corporate social responsibility (CSR) policy.
British Telecom (BT)	UK	Telecom services	BT is one of the world's leading providers of communications services, operating in 170 countries with long-standing commitment to sustainability.
Canadian Hydro	Canada	Energy	Canadian Hydro is Canada's premier independent developer of EcoLogo® certified low-impact renewable energy.
Canon	Japan	Electronics	Canon is a major producer of electronic equipment and is driven by its kyosei philosophy: 'all people harmoniously living and working together into the future'.
Conergy	Germany	Energy	Conergy is a leading European solar enterprise.
Gamesa	Spain	Energy	Gamesa specializes in sustainable energy technologies, mainly wind power, with 15% of the global market in 2007.
Geberit	Switzerland	Sanitation technology	Geberit is the European market leader in sanitation technology with a focus on water conservation.
ING	The Netherlands	Insurance	ING is a global financial services group, with a focus on the development of sustainable products and services.
Itron	US	Utilities technology	Itron is a leading provider of metering technology that improves the efficiency of energy and water use.
Nokia	Finland	Telecoms equipment	Nokia is the world's leading mobile communications group, with a commitment to environmental leadership.
Novozymes	Denmark	Biotech	Novozymes is the world leader in bio-innovation, and its products contribute to saving considerable amounts of raw materials, energy, water and/or chemicals.
SolarWorld	Germany	Energy	SolarWorld is an integrated solar technology company that takes economic, ecological and social factors into consideration on an equal footing.
Veolia Environnement	France	Environmental services	Veolia Environnement is the world leader in environmental services, with interests in water, waste, energy services and public transport.
Vestas	Denmark	Energy	Vestas is the world's leading producer of wind turbines with a 23% market share in 2007.

Source: Cary Krosinsky, using fund company websites and public disclosures websites such as www.sec.gov, compiled April and May 2008.

Looking a bit more closely at funds with a sustainable investing approach over the last five years, it is interesting to examine what companies these funds own in common in order to get a gauge of what a 'most sustainable' company looks like. In Table 2.3, these companies represent the most commonly held companies from an independent review of the ownership of these funds, and represent an equal weighted consensus view of these sustainability-minded managers.

All of the above have been cited either for their advanced technologies, which aim to capitalize on the apparently changing world before us, or for their efforts at building maximum efficiencies in traditional sectors. Slightly further down the list are other companies that many will recognize, such as Allianz, BG Group and Philips Electronics – companies in traditional industries being recognized for positioning themselves competitively for the future.

THE IMPORTANCE OF TIME HORIZONS

Another critical dimension to sustainable investing is time horizon. Looking at the funds analysed in the study, those with the lowest turnover performed best (see Figure 2.1). Turnover is the average period of time in which a fund completely changes its holdings. For example, a high turnover would mean that the fund in question changed its entire portfolio at least once over the course of a year. 'Low' indicates a portfolio that makes infrequent changes within the

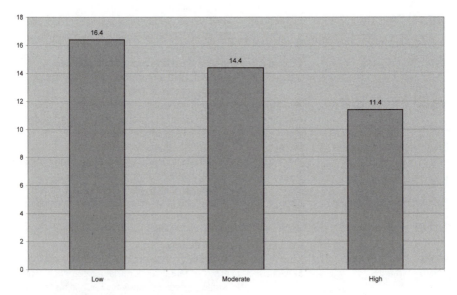

Note: Average five-year return of studied funds by turnover range.
Source: Cary Krosinsky, using fund company websites and public disclosures websites such as www.sec.gov, compiled April and May 2008.

Figure 2.1 *Average five-year return (per cent) of studied funds by turnover range*

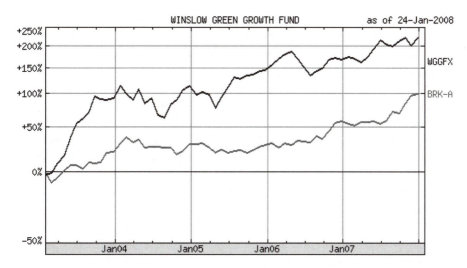

Source: Yahoo! Finance

Figure 2.2 *Winslow versus Warren Buffett*

course of a year, and that such portfolios might take three to five years to completely 'turn over'. Performance drops unambiguously as turnover increases on a directly sliding scale.

Interestingly, a higher percentage of sustainable investing funds had a low turnover (76 per cent of such funds), as opposed to their purely ethical peers (only 49 per cent). The combination of the potential *alpha* gained from a sustainability tilt along with a long-term time horizon serves to create the potential for a Warren Buffett of Sustainable Investing, and the more skilled and experienced sustainable investors have already been outperforming as demonstrated.

Looking back at the Winslow Green Growth Fund once more, it has significantly outperformed even the Oracle of Omaha himself (see Figure 2.2). Over the five years to the end of 2007, Berkshire Hathaway has increased by a nice 100 per cent, while the Winslow Green Growth Fund has seen over 200 per cent growth, over double the performance of Buffett's holding company.

WHAT'S HOLDING BACK THE MAINSTREAM?

These results are reflected in the investment marketplace, where a clear shift is under way from ethical and socially responsible approaches towards sustainable investing. For example, in 2005, Henderson Global Investors in the UK re-launched its ten-year-old ethical fund as the Industries of the Future Fund, a multi-thematic sustainability growth fund. And in 2006, Pax World in the US moved away from its long-standing zero-tolerance approach to ethical investment, heralding the adoption of a sustainable investing strategy. In

Chapter 3, Julie Fox Gorte outlines the rationale for Pax World's move. Many more classic SRI funds are likely to follow a similar path. But a much wider question is whether or when the investment mainstream will be drawn to this potential for superior returns, while keeping risk at bay.

It is time for strategic reflection on the state of the investment management industry. The total value of global equity continues to soar and the trend is clear – more potential influence is held by institutional investors owning the world's largest companies, and there is also more of a stake in this for the ultimate beneficial owners of this equity. Overall, in 2005, institutional ownership accounted for 67.9 per cent of the largest 1000 global companies, up from 61.4 per cent in 2000 (Conference Board, 2007). All of these investors, in theory, should share in the desire to outperform while mitigating as much risk as possible. Given the success of sustainable investing practices, and the predominance of institutional investors today owning global public companies, it is perhaps surprising that the largest global investors continue to pay little heed to sustainable investing. Why have so many mainstream investors and asset owners failed to factor this more fully into their allocations? Old, staid ways of thinking? Perhaps they simply aren't aware that there is money to be made. Perhaps they are unwilling to invest in the necessary skills. Sustainable investing can outperform, but it needs to be achieved through diligent, extensive research and careful consideration, and it requires breaking down old patterns of behaviour.

Some of the largest investment institutions, such as Barclays and State Street, have started to build expertise and offer relatively small but growing SRI portfolio options. However, the majority of their equity is invested directly against mainstream indices such as the S&P 500 and FTSE 100, which, by definition, are neutral to sustainability measures. The rest of the top global institutions include the likes of Fidelity Investments and the Vanguard Group, where the vast bulk of investment is housed in mutual funds that have never taken any approach towards sustainability factors.

Most individual investors engage in equity investment via their retirement accounts – 401(k) plans in the US, individual savings accounts (ISAs) and pension funds in the UK, and similar structures globally. Of the US$4.1 trillion in mutual fund retirement assets held in individual retirement accounts (IRAs), 401(k) plans and other retirement accounts at year end 2006, US$2.8 trillion, or 70 per cent, were invested in domestic or foreign equity (ICI Investment, 2007). And there are growing incentives to leave such retirement funds static. Investors in the US are usually penalized for short-term selling of fund shares recently purchased. For this and other reasons, retirement investments have, on average, a lower turnover. Sustainable strategies are infrequently available to such plan members, meaning that much US equity investment is locked into programmes without any sustainability-minded option whatsoever. For example, at the time of this writing, Fidelity does not manage any SRI funds whatsoever, let alone one with a sustainable focus. Vanguard themselves oversee only one SRI portfolio, the Vanguard FTSE Social Index Fund, which invests in US stocks only. At present, among this fund's top ten holdings are McDonald's and Disney. Given that European companies (see Table 2.3) have often been leaders in sustainability, limiting 401(k) participants to a US-only option is questionable.

Currently, just under 20 per cent of defined contribution (DC) pension plans in the US include an SRI option (generally of the ethical variety). However, a Mercer survey from 2007 suggests that a further 41 per cent of all DC plan sponsors expect to be offering a SRI option within the next three years. This would translate to 60 per cent market penetration for SRI options in DC retirement plans by 2010 (Mercer and Social Investment Forum, 2007). If this welcome advance is to benefit both plan beneficiaries and the planet, then careful scrutiny will be required to ensure that integrated sustainable investing strategies are selected.

It is now imperative that interested retirement participants insist on more sustainability-minded options. If a large enough percentage of US investors demanded such choices, a dynamic could be generated that would encourage companies to improve their management of sustainability risks and opportunities, or risk being dropped by such funds. Without this demand for sustainable investing, there exists, in effect, a large, unwittingly passive block of equity ownership, preventing progress towards what could be the most efficient possible corporate behaviour. In the UK, pension funds are the largest similar actors, but in many cases are managed by trustees not focused on sustainability. One notable and positive exception would be the responsibility overlay strategy deployed by the UK Environment Agency, who actively encourages its appointed fund managers to behave in a sustainable manner (Krosinsky, 2007).

CONCLUSION

Of course, no two sustainable portfolios or approaches will give identical results, nor should they. As with any portfolio or allocation decision, there will be differences of opinion, and quality managers are paid to provide the best advice they can give. No matter the strategy, no matter the past performance, there can be no guarantee of future success, whether via mainstream strategies, hedge fund investing or attempting to invest in the most sustainable manner possible. The question is how to best position yourself for the changed future that now seems inevitable. Many long-term investors have obtained a false sense of security about equity markets and investing, in general, based on a combination of myth, perceived past performance and a desire for a sense of comfort. As mentioned, many global mutual funds, large governmental and corporate pension funds and insurance portfolios are often positioned in a passive fashion against benchmark mainstream indices, such as the S&P 500, FTSE 100 and the MSCI World. These have been reasonably safe and effective ways of deploying equity strategies in the past. Looking forward, though, it is less clear that flat index investing will be successful in the coming decades. The world is changing rapidly, and long-term investors now need to at least start to consider many new and potentially hard-to-quantify dynamics. Given the outperformance of sustainable investing that we have demonstrated, that time is not only now, but was apparently already the case years ago.

REFERENCES

Conference Board (2007) *The 2007 Institutional Investment Report*, www.conference-board.org/utilities/pressDetail.cfm?press_ID=3046, accessed 12 May 2008

Eurosif (2006) *European SRI Study*, Eurosif, Paris, France

Graziadio Business Report (2007) *The Moral and Financial Conflict of Socially Responsible Investing*, Pepperdine University, Graziadio School of Business and Management, vol 10, issue 1, http://gbr.pepperdine.edu/071/sri.html, accessed 12 May 2008

Hamilton, S., Jo, H. and Statman, M. (1993) *Doing Well While Doing Good? The Investment Performance of Socially Responsible Mutual Funds*, www.pensionsatwork.ca/english/pdfs/scholarly_works/sw_edition3/HamJoStat.pdf

Hong, H. and Kacperczyk, M. (2006) *The Price of Sin: The Effects on Social Norms on Markets*, Princeton University, Princeton, NJ

ICI Investment (2007) *ICI Investment Company Factbook*, www.ici.org/statements/res/2007_factbook.pdf, accessed 12 May 2008

Jewson, E. (2008) 'The costs of ethical investing', *Investment Week*, 21 April

Krosinsky, C. (2007) 'Shifting Tides', *IR Magazine*, December, www.thecrossborder group.com/ir_archive/pages/1657/December+2007.stm?article_id=12274, accessed 12 May 2008

Mercer and Social Investment Forum (2007) *Defined Contribution Plans and Socially Responsible Investing in the United States*, Mercer and Social Investment Forum, www.calvert.com/pdf/mercer-survey.pdf, June

Sparkes, R. (2002) *Socially Responsible Investment: A Global Revolution*, John Wiley & Sons, Chichester, UK

Tyrrell, M. J. and Brown, M. (2007) *Crossing the River II*, Citigroup, London, 5 January

UNEP FI (United Nations Environment Programme's Finance Initiative) (2007) *Demystifying Responsible Investment Performance*, UNEP FI, Geneva, Switzerland, www.unepfi.org/fileadmin/documents/Demystifying_Responsible_Investment_Performance_01/pdf, accessed 12 May 2008

US SIF (Social Investment Forum) (2007) *Report on Socially Responsible Investing Trends in the United States*, SIF, Washington, DC

Investors: A Force for Sustainability

Julie Fox Gorte

There may well be no truly sustainable company on Earth at the moment. That may sound like a daunting statement. However, in aggregate, we are dipping into the Earth's endowment of useful resources, drawing down the capital of minerals, fuels, fertile soil, clean water, and fresh air. It is essential, therefore, not only for investors, but for mankind, that we learn how to operate within that carrying capacity, and that will require the efforts of everyone – communities, families, corporations: everyone. Being a large part of the equation, it is essential to change the behaviour of corporations. Centuries ago, no matter how powerful the corporation, it was difficult to have a truly global impact. Today, it is difficult not to. Turning on the lights, using a computer, driving a car, even eating dinner puts all of us at the end of a long supply chain that emits greenhouse gases and air pollution, spreads pesticides and persistent organic pollutants as far as the Arctic circle, and strains a freshwater system that puts nearly half the world's population at risk of serious water shortages.

Happily, there has never been greater interest in corporate sustainability than there is now. In addition, investors are becoming a more significant force in driving sustainability. Sustainable investing is a new style of investment, led by investors such as Generation and Pax World, which relates the concept of sustainable development to financial prosperity seamlessly. Sustainable and responsible investing (SRI) has been around, in a wide variety of forms, for over three decades. Many of these funds were shaped initially by the concerns of faith-based investors, whose objections to certain activities such as the use of alcohol and tobacco, gaming, and armed conflict to settle differences led them to create screens that eliminated corporations involved in tobacco, alcohol, gaming and weapons from their portfolios, and these will probably retain their niche in the market.

Whatever the fate of SRI, it is not the same as sustainable investment (Keefe, 2007). The single most important distinction is that sustainable investment has a strong underlying premise – that sustainably managed enterprises are better able to add value over the long run – which makes sense in the context of investment. Social responsibility is most often defined in the context of values; the tag line 'invest with your values' usually comes up one way or another in most related presentations. No matter how 'values' are stitched together with investment, the seam always shows. Whose values matter? Many would define the 'values' of socially responsible investors as liberal or progressive: pro-workers' rights, pro-environment, anti-nuclear and so on. But the roots of such investing methodologies were in the values of faith, which tended to view smoking and drinking as tools of the devil. But other faith-based values, such as pro- or anti-abortion, have been more of a third rail, and still others, such as protection of the rights of gay, lesbian, bisexual and transsexual employees, are embraced in some funds and shunned by others. But if SRI is about investing with values, then why wouldn't a fund that invests with the 'value' of 'the purpose of business is business' and the right to keep and bear arms be considered responsible? In short, there is no encompassing *financial* discipline or deep logic to social responsibility. Sustainability, on the other hand, is transparent and makes financial sense: companies that have lighter footprints and treat people and communities with respect aren't painting targets on their chests for regulators or activists, or spending profits that could otherwise be used for reinvestment (improved share price) or disbursal (dividends) defending lawsuits and paying fines.

Moreover, sustainable investing is defined positively by seeking to invest in companies whose practices and policies include sustainability goals, where classic SRI was often defined negatively by what industries or companies were excluded. Such defensive investment behaviour has been performed not because its practitioners wished to be negative, but because they were often painted into that corner by the disciples of modern portfolio theory, who hold that by excluding parts of the investment universe it cannot (theoretically) be possible to construct the most efficient portfolios. Sustainable investment seeks outperformance by investing in companies with the greatest fidelity to *long-term* drivers of outperformance, or superior sustainability. The growing investor interest in sustainability is usually the scion of growing awareness of risks to brand, new market requirements and the forces of competition.

The value of a corporate brand, or a reputation, has never been greater. According to a recent white paper from the Economist Intelligence Unit, reputation is widely viewed as a major source of competitive advantage, a key corporate asset – and one of the most difficult assets to protect (Economist Intelligence Unit, 2005). An earlier survey by Templeton College reported that 85 per cent of all respondents believed that their brand was their most important asset, growing in importance even as straight price-based competition has waned

(Knight and Pretty, 2000). As the value of intangible assets of all types captures an ever larger share of the average value of the publicly traded company, the financial importance of brand, reputation or any other factor that embodies the concept of *trust* has increased in tandem. But public trust in business is low. A June 2007 Gallup poll, for instance, reports than only 7 per cent of US adults have 'a great deal' of confidence in big business, while 38 per cent reported that they have 'very little' confidence. With so many people apparently mistrustful of business, it is little wonder that the lion's share – 84 per cent – of respondents to the Economist's survey in 2005 reported that reputational risks had increased significantly since 2000, a more significant threat to business than any other type or risk identified (Economist Intelligence Unit, 2005, pp2–6).[1]

It is no surprise, then, that the number of companies reporting on their sustainability, and taking action to improve it, has gone up. The days when it was possible to create a warm and fuzzy feeling about corporate sustainability through talk and spin alone are numbered. As an important contributor to intangible value, reputation and the social licence to operate have become an important factor for sustainability analysis and engagement.

The increasing power of sustainability to shape corporate, regulatory and investor strategy is illustrated by the rapidly changing agenda related to climate change and, specifically, coal-fired power stations in the US. The Kyoto Protocol was agreed in late 1997 and entered into force in February 2005, when Russia's ratification meant that countries representing at least 55 per cent of 1990 emissions had ratified the proposed treaty. As of 2007, 174 countries or governmental entities had ratified the protocol, with the US being the lone major holdout against ratification. Even without US federal action or ratification, however, the momentum for regulating greenhouse gas (GHG) emissions has grown stronger as state governments move forward with regulatory schemes. Seven northeastern and mid-Atlantic states established the Northeast Regional Greenhouse Gas Initiative (RGGI) in 2005, committing to establish a cap-and-trade system to regulate carbon dioxide emissions from power plants. Since then, three more states have joined RGGI. In 2006, the governors of Arizona and New Mexico agreed to create the Southwest Climate Change Initiative, aimed at reducing greenhouse gas emissions and addressing the impacts of climate change in the US Southwest. In 2007, the governors of California, Arizona, New Mexico, Oregon, and Washington created the Western Climate Initiative, and shortly after its creation Utah, Manitoba and British Columbia joined. California recently announced its intention to sue the Environmental Protection Agency for denying the state a waiver to establish a state programme limiting GHG emissions from cars, trucks, and SUVs that would be stronger than federal requirements. Early in 2008, California did just what it promised, filing a lawsuit in the federal court challenging the Bush administration's refusal to allow it to regulate vehicular emissions of greenhouse gases. Moreover, California was joined by 15 other states and 5 environmental groups (Egelko, 2008).

These are only some of the moves being made to establish a regulatory regime governing emissions of greenhouse gases in the US, and all of this ratchets up the pressure for national regulation. It is now a common expectation of Wall Street analysts that national regulation is coming. Goldman Sachs's 2007 utilities report states: 'We believe US carbon emissions legislation is likely, but no earlier than 2009 and with regulations that contain a ceiling on emissions costs' (Goldman Sachs, 2007, p4). JPMorgan Chase agrees: 'Given the recent sharp increase in rhetoric surrounding greenhouse gas emissions, we believe some form of national greenhouse gas emissions limits are likely in the next 12 to 24 months' (JPMorgan Chase, 2007). In December 2007, for the first time, a bill requiring national cuts in GHG emissions passed in a senate committee vote (Myers, 2007). Since financial markets price what investors believe will happen *in the future*, the expectation of a stronger emissions regulatory regime in the US has created a sense that high emissions represent a liability, and carbon efficiency or low-emissions technologies should be a competitive advantage. Exactly how much of an advantage or a liability is unknown – markets have a great deal of trouble pricing risks (or opportunities) that are non-linear, and a major change in a regulatory regime is a poster child for non-linearity. But the direction of the impending change is all but certain, and the corporate response has been strong. AEP, one of the largest emitters of greenhouse gases through its many coal-fired power plants, has become a leader in calling for national regulation of greenhouse gases, working to develop low-emission technologies for coal power, and developing technologies for carbon capture and sequestration. Five years ago, it was rare to see a company sustainability report with greenhouse gas emissions reported in the US; now it is rare to see one that does not.

Coal is the dirtiest of all the fossil fuels, in terms of the environmental consequences of its combustion: it emits more air pollution and carbon dioxide than any other fossil fuel. But until the last year or two, the greenhouse gas emissions of coal plants were treated as unfortunate but not deal-killing footnotes by most power regulators and utilities, and most of the opposition to coal plants came from environmental groups. As the consequences of climate change grew more apparent, however, public utility commissions, investors, citizens and utilities themselves have joined with environmentalists in seeing coal not as a secure supply of fuel for producing electricity, but as a long-term source of emissions that can have profoundly jarring effects on the economy and on society.

The first drama in the story of changing attitudes towards coal-fired power came in early 2007, when the publicly traded Texas utility TXU announced that it had accepted a takeover bid from Kolhberg Kravis Roberts to go private. For the first time, part of the negotiations in the buyout were over emissions, and the environmental group Natural Resources Defense Council had participated in confidential discussions with KKR over the purchase. The utility had proposed to build 11 new coal-fired power plants, and that decision had created a controversy large enough to affect the stock price:

> *Within TXU, the controversial plan to build a raft of coal plants had become so damaging to its stock price that its board had been privately weighing a plan to scrap part of the project, said people involved in the talks, bringing the number of new plants to 5 or 6 from 11. Shareholders had sent the stock on a roller coaster ride from more than US$67 a share to as low as about US$53 over concerns about the risk and vast expenditure; the stock closed at US$60.02 on Friday.* (Ross Sorkin, 2007)

As a result of the buyout, the company's new owners agreed to scrap plans for 8 of the 11 proposed new plants, and put former Environmental Protection Agency (EPA) administrator William Reilly on the board.

The next chapter was written in the unlikely state of Kansas. In October 2007, the state's Department of Health and Environment refused to issue a permit for a proposed new coal plant, citing carbon dioxide emissions. But even before October, financial analysts were seeing handwriting on the wall. An April report from Goldman Sachs stated:

> *Government statistics highlight about 68GW in new coal powered plants in development and expected to come online in 2009–2015, while we expect about 31GW... For various reasons, we believe many of the announced potential coal plants will not actually be built. The National Energy Technology Laboratory (NETL) forecast, a 68GW new-build of coal-fired power plants, is too aggressive in our view, due to costs/financing issues and concerns regarding environmental ramifications. On the latter, some concerns are a function of popular displeasure with potential pollution increases (we believe this was a major influence in Texas) as well as state government opposition (Illinois and Pennsylvania).* (Goldman Sachs, 2007)

Investors themselves are important catalysts for change as amply demonstrated by the long histories of advocacy on governance issues by TIAA–CREF and CalPERS, among others. Religious and social investors have also often led efforts to improve corporate performance and policy on social and environmental scales, as well as corporate governance. The Interfaith Center for Corporate Responsibility (ICCR) tracked 306 shareholder proposals filed with 205 companies in the 2006 to 2007 shareholder season, up from 285 resolutions on 84 corporations two seasons earlier (2004 to 2005). Resolutions ranged from fairly standard governance matters such as declassifying boards and separating the board chair role from that of the chief executive officer (CEO), to social resolutions such as curtailing violence in video games, sustainability reporting and emissions reduction. According to ICCR's account, nearly 40 per cent of the resolutions filed in the 2004 to 2005 season were withdrawn, meaning that the filers were able to reach some kind of agreement with the target company after negotiation.

Many investors now choose to engage and negotiate with companies whose stock they own on matters ranging from narrowly defined corporate governance to public policy to environmental, social and governance (ESG) performance and policy. In one study of CREF's engagement activities, the authors found that CREF was able to reach agreement with management in more than 70 per cent of the cases in which the large institutional investor attempted to influence management (Carleton et al, 1998). My own experience in engagement with corporate management on governance and ESG issues is peppered with examples of successful encouragement of corporations to improve their performance and/or policies governing social or environmental conduct. Where shareholders and management reach agreement privately, there are many winners: improved company performance benefits not only the companies but their shareholders. Academic studies of the impact of shareholder engagement reach very different conclusions on whether engagement or advocacy is effective at improving financial performance, at least with regard to governance-related advocacy. Limitations of method may account for this: for the most part such studies are almost invariably confined to a relatively modest subset of all engagements, and most employ the event-study method, which may not be the best tool for judging the impact of shareholder pressure (see Hawley and Williams, 2000). Even in cases where event studies or other academic techniques do not find an increase in shareholder wealth, however, it is clear that quiet engagement can be effective at changing corporate behaviour or policy, or both.

Competition can also be a powerful force for change of any kind. We are accustomed to thinking of competition as forcing a race to the bottom when the topic is sustainability, and there are many instances where this truth is painfully apparent. In many manufacturing industries where assembly operations do not require greatly skilled labour (e.g. apparel, footwear and toys), it has become nearly impossible to remain competitive without joining the rush to low-wage countries for a labour force. But competition can work the other way as well. When Home Depot announced its intention to curtail purchases of wood sourced from ancient forests, Lowe's followed with a similar initiative a year later (Socialfunds.com, 2000). Office Depot announced its own environmental initiatives about 16 months after Staples came out with its first environmental initiatives (*Forest Ethics*, 2004). Nike's publication of the names of its contract supplier facilities came on the heels of Gap's groundbreaking sustainability report.

Investor interest in sustainability solutions is also driven by competition. Alternative energy has become one of the largest categories of venture capital, and Morgan Stanley announced a new green energy index in August 2007, the latest in a growing list of clean financial indices that includes the S&P Global Clean Energy Index, the WilderHill Clean Energy Global Innovation Index, the

NASDAQ Clean Edge US Index, and the KLD Global Climate 100 Index (Moore Odell, 2007). Even the hedge funds have started dipping toes in the waters; Arch Investment Group began marketing an absolute return fund based on long-term environmental, infrastructural and socio-economic themes during the summer of 2007 (McIntosh, 2007).

What differentiates today's leading corporate sustainability programmes is the integration with corporate strategy, which is why investors are increasingly interested in the links with long-term value creation. Instead of taking an environmental step or inventing a social programme to burnish an image or satisfy a philanthropic impulse, much of what corporations are doing in sustainability today is driven by competition. Dow Chemical's CEO, Andrew N. Lewis, states that: 'There is 100 per cent overlap between our business drivers and social and environmental interests', and this is backed up by the evidence: Dow is ploughing money into R&D on initiatives such as solar power and wastewater treatment, as well as working to reduce its own environmental footprint (energy intensity and environmental emissions), which the company estimates will create value of US$3 billion to US$5 billion (and cost an estimated US$1 billion) (see the Dow Chemical website, www.dow.com/commitments/stewardship/case.htm, accessed 28 August 2007. Likewise, Chad Holliday, CEO of DuPont, states:

> *In the 1970s and 1980s, our focus was on internal safety and meeting environmental regulations. In the late 1980s and 1990s, we added voluntary footprint reductions, going beyond regulatory requirements. We looked to increase shareholder value with a goal of zero safety and environmental incidents as we decreased raw material and energy inputs into our products and reduced emissions at our manufacturing sites. Now we see ourselves in a third phase of sustainable growth, characterized by a holistic approach that is fully integrated into our business models. In this phase, sustainability is broadened to include human safety as well as environmental protection, and it becomes our market-driven business priority throughout the value chain. The transition to products that meet the definition of 'sustainable' will take place over time, for DuPont as well as for other companies such as General Electric and Wal-Mart. But the pace will quicken as the synergistic effects of market demand, societal expectations and product innovation create collaborations up and down the value chain. Sustainability will increasingly become central to the total value proposition. This will impact not only our business, but every customer and – through their products – every consumer we touch.* (Holliday, 2006)

Sustainability is still a destination so distant that we don't know exactly what it looks like. The vast majority of the world's energy is taken from altogether unsustainable resources bases such as coal, oil or gas; while experts debate whether oil production has already peaked, emissions from the combustion of all fossil fuels have given us global warming at an unprecedented pace. The Millennium Ecosystem Assessment points out that 25 per cent of the world's coral reefs and 35 per cent of its mangrove stands have been lost since 1980, together with their ability to help protect coastal inhabitants from storms. Half the synthetic nitrogen fertilizer ever made has been used in the last 20 years, contributing to nitrate concentrations in rivers and lakes that can result in dead zones: areas where marine life cannot survive. The assessment warns starkly:

> *A large and growing number of people are at high risk of adverse ecosystem changes. The world is experiencing a worsening trend of human suffering and economic losses from natural disasters. Over the past four decades, for example, the number of weather-related disasters affecting at least 1 million people has increased fourfold, while economic losses have increased tenfold. The greatest loss of life has been concentrated in developing countries. Ecosystem transformation has played a significant, but not exclusive, role in increasing the vulnerability of people to such disasters. Examples are the increased susceptibility of coastal populations to tropical storms when mangrove forests are cleared and the increase in downstream flooding that followed land-use changes in the upper Yangtze River.* (Hassan et al, 2005, p2)

In order for our species to live sustainably on Earth, we will have to change our behaviour far more deeply than we have. In order to stabilize the climate, for example, emissions of greenhouse gases must be reduced *70 per cent* below the levels of 1990 – a profoundly greater step than the 5 to 8 per cent reductions called for in the first commitment period of the Kyoto Protocol (Flannery, 2005). Restoring damaged coral reefs, collapsed ocean fisheries or high-graded forests will take decades, if not centuries.

So, while it is clearly possible to change corporate behaviour and graft sustainability onto corporate strategies, the pace must pick up in order to avoid some of the more dire outcomes of continuing to run through our resource endowments as quickly as we are now. There is reason for hope, mainly because the new wave of business consciousness of sustainability is more strategic than philanthropic. But we must also be conscious of thresholds: milestones that mark the outer boundaries of reversible changes. As we grow to understand many of the systems that govern life on Earth, we have become aware of more of the so-called tipping points, or places where changes become irreversible, and the effects may be abrupt or profound enough to be calamitous. In earlier eras, some forms of business that were regarded as permissible, or at least possible, are now beyond the pale: for example, most companies no longer engage in slavery or do not admit it if they do. Similarly, we must get to the point where corporate operations routinely consider the impacts upon the planet and communities and supply chains, and take steps to maximize the benefit and minimize the harm.

Investors have a unique role to play in shifting the engine of commerce into sustainability gear. For far too long, the attitude of many business people – and, indeed, still the attitude of many foundation and endowment trustees – is that one should do whatever is necessary to make money and then, if one is interested in sustainability, donate one's profits or income to organizations whose missions encompass environmental impact or diversity or human rights. But this is a strategy doomed to failure if sustainable business is the goal. For decades, the average profit margin in the US hovered around 8 per cent. The simple arithmetic of this is that the amount corporations and investors have to spend on saving the planet is less than 10 per cent of what they spend to get that power, which is largely responsible for creating the problems in the first place. We have shown that we are capable of transforming our planet; but we are accustomed, over the centuries of human habitation on Earth, to thinking that our transformations all (or mostly) make things *better* for us. But we may also be at the threshold of a transformation that makes things profoundly worse, at least for the two or three generations whose faces we will see during our allotted spans.

In short, climate change, as well as the many inequities and damages caused by pursuing commerce as we know it, is a black swan, an occurrence that we have never experienced and many people cannot even imagine (and are determined not to imagine, through denial). If we wish to avoid this outcome, we have in our solutions toolkit a tool whose power is largely untested: the power of owners. Investors never speak with a single voice; but the markets turn the millions of decisions and preferences expressed by investors into a set of statistics (price, volatility, etc.) that represent an average, if not a consensus, of how investors feel about corporate management. The number of investors who care about sustainability is growing, as indicated by higher votes for sustainability-oriented shareholder resolutions and the increase in assets in all of the various socially responsible asset classes, as well as the growing interest and participation of institutional investors in coalitions such as the Carbon Disclosure Project and the Principles for Responsible Investment. Investors are capable of creating a sustainability revolution, and there are signs that many – though not enough – are already aboard. Imagine what could happen if most investors saw sustainability as an indicator of good management. This Sustainability Revolution in investment thinking is under way – the only question is whether it can grow fast enough to avoid the unmanageable consequences of unsustainable operations.

NOTE

1 Other risks included regulatory risk, human capital risks, information technology (IT) network risk, market risk, credit risk, country risk, financing risk, terrorism, foreign exchange risk, natural hazards, political risks and crime/physical security.

REFERENCES

Carleton, W. T., Nelson, J. M. and Weisbach, N. S. (1998) 'The influence of institutions on corporate governance through private negotiations: Evidence from TIAA-CREF,' *Journal of Finance*, vol 53, p4

Economist Intelligence Unit (2005) *Reputation: Risk of Risks*, Economist Intelligence Unit, London, December

Egelko, B. (2008) 'State sues EPA to force waiver over greenhouse gas emissions,' *San Francisco Chronicle*, Thursday, 3 January

Flannery, T. (2995) *The Weather Makers*, Grove Press, New York, NY, p168

Forest Ethics (2004) 'Office depot agrees to endangered forest and recycling policy – environmental campaign against the company ends,' *Forest Ethics*, 25 March

Goldman Sachs (2007) *Americas: Energy*, Goldman Sachs, 9 April

Hassan, R., Scholes, R. and Ash, N. (2005) *Ecosystems and Human Well-Being: Current State and Trends, Vol 1*, UN Millennium Ecosystem Assessment, Island Press, Washington, DC, p2

Hawley, J. P. and Williams, A. T. (2000) *The Rise of Fiduciary Capitalism: How Institutional Investors Can Make Corporate America More Democratic*, University of Pennsylvania Press, Philadelphia, pp110–123

Holliday, C. (2006) 'An expanded commitment', www2.dupont.com/Sustainability/en_US/Newsroom/speeches/coh_101006.html, accessed 12 May 2008

JPMorgan Chase (2007) *Global Utilities – Trading Climate Change*, issue 1, 5 March

Keefe, J. F. (2007) 'From SRI to sustainable investing,' *Green Money Journal*, summer, www.ens-newswire.com/ens/aug2007/2007-08-06-03.asp

Knight, R. F. and Pretty, D. J. (2000) *Brand Risk Management in a Value Context*, Templeton Briefing sponsored by Marsh, June

McIntosh, B. (2007) 'Arch investment launches sustainable finance fund', HedgeWorld.com, 27 July

Moore Odell, A. (2007) 'Merrill Lynch offers new energy efficiency index', Socialfunds.com, 8 August

Myers, J. (2007) 'Bill would set aside billions for conservation', *Duluth News-Tribune*, 7 December

Ross Sorkin, A. (2007) 'A buyout deal that has many shades of green,' *New York Times*, 26 February

Socialfunds.com (2000) 'Lowe's launches forest protection initiative,' Socialfunds.com, 11 August.

4

Sustainability Analysis

Valery Lucas-Leclin and Sarbjit Nahal

A key question, in our view, is determining the underlying purpose of sustainability analysis. We propose to do this first by briefly reviewing the current state of sustainable and responsible investing (SRI) before moving on to consider the potential for sustainability to contribute to mainstream financial analysis. We will then investigate one possible way of integrating sustainability within mainstream analysis – as a factor modulating the risk premium used in dynamic valuation models, such as discounted cash flow. We believe that a financial basics-centred approach – notably an approach that focuses on calculating beta, or β, can provide a basis for the risk assessment of the long-term sustainability of companies.

THE HISTORY OF SRI ANALYSIS

Looking at the growth of SRI in France, the seeds were spread for the first time in 1997 when Geneviève Ferone founded Arèse (the first French SRI rating agency) with the support of Caisse des Dépôts et Consignations (CDC) and Caisse d'Epargne, and the conviction that it was only a matter of time before all investors would need to become informed on environmental, social and governance (ESG) issues. The evolution of SRI since that time has been remarkable – from one small agency with three junior analysts and a total value of US$75 million in assets under management (AUM), there are today 175 SRI funds available in France with over US$33 billion (end 2007, ex-mandates). There is now a plethora of research and ratings providers, such as Vigeo, as well as a growing body of sell-side teams to service the French buy-side community, with almost all buy-sides – small and large – tackling SRI today in one fashion or another.

The developments and evolution in terms of SRI research and asset management in France have been mirrored across all of the major European markets, and we are seeing growing mainstream interest from the US and Japan as well.

EXTRA-FINANCIAL ISSUES STILL ON THE OUTSKIRTS OF FINANCIAL ANALYSIS

In spite of, or perhaps because of, this rapid growth, the time has come to ask if the borders between SRI and so-called mainstream analysis are still intangible (e.g. is it still worth keeping track of SRI funds, SRI analysts and SRI fund managers?). Fundamentally, the objective of SRI was to add new perspectives and criteria to mainstream analysis, and not to abolish mainstream analysis or to develop sustainability analysis on a stand-alone basis.

This question worth debating is whether it is from a pure marketing standpoint or from a philosophical perspective. On the one hand, one can argue that it is better to have a clearly identified set of funds and research-tagged SRI in order to facilitate client choices. On the other hand, one could also argue that if extra-financial factors have achieved a certain degree of materiality, their true place should be in mainstream financial research.

However a Yalta-like gap exists in the world of SRI research between different actors. For instance, many SRI research and rating agencies still cling to good old corporate social responsibility-influenced analytical frameworks with systematic annual sector reviews and compliance assessments based on best practice standards. In contrast, as brokers working on sustainability, our main task is to try to bring material ESG trends, practices and technologies to the forefront of the mainstream investment picture (whether as opportunities or risks) so that investors can outperform their relative benchmarks. It is, in effect, a permanent race to tackle often yet to be addressed issues that could have an impact in the short to medium term. Such issues include new automobile regulations scheduled in Europe for 2012, carbon capture and storage, green buildings, and the lack of skills in many sectors, among many other issues.

As things stand today, it takes a lot of time and a very strong case to convince the mainstream financial community to consider integrating ESG factors. It can happen in a straightforward manner when risks or accounting rules lead to material provisions on issues such as industrial safety and asbestos. It is much more complicated when analysts have to deal with corporate governance or human resources issues.

INTEREST AND SELF-INTEREST
ON THE SELL SIDE

With regard to day-to-day work at brokerage houses, the frontier between sustainability and the mainstream is not easy to identify. With so many buy-side institutions eager to explore sustainability – and quite busy building up their own credentials in the field – demands vary enormously regarding investment universes, sectors, stocks, themes, criteria, qualitative versus quantitative approaches, financial perspectives, and investment horizons. Sell-side research is very much dependent upon client requests – if the client wants it, 'I'll dance on the table' as one senior colleague once told us when asked his views on sustainability.

But in this sell-side sustainability twilight zone of perhaps not yet material ESG factors, one never knows where and for how long to commit one's efforts. In a typical day, we can look at issues as diverse as calculating our own quantitative sustainability ratings; identifying long-term ESG considerations for the luxury goods sector; identifying the carbon footprint of a car manufacturer; arguing over a utility company's carbon dioxide-derived windfall profits; screening companies with potential involvement in producing cluster bombs; debating the nutritional benefits of a certain range of margarines; and assessing the consequences of the last European Court of Justice ruling on the minimum wage in Germany. And, of course, one must not forget to tailor one's work according to the commission fees paid by clients (always carefully monitored by the client's account manager).

The diverse range of requests is quite informative about the differing priorities of the so-called SRI community. In the long run, most brokers will probably agree that the best sustainability service is one that could be provided by mainstream financial analysts themselves. After all, if ESG factors really turn around financial analysis like Saturn's rings, the best place to analyse them is very likely on Saturn itself.

But we do believe that the day will come when all financial sector analysts will need to know the ESG consequences of the companies that they cover. Financial analysts, especially on the sell side, have an immense knowledge of their sectors and stocks, along with a solid grounding in the quality of their company's management. The reason is very simple – a financial analyst covers a maximum of four to eight stocks and often has as much as 10 or 20 years' experience in doing so. In contrast, many SRI analysts cover up to 50 stocks, with far less experience and an often limited financial background. It does not take a rocket scientist to see that extending ESG issues into a mainstream financial analyst's coverage would be easier and faster. Some recent initiatives by institutional investors (such as the Enhanced Analytics Initiative launched in 2005) are pushing in this direction towards better integration and appropriation by financial analysts.

It seems so obvious that outsiders might wonder why this is not already the norm. It is not so much a lack of necessary training or understanding of ESG criteria that poses the difficulty, but rather the way in which mainstream brokerage is organized. In that vein, brokers are largely organized to provide instant reactions and short-term analysis to corporate moves: the faster the better, as the market immediately integrates information and rewards brokers. In our experience, long-term analysis is almost always sacrificed in favour of short-term profits by both investors and brokers. At the end of the day, the long-term profitability of a broker is largely the result of a short-term profit focus by investors. If long-term investors asked for and rewarded a different kind of research, things would be much easier.

This poses an interesting paradox: is it better to play a long-term stock trend or to anticipate short-term cyclical variations? From a classical broker perspective, the cyclical variations will definitely drive more trading and, thus, superior commissions – self-interest will prevail and the preference will always be for an active buy–sell rotation. For investors, other factors are also at play, especially investment horizons and liquidity.

SUSTAINABILITY RISK ADJUSTMENT OF FINANCIAL VALUATION

If we imagine that investors might really spend more time and energy on long-term issues, it is possible to propose novel ways of integrating ESG issues within financial research. At Société Générale (SG), since 2005, we have proposed a model to integrate sustainability effects within risk assessment. We have based our model on correlations drawn between beta (the market risk factor, or the sensitivity to market reactions) and sustainability ratings as we can infer them from various external recognized sources (namely, sustainability research and rating agencies). We first measured the sustainability financial impact based on the beta variations observed from 2004 to 2006 for a large panel of European companies. Over the past two years, our best rated stocks (A+) have had below-average betas (approximately −8.5 per cent), and our lowest rated stocks have had higher betas (approximately +7.7 per cent). In our view, at the very least, this suggest that there is a 'minimum' sustainability impact at play, notwithstanding any direct positive–negative impacts on sales, brand value, provisions and long-term growth due to new opportunities for active companies.

STAKEHOLDER PRESSURE: IGNORE IT AT YOUR PERIL

Our findings were derived by using the SG *SRI Rating Matrix* report from October 2006 (Société Générale, 2006b), which helped to interpret which part of CSR management might be explained by stakeholder pressure (i.e. industrial sector, size of the company, country of origin, percentage of free float market capitalization, etc.).

In order for companies to reduce the financial risks (i.e. beta) associated with extra-financial issues, management must identify and address *stakeholder pressure*. In our view, stakeholder pressure increases risk, especially for large cap companies. A company's ability to deal with stakeholder pressure is thus a clear proxy for good management. But measuring a standard for stakeholder pressure is also a prerequisite before praising any company for their achievements.

Every company has to deal with stakeholders, whether directly or indirectly. While it is true that a dialogue with stakeholders is already being addressed and pursued by most large cap companies, stakeholder pressure must be interpreted in a broader sense as part of the full range of interactions and constraints that directly and indirectly shape the day-to-day business of any company.

Growing body of stakeholder pressure

We believe that companies face ever-growing stakeholder pressure. Increasingly, this pressure is manifested in the form of different sets of formal and informal rules and standards put forward by a wide range of stakeholders, which include:

* *Legal pressure* – national, regional and international laws and regulations and related jurisprudence, such as the European Union (EU), the Organisation for Economic Co-operation and Development (OECD), the United Nations (UN), the Kyoto Protocol and the Foreign Corrupt Practices Act (FCPA).
* *Professional pressure* – professional and sector guidelines and rules, International Organization for Standardization (ISO) certifications, and widely accepted business practices.
* *Best practice pressure* – non-binding national, regional and international standards and guidelines, such as the Global Compact, the Global Reporting Initiative (GRI), the Carbon Disclosure Project, the Extractive Industries Transparency Initiative, the Equator Principles and Responsible Care.
* *Ethical pressure* – campaigns and pressure applied by stakeholders such as non-governmental organizations (NGOs), local associations, and communities and individuals, as well as the growing force of public opinion (and its long-term influence on legal standards).
* *Investor pressure* – sustainability and mainstream investors' growing interest and activity in long-term extra-financial issues from a risk reduction perspective, such as the Enhanced Analytics Initiative (EAI), the Institutional Investors Group on Climate Change (IIGCC) and the Marathon Club.

QUALITY OF MANAGEMENT IS STILL KEY: LOOK FOR TRACES RATHER THAN CLUES

The most important factor that investors and analysts look at when judging a company is the quality of its management, according to reports such as the 2005 December Investor Relations Society (IRS) report based on MORI research. This factor alone leads all other measures by 34 per cent and was the top criterion for the third year running.

Investors know perfectly well that the bigger the company, the more management can make a difference, leading the way, tightening internal links, providing a clear vision, accelerating change and making sure that policies are consistent across the board. Other factors such as changing business models, disruptive technologies and greater competition from emerging markets can put reactivity and responsiveness to the test.

Investors are giving ever greater importance to the value of good management. High-quality management does not automatically create tangible value, but is nonetheless a reassuring sign for a company's growth and risk mitigation.

Sustainability: A proxy for quality management

From an external perspective (i.e. from outside the company), sustainability is essentially a qualitative signal or, rather, a series of signals vis-à-vis a company's stakeholders. These signals come in a number of different forms:

- public commitments to apply policies or codes of conduct;
- changes to corporate governance and executive remuneration structures;
- management systems on environmental, human resources (HR), and quality and safety issues;
- rewards and sanctions by stakeholders (i.e. complaints, boycotts, class actions, etc.);
- legal and regulatory fines and sanctions;
- performance indicators on customer service, quality, environmental performance and safety;
- anti-competitive business practices such as corruption, money laundering and fraud;
- violations of international norms and standards such as human and labour rights.

QUALITATIVE AND QUANTITATIVE SIGNALS

It is self-evident that these signals are not homogeneous or easily comparable (which is more often the case with financial signals). However, if we attempt to assess the exhaustive body of information and data on these signals, we can try to translate the qualitative perception and evaluation of a company's behaviour vis-à-vis its stakeholders into a quantitative signal, even though it will inevitably be incomplete.

Sustainability and quantification: Valuation

From an investor's perspective, quantifying sustainability means talking about the possible impacts of ESG factors upon the valuation of companies. Just as an insurer evaluates the quality of his or her portfolio on the basis of the frequency of claims, we believe that the best way to quantify sustainability is to measure the impacts of ESG criteria on financial performance.

MATERIALITY OF EXTRA-FINANCIAL FACTORS

From any investor's viewpoint, the key question is whether extra-financial factors are material – in other words, whether they impact upon financial valuation. We believe that there are a number of possible ways to try to make this link:

- A cost–benefit approach works in a number of cases, such as asbestos-related provisions, carbon dioxide (CO_2) emission quotas and outsourcing to lower-cost countries. For example, in the electric utilities sector, we believe that CO_2 prices post-NAP2 are virtually certain to be at high levels (35–40 Euros per tonne) following the EU's new targets for reduction in greenhouse gases (GHGs) – and that this will play a key role in creating a potential 20 per cent upside for wholesale base-load prices by 2012 to at least US$112 per megawatt hour (MWh). Among many other impacts, this will probably boost the competitiveness of nuclear power. It has allowed new European pressurized reactors (EPRs), with production costs estimated by Electricité de France (EDF) at US$69 per megawatt hour, and at lower levels by others, to be built with confidence. Without the 'help' of the CO_2 factor, the new Flamanville EPR would have lagged behind new combined-cycle gas turbine plants (CCGTs) based on oil at or below US$60 per barrel and coal at or below US$125 per tonne, if we assume EDF's per megawatt hour cost estimate.
- A long-term growth approach that works in cases such as sustainable trends (e.g. growing demand for hydrogen or changing demographics and retirement-related services). For instance, with regard to the photovoltaic (PV) solar market, we recently conducted an analysis of the reasons for their current high valuations:
  - prospective growth in installed capacity out to 2030 based on European Photovoltaic Industry Association forecasts;
  - the expected trend in installed module prices;
  - the cash conversion to sales ratio; and

Table 4.1 *Different ways of addressing the financial materiality of extra-financial issues*

Cost–benefit analysis	Long-term growth analysis	Risk mitigation approach
Environmental provisions	Sustainability themes (e.g. water scarcity, food scarcity, waste management, energy needs, etc.)	Internal policies and processes (quality, productivity and adaptability)
Cost of litigation and fines		Human resources and human capital practices (staff motivation, retention, recruitment and training)
Cost of product withdrawals	Demographics (i.e. aging population)	Environmental management systems
Internalized externalities (CO_2)	Eating patterns (i.e. obesity)	Corporate governance practices
Lay-offs and staff reductions	Renewables (i.e. hydrogen demand)	Stakeholder dialogue
		R&D and product and service design
Costs associated with complying with new regulations	Developing world market growth	Customer orientation
Legal costs	New services designed for new emerging needs (niche markets at the beginning)	
Taxes		

Source: SG Equity Research

 — a 12 per cent discount rate with a beta of 1.4 to reflect the risks surrounding the development of the PV solar market, including technological and regulatory risks.

Using this approach we found that PV solar energy stocks were overvalued compared with prospective growth in their market out to 2030. Based on an estimated market value of 65 billion Euros and looking only at companies with silicon-linked operations, we found that PV solar stocks were overvalued by some 20 per cent. This factor, together with the weak visibility created by potential silicon overcapacity, led us to adopt a more conservative valuation approach.

COST–BENEFIT AND LONG-TERM GROWTH CAN'T EXPLAIN EVERYTHING

However, the ability of either of these methods to capture financial impact is extremely limited when it comes to a wide number of ESG issues, such as human resources and human capital, corporate governance practices, environmental management systems, community involvement and dialogue with stakeholders.

IS SUSTAINABILITY ANALYSIS A USEFUL FORECASTING TOOL?

A dynamic valuation approach based on future flows – dividends or cash flows – seems to us the most appropriate method in many cases, both for understanding sustainability analysis and for examining its possible contribution to mainstream financial analysis. Clearly, all analysis must be explicative and normative (i.e. what has happened and why); but to be really useful for investors, it must also have predictive capacity (i.e. what will happen). Financial analysis allows us to forecast future flows relatively accurately (although not perfectly) and thus obtain an accurate net present value. One could say that accounting is concerned with the past, while financial analysis attempts to predict the future. Sustainability analysis, if it is to survive and prosper, must do the same.

THE PREDICTIVE CAPACITY OF SUSTAINABILITY RATINGS IS LARGELY UNEXPLORED

To date, there has been little comprehensive work on the financial predictive capacity of sustainability ratings, either by agencies or investors. The main reason for this is the lack of historical ratings, with the first ESG ratings dating back only to the mid 1990s. We look forward to the time when a set of historic rating tables will be available and can be compared with financial performance for later years, similar to the tables produced by financial rating agencies for bankruptcies (credit risk). It would be particularly interesting to see if sustainability ratings do have predictive capacity with respect to economic or financial returns, or, more precisely, with regard to the beta for listed companies. However, we cannot just assume, *a priori*, that ESG risks can directly replace a stock's risk for the purposes of valuation. Strictly speaking, if a link does exist between financial risk and extra-financial risk (from ESG factors), this should first be established before routinely applying it to financial valuation formulas. This brings us to the heart of the subject under review: sustainability's potential contribution to financial analysis.

SUSTAINABILITY MANAGEMENT AS A FACTOR MODULATING RISK SENSITIVITY

Fundamentally, one of the most promising areas in determining the sustainability–financial link is that of risk modulation. Those striving to defend or promote the interests of stakeholders correctly assess that a company which stubbornly refuses to take on board their implicit and explicit requests will sooner or later run into serious problems in terms of negative publicity, brand image, fines, provisions for damages, technology rendered obsolete by stricter legislation, recruitment difficulties, or even loss of market share. On the other hand, a company that is actively tuned into – or even anticipates – its stakeholders' views, can lower its exposure to business risk and gain a competitive edge.

However, we need to avoid the temptation to oversimplify things. While the idea of operational ESG risk and all of its consequences are systematically bandied about by stakeholders, it is still difficult to calculate an accurate breakdown of all potential impacts (i.e. sales shortfalls, provisions, loss of key employees, etc.).

OUR PROPOSAL: TWOFOLD RISK MANAGEMENT AND COMPANY BETA APPROACH

We believe that the materiality and financial impact of extra-financials can best be made by two complementary approaches focusing on risk and risk management, and via potential deviations in fair value assessments.

The first method involves directly identifying the direct costs of risk and their impact upon earnings and share price. The difficulty lies in assessing the underlying costs of risk linked to sustainability and extra-financial issues – even if they are identifiable, many of them may be difficult to quantify with any degree of precision.

Cost of capital and beta approach

The second method is a cost of capital and beta approach, which makes it possible to evaluate the financial impact of extra-financials on the basis of an evaluation of risk reduction efforts based on sustainability ratings (all else being equal). Materiality can be indirectly calculated as the potential deviation in fair value. For the time being, our preference is for this beta-based method. This method is both systematic and systemic, and should, therefore, more accurately reflect the routine risks associated with corporate behaviour over the long term.

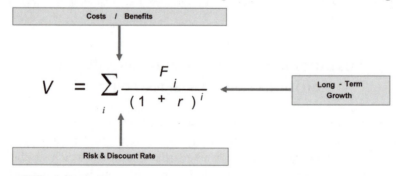

Source: SG Equity Research

Figure 4.1 *Three distinct approaches to analysing the financial materiality of extra-financials*

One small step forward from sustainability risk to the Capital Asset Pricing Model (CAPM)

We believe that the risk approach is promising. In the Capital Asset Pricing Model (CAPM), a stock's risk is measured by its beta – that is, its sensitivity to market fluctuations. The usual equation, in its simplified form is:

$$Ri = Ro + \beta \times (Rm - Ro)$$

where Ri is the expected rate of return from stock i, Ro is the risk-free rate, Rm is the expected return on the overall equity market, and β is stock i's sensitivity to market fluctuations. Ro is the rate of return on a risk-free investment and (Rm – Ro) is the risk premium.

From β observed *ex-post*, we can calculate a forecast β, either by assuming that β remains stable throughout the investment return period or by breaking down β into 'sector β,' or activity β, (being the average, weighted or not, of beta for companies working in the same sector, or even the same activity) and multiplying this by a coefficient specific to the company, called 'company β'. Excluding debt and assuming that company i is present in just one fairly homogeneous sector of activity, then:

Share i's β = activity i β × company i β.

This breakdown is commonly used by financial analysts because, in contrast to a portfolio β, the β for an individual share is relatively volatile (strong standard deviation for various samples) to sector β. To obtain more stable forecast β, it is therefore useful to introduce an intermediary step.

What bearing does this have on sustainability analysis?

In predicting expected returns, we can always marginally adjust the company or sector β applied if there is some doubt about the sector or company, or, conversely, considerable confidence. Analysts frequently modulate the company β by applying a quality of management coefficient. This assessment is generally based on the management team's ability, whether proved or not, to meet or even surpass strategic business objectives.

If a management team's forecasts on growth, company sales and earnings are repeatedly incorrect, it would seem justified for an investor to apply a quality of management β greater than 1 to the company β. In other words, if certain managers have an inability – for good or bad reasons – to keep their promises or fail to meet certain minimum requirements, this constitutes additional uncertainty for an investor and warrants a higher rate of return (via the discount rate). For any stock i, and excluding debt, the equation would then be:

Share i's β = activity i β × company i β × quality of management i β.

A quality of management β greater than 1 (> 1) simply signifies that compared to the average for the different management teams observed, company i's management is more likely to fall short of its 'deliverable' targets. By extension, it is clear just how relevant the corporate governance factor is, given that it has a direct bearing on assessing the future quality of management. This quality of management β is therefore quite similar to a possible corporate governance β (or a series of sub-governance β). Could the governance β replace the quality of management β? Not necessarily, as the two factors may be considered sufficiently different for them to be assessed separately and for both to be integrated. Practice will probably determine how such a corporate governance β is calculated (i.e. what added value can be brought to the accuracy of the final β given the cost of obtaining the information and then calculating the governance β).

As corporate governance is one of the pillars of sustainability, it is clear that the sustainability approach can contribute to financial analysis.

WORKING ON THE FINANCIAL–EXTRA-FINANCIAL LINK

In our work over the last three years, we have explored the possible sustainability–financial risk approach (compare Société Générale, 2005, 2006a, 2007, 2008). We established a number of basic premises for the financial–extra-financial link and for sustainability-related risk reduction, and concluded that:

- Managing extra-financial issues should be part of overall corporate risk management systems.
- Sustainability risks may have a financial impact as measured by beta (i.e. as a measure of financial risk or a sensitivity to market risk).
- Sustainability risks can and should be mitigated through an approach that attempts to strike a balance between stakeholder pressure (i.e. on companies) and stakeholder management (i.e. a company's efforts to meet these pressures), rather than on an absolute risk basis.

We believe the last point is crucial, as stakeholder pressure varies widely depending upon a company's industry sector, country of origin, market capitalization, level of free float and financial resources (i.e. 'deep pockets syndrome').

SUSTAINABILITY ISSUES: THE BETA LINK

We believe that sustainability issues can have material financial impacts both from risk and opportunity perspectives. However, if they are to be useful, they need to be factored into established financial valuation models, rather than constantly trying to reinvent the wheel. Opportunities involve new markets, new innovations, new technologies, and are easier to understand. Sustainability-related risks, however, are not as self-evident.

Calculating a sustainability beta?

If we accept the principle that it is appropriate to marginally adjust beta, the level and extent of the modulation still has to be determined. In this respect, scoring techniques would appear relevant. If all the good practice data can be put on a scale from worst to best performer, it must surely be possible to attribute scores to each and then to deduce averages and standard deviations from which to centre and standardize the variables obtained. This would gives us the percentage variation from the average for the practices observed (framework of best-in-class approach), which could then serve as an inverse governance β (1 for the sample average, > 1 for those bottom of the class, < 1 for those at the top). As for the scope and extent of governance β, it is still too early to say.

Our first sets of tests on the idea at SG showed that our best rated stocks on ESG issues (A+) compared very favourably with our worst rated stocks (D–) with regard to beta levels and their fluctuation over a four-year period (2002 to 2006). Over the long term, we believe that the beta variation gap between best and worst rated stocks could widen as stakeholder expectations increase and more pressure is placed on companies regarding sustainability issues.

Table 4.2 *Sustainability effect on historical beta (2004 to 2006)*

Sustainability rating	Company sustainability type	Company sustainability status	Observed sustainability effect on beta
A+	Proactive	Hidden stars	−8.5%
A−	Proactive	Leaders	0.4%
B+	Active	Hidden stars	−2.2%
B−	Active	Leaders	0.8%
C+	Reactive	Laggards	7.7%
C−	Reactive	Free-riders	−1.2%
D+	Negative	Laggards	−5.0%
D−	Negative	Free-riders	7.5%

Note: Average rolling two-year beta on weekly data versus DJ STOXX 600 as a benchmark.
Source: SG Equity Research

BACK TO BASICS: PERCEPTION OF RISK PREMIUM
AND QUALITY OF MANAGEMENT

Our most recent analysis (see Société Générale, 2008) focuses on a new risk assessment tool that does not depend upon our own views or those of SG or other sector analysts, but rather upon calculating a 'market'-implicit beta based on market consensus. We have recently dropped the historical beta and moved to an implicit beta based upon a reverse price-to-earnings (P/E) ratio. From a financial perspective, the historical beta is too dependent upon stock price variations and does not reflect forward risk as seen by investors. The P/E consensus drives to a consensus cost of equity level (*modulo* long-term growth rate) and, in turn, an implicit beta that provides a common ground for long-term risk assessment. Our analysis of the potential beta variations led to sustainability impacts of up to ±10 per cent on the target prices of companies in the broad industrial sectors.

Table 4.3 *Potential sustainability effect on valuation through ESG risk management*

	Sustainability rating				
	A	B	C	D	Average
Average COE–g	7.70%	8.20%	8.20%	8.40%	8.10%
Standard deviation COE–g	±0.33%	±0.30%	±0.24%	±0.55%	±0.28%
Financial upside/downside	5.50%	−1.50%	−1.50%	−3.50%	0.00%

Note: Standard deviation is calculated according to the number of companies per subclasses, average (cost of equity minus growth rate) COE-g calculated over April 2003 to April 2008.
Source: SG Equity Research

CONCLUSION: MOVING THE SUSTAINABILITY
FINANCIAL DEBATE FORWARD

We believe that our analysis shows that investors already give preference to companies that manage ESG issues well through a lower level of risk (in terms of beta). It is likely that this is not the only possible effect as we still believe that ESG factors can, for instance, also contribute to mid- and long-term growth. As to whether sustainability is already priced in by the market, this is a more difficult question. Here we propose to consider that if a company already has an implicit beta significantly deviating from the sustainability-adjusted sector equivalent, then it is very likely that investors have already integrated the sustainability signal.

Going forward, we believe that the key focus of the sustainability–financial link debate needs to be placed on the financial fundamentals. As our beta-sustainability analysis shows, sustainability issues can have an impact. However, further focus needs to be placed on emerging areas, such as:

- Sustainability will be a luxury for some. For highly profitable companies – earnings before interest and tax (EBIT) margins greater than 15 per cent – investors can always afford to opt for high margins with sustainability simply being an additional luxury (i.e. Porsche or the luxury goods sector). For such companies and sectors, the key indicator will lie with beta (or cost of equity) levels and profitability (as measured by EBIT margins), rather than sustainability ratings. Despite poor ESG performance, high levels of the former will paradoxically mean that investors will consistently attach a lower risk premium to such stocks.

- Sustainability really matters for financially needy companies. Sustainability is more likely to play a material role in stock valuation when companies are under financial pressure regarding their absolute and sector-relative profitability. The link between sustainability ratings and the level of risk (as measured by our implicit beta indicator) is only really respected when we consider sectors with 'low' profitability as measured by EBIT margins (less than 15 per cent). In our view, these are the companies which investors need to be targeting to realize a profitable sustainability strategy.

- Determining whether sustainability is in line with market perceptions. In our view, this should be a key focus area for investors. We believe that properly managing ESG issues can help to reduce total risk levels; but the key question is whether or not these issues are already priced in. Comparing the expected effect of sustainability on levels of risk and market consensus on beta levels will give us a good clue.

The convergence of sustainability analysis and financial analysis has only really just begun; but it will be a key goal if we are to advance our belief that ESG factors can affect a company's valuation.

REFERENCES

Bauer, R., Koedijk, K. and Otten, R. (2005) 'International evidence on ethical mutual fund performance and investment style', *Journal of Banking and Finance*, vol 29, no 7

De Brito, C., Desmartin, J. P., Lucas-Leclin, V. and Perrin, F. (2005) *L'Investissement Socialement Responsable*, Editions Economica, Paris, France

Derwall, J., Guenster, N., Bauer, R. and Koedijk, K. (2005) 'The eco-efficiency premium puzzle', *Financial Analysts Journal*, vol 61, no 2, March/April

Friedman, M. (1970) 'The social responsibility of business is to increase its profits', *New York Times Magazine*, 13 September

Guerard, J. B. (1997) 'Is there a cost to being socially responsible in investing?', *Journal of Investing*, vol 6, no 2, summer

Le Sourd, V. (2008) *The Performance of Socially Responsible Investment: A Study of the French Market*, EDHEC Business School, February

Margolis, J. D. and Walsh, J. P. (2001) *People and Profits? The Search for a Link Between a Company's Social and Financial Performance*, Lawrence Erlbaum Associates, Mahwah, NJ

Revue d'Economie Financière (2006a) 'La performance de l'ISR', *Revue d'Economie Financière, L'Investissement Socialement Responsible*, no 85, September

Revue d'Economie Financière (2006b) 'Qu'apporte l'analyse ISR à l'analyse financière?', *Revue d'Economie Financière, L'Investissement Socialement Responsible*, no 85, September

Revue d'Economie Financière (2006c) 'Pourquoi l'ISR est déjà un enjeu économique et financier', *Revue d'Economie Financière, L'Investissement Socialement Responsible*, no 85, September

Société Générale (2005) *SRI Impact on Valuations*, Société Générale, April

Société Générale (2006a) *The Missing Link?*, Société Générale, April

Société Générale (2006b) *Introducing the SRI Rating Matrix*, Société Générale, October

Société Générale (2007) *SRI Rating Matrix*, Société Générale, October

Société Générale (2008) *Back to Basics*, Société Générale, April

Vermeir, W., Van De Velde, W. E. and Corten, F. (2005) 'Sustainable and responsible performance', *Journal of Investing*, vol 14, no 3, fall

Part II

Confronting New Risks and Opportunities

5

Observations from the Carbon Emission Markets: Implications for Carbon Finance

Abyd Karmali[1]

OVERVIEW

Much analysis has been undertaken on carbon emission markets, but very little of it from the perspective of investment banks and other practitioners of carbon finance. It is critical that those with responsibility for designing market-based mechanisms also view issues through a financial lens in order to appreciate the inextricable links among climate change policy, carbon markets, incentives provided for low-carbon technology and signals for carbon finance.

A very significant scaling-up of carbon finance is required to deliver the low-carbon technologies necessary over a timeframe that can limit the adverse impacts of climate change. The United Nations Framework Convention on Climate Change (UNFCCC, 2007) estimates that 86 per cent of the incremental investment and financial flows of around US$200 billion per year required by 2030 will need to come from the private sector. While the scale of capital required does not appear to be a barrier, the World Business Council on Sustainable Development (WBCSD, 2007) suggests that the real challenge is directing capital towards the development, demonstration and deployment of low-carbon technologies, such as those included in Table 5.1. The private sector mobilizes capital best when there are unambiguous market signals. This chapter explores the signals currently being provided by the rapidly maturing carbon emissions markets and explores how the markets are gradually contributing to a new generation of innovative financial instruments that can help scale up carbon finance.

Table 5.1 *Greenhouse gas emission mitigation technologies*

Energy supply	Efficiency; fuel switching; nuclear power; renewable (hydropower, solar, wind, geothermal and bioenergy); combined heat and power; early applications of CO_2 capture and storage
Transport	More fuel-efficient vehicles; hybrid vehicles; biofuels; modal shifts from road transport to rail and public transport systems; cycling, walking; land-use planning
Buildings	Efficient lighting; efficient appliances and air conditioning; improved insulation; solar heating and cooling; alternatives for fluorinated gases in insulation and appliances
Industry	More efficient electrical equipment; heat and power recovery; material recycling; control of non-CO_2 gas emissions
Agriculture	Land management to increase soil carbon storage; restoration of degraded lands; improved rice cultivation techniques; improved nitrogen fertilizer application; dedicated energy crops
Forests	Afforestation; reforestation; forest management; reduced deforestation; use of forestry products for bioenergy
Waste	Landfill methane recovery; waste incineration with energy recovery; composting; recycling and waste minimization

Source: IPCC (2007)

INTRODUCTION TO THE CARBON MARKETS

Though initially treated with suspicion by some environmentalists, market approaches for promoting sustainability are now widely understood to be an effective means of promoting environmental protection goals through what economists refer to as the internalizing of environmental externalities. Until recently, market instruments focused mostly on regional- or national-scale environmental problems, with the US acid rain programme (built around a system of trading sulphur and nitric oxide emissions) perhaps the best-known example. Based on the success of the US experience in reducing acid rain and other similar pioneering programmes, such as the Singapore tradable quota and allocation system for phasing out ozone-depleting substances and the New Zealand programme on transferable fishing rights to address overfishing, in 1997 the negotiators of the Kyoto Protocol pushed for incorporating several market measures in the international agreement, including emissions trading and project-based emissions reductions (also known as carbon credits). They rightly recognized that the challenge of climate change is so vast that it requires a whole suite of complementary policy instruments in order to meet the environmental target in a cost-effective manner.

The theory behind emissions trading is relatively straightforward. By setting a quantitative limit (emission cap), policy-makers can have high confidence that the environmental objective will be met. For those subject to the emission cap, emission trading allows more flexibility in meeting the target by ensuring that companies with relatively high marginal abatement costs can purchase emission reductions from those companies with relatively low marginal abatement costs, and never pay more than the market-clearing price of emissions. This lowers overall system costs for all participants in the market and provides incentives for companies with lower marginal costs of abatement to reduce emissions to a level lower than would have been undertaken via a blunt command-and-control or tax approach.

At the time of writing, the World Bank and International Emissions Trading Association (IETA and World Bank, 2007) estimated the global carbon market to be worth US$31 billion in 2006, with analysts forecasting growth to US$70 billion in 2007, making carbon emissions one of the fastest-growing commodity markets globally. UK Prime Minister Gordon Brown suggested that the global carbon market could be worth US$600 billion by 2030. The early growth of the carbon market has undoubtedly exceeded the government negotiators' expectations, particularly given that the US government has, by virtue of its *volte face* on the Kyoto Protocol in 2000, not been directly involved in the market's formative years. Other US private-sector participants have, however, been involved. Global investment banks have been among the biggest liquidity providers to participants in the emissions markets and US technology providers have been among the leading suppliers of low-carbon technologies for carbon credit projects that reduce emissions.

There are, in fact, multiple carbon markets that can be categorized in a variety of ways (see Table 5.2). The first and most important distinction is between the emission allowance markets and project-based emissions reduction markets. In allowance markets, the entity or entities responsible for market oversight issue a fixed amount of property rights in the form of emission allowances. By contrast, carbon credits are project-based emission reductions created through implementing technology (raw material or fuel change, process improvement, gas capture or product modification) that reduces emissions against a counterfactual hypothetical baseline scenario.

The second distinction is between mandatory and voluntary markets. The mandatory carbon markets currently represent more than 99 per cent of the market of the value transacted; but, according to consultancy ICF International (2008), the voluntary segment of the carbon market had reached more than US$300 million in 2007 and is forecast to grow to between US$1 billion to US$4 billion by 2012. The drivers for growth in the voluntary market are numerous and include individual and corporate social responsibility, as well as companies seeking to learn from early action in advance of being included in a mandatory cap-and-trade scheme. There are now numerous companies who are using voluntary emission offsets as part of an overall strategy to minimize their carbon emissions footprint and, in some cases, to become 'carbon neutral'.

As highlighted in Table 5.2, much of this transactional value in the global carbon market can be attributed to the launch of the European Union Emissions Trading Scheme (EU ETS) in 2005, the world's first international carbon market that now covers five sectors and 27 countries.

Table 5.2 *Value and volumes in the carbon markets*

	2004		2005		2006		2007	
	CO_2e (million tonnes)	US$ (millions)	CO_2e (million tonnes)	US$ (millions)	CO_2e (million tonnes)	US$ (millions)	CO_2e (million tonnes)	US$ (millions)
Allowance markets								
Mandatory								
EU ETS	8.5	NA	321	7908	1104	24,436	2,061	50,097
New South Wales	5	NA	6	59	20	225	25	224
UK ETS	0.5	NA	< 1	1	–	–	–	–
Mandatory total	14	NA	327	7968	1121	24,661	2086	50,321
Voluntary (Chicago Climate Exchange)	2.2	NA	1	3	10	38	23	72
Allowance markets total	16.3	NA	328	7961	1134	24,699	2109	50,393
Project-based transactions								
Compliance								
Clean Development Mechanism	97	485	351	2638	537	5804	551	7462
Joint Implementation	9.1	54	11	68	16	141	41	499
Other	1	4.4	20	187	–	–	–	–
Compliance total	107	544	382	2894	–	–	–	–
Voluntary	2.9	5.6	6	44	10+	100	–	–
Project-based total	110	549	388	2937	611	6536	874	13,641

Source: IETA/World Bank (2007)

Seven observations are listed below on the impacts of carbon markets with a view to providing insights to those designing new emissions trading schemes and mechanisms for scaling up carbon finance.

OBSERVATION 1: CARBON MARKETS ARE EFFECTIVE IN REDUCING EMISSIONS

There has been much written in the last few years about the early years of the EU ETS, much of it in the form of premature obituaries. What is not in dispute is that the pilot phase of the EU ETS was intended to provide a learning-by-doing environment during 2005 to 2007 in a period when no annual emission reduction targets existed for the countries of the EU. The first commitment period of the Kyoto Protocol runs from 2008 to 2012. Many market commentators have articulated a thesis of unadulterated market failure based on the fact that some member states unquestionably provided installations in the scheme with too many emission allowances ('over-allocation' in the jargon), and that as a result the spot price of December 2007 European Union Allowances (or EUAs, the tradable carbon instrument) is now close to zero as the end of the pilot phase approaches. In some quarters it has even led to calls for the scheme to be scrapped and replaced by a carbon tax. What is often not understood is that the EU ETS has, in fact, resulted in reduced carbon emissions in the EU ETS and that by explicit design no banking of allowances from the pilot phase was permitted during the period of 2008 to 2012. It also ignores the important political calculus that the European Commission had to weigh in trading off a prompt start to the EU ETS with deeper cuts in emissions.

A study by Danny Ellerman from the Massachusetts Institute of Technology (MIT) and Beatrice Buchner from the International Energy Agency (IEA) (Ellerman and Buchner, 2006) concluded that the EU ETS has successfully reduced emissions in the five sectors covered by the scheme by around 80 million to 100 million tonnes of CO_2e per year. In addition, the price signal presented during the first 16 months of the EU ETS and the robust forward price signal provided by the futures market for 2008 to 2012 EUAs have contributed to an unleashing of carbon entrepreneurialism in developing countries as companies seek to monetize project-based emission reduction earning carbon credits through the Clean Development Mechanism (CDM). Of note is the fact that this is occurring without developing countries having any emission reduction targets under the Kyoto Protocol. The CDM awards carbon credits in the form of certified emission reductions (CERs) for eligible projects taking place in countries without emissions reduction targets. The quantity of CERs is defined as the verified yearly difference between the with-project scenario and a hypothetical counterfactual baseline scenario. The United Nations Environment Programme (UNEP) (2007) estimates that the pipeline of projects in the CDM will deliver emission reductions on the order of 2.5 billion tonnes of CO_2e over 2008 to 2012.

Much has also been made by commentators about the ability of power generators to pass on the opportunity costs of the EUA in some electricity markets across the EU. Because the allowances were received for free, this has resulted in accusations from some quarters of the allowances representing handouts of windfall profits. In fact, it can be argued that the increased electricity costs now faced by the broader industry, commercial and residential sectors has led to a growing sensitivity of the importance of energy efficiency resulting in behavioural change and increased general awareness about climate change. One means of addressing windfall profits is to have an increasing proportion of allowances distributed via auctioning as opposed to grandfathering for free. It is now widely expected that auctioning will play an ever more prominent role in allowance distribution in future phases of the EU ETS.

OBSERVATION 2: GREATER LINKAGE BETWEEN EMERGING CARBON MARKETS WILL INCREASE LIQUIDITY AND REDUCE OVERALL FINANCING NEEDS OF MEETING THE CLIMATE CHALLENGE

As explained earlier and illustrated in Table 5.2, carbon markets are currently fragmented. In the short term, this is an understandable outcome given that countries are pursuing different portfolios of policies and some large emitter countries are still outside the Kyoto Protocol. Each approach pursued by government creates a direct (in the case of a cap-and-trade scheme) or indirect (in the case of other policies and measures) cost of carbon for the targeted sectors and, thus, an incentive to reduce emissions. As economic theory suggests, overall emission abatement costs generally fall for all participants as the number of participants in a cap-and-trade scheme increase. A global carbon market that links national or regional cap-and-trade schemes is a desirable policy objective since it will establish one carbon price and ensure that companies focus first on the lower emission-abatement cost opportunities. From a financial perspective, more liquidity with a smaller set of different carbon emission commodities instead of less liquidity with a larger set of different carbon emission commodities means that the markets will perform in a more efficient manner. In some cases, emerging carbon markets that are unlinked to the broader carbon markets may fail to attract market intermediaries if the perceived liquidity is too low. For example, the pilot voluntary UK Emission Trading Scheme that predated the mandatory EU ETS was a worthy effort to encourage UK companies to undertake early projects to reduce emissions, but was an illiquid market. Bid-offer spreads were wide since trading volume was extremely low. As various countries contemplate the design of their national emission trading scheme (e.g. the US, Canada, Australia, New Zealand and Japan), it will be increasingly important for carbon markets to be linked.

Linkage occurs when one cap-and-trade system recognizes the compliance instrument being used in another system. If this recognition is reciprocated, full linkage is possible since the two compliance instruments could be used in either scheme. Indirect linkage between schemes is also possible via Kyoto-compliant carbon credits (based on the CDM). The national or regional cap-and-trade scheme can allow companies to import carbon credits into the scheme for the purpose of meeting their compliance obligation. Some important considerations for linkage between schemes include the following:

*   Ensuring that different countries do not establish their own rule-books for what constitutes an eligible project-based carbon credit. Such an approach would increase transaction costs considerably and would unnecessarily duplicate the extensive efforts being taken by the United Nations through the CDM.

- Some countries have proposed price caps for their domestic emissions trading schemes as a means of cost control. In practice, such price caps, if set at too low a level, can act as a carbon tax and provide little incentive for innovation. Moreover, if schemes are linked, the price cap would effectively be transferred through to the other schemes, affecting the incentive for emissions reductions in the linked schemes. Finally, price caps greatly reduce the incentive for financial intermediaries to provide risk management and liquidity services.

- Banking and borrowing provisions should be harmonized across linked emission trading systems since limits in one system can be bypassed by taking advantage of unused limits in another scheme.

- On other design issues, such as penalties for non-compliance, approaches to allocation of allowances and the degree of linkage via imports of carbon credits, there is less of a need for harmonization across schemes.

OBSERVATION 3: ROBUST CARBON MARKETS ARE A KEY ENABLER FOR THE DESIGN OF INNOVATIVE SOLUTIONS

One sign of the health and growing maturity in carbon emissions markets during 2007 has been the increase in the use of derivatives (futures and options contracts) in order to increase liquidity and provide additional risk management services for participants in the market. Such instruments were largely absent during the first phase of the EU Emissions Trading Scheme but are now increasingly used to hedge participants' financial risks in the market for 2008 to 2012. Examples include basis arbitrage (e.g. to take advantage of possible differences between the price of the spot EUA contract and the price of the future EUA contract minus its cost of carry); inter-market spread contracts (where participants take simultaneous positions in two or more related contracts, such as UK natural gas, UK power and EU emissions in order to hedge potential spread risks among contracts); repo contracts (where an investment bank buys emissions contracts from a seller in order to monetize the allowances up front, and then sells back the emissions to the original counterparty at an agreed future date and price reflecting differences between the implied emissions market and financial market costs of carry); and swap contracts (to reflect the difference in price and risk characteristics of EUA and CER). Investment banks have become important participants in the carbon credit market where each project has different risk profiles (see Figure 5.1), thereby presenting an opportunity for banks to help counterparties hedge their carbon credit delivery risks for individual projects as well as for portfolios of projects.

Investment banks are also succeeding in attracting new participants to the carbon market by deriving synergy from their wealth management businesses. Increasingly, individual investors wish to have some exposure to the carbon

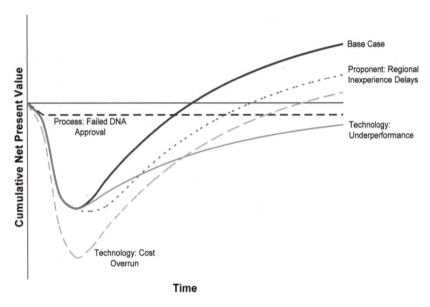

Source: IETA (2007)

Figure 5.1 *Carbon credit projects have different risk–reward profiles*

market. This can be accomplished by designing structured emission products (using put or call options to create an investment note that provides an agreed level of principal protection and capital participation) based on underlying EUA or CER futures contracts. The increase in numbers of exchanges, including EUA and CER futures contracts, facilitates the development of such products even in markets not hitherto under emission caps. For example, in December 2007, Merrill Lynch became one of several investment banks to invest in a new 'Green Exchange' to be launched by NYMEX in 2008. The launch of emissions contracts in the US should help to increase global liquidity in the carbon market.

More generally, there are now a multitude of investment products with a carbon market or climate change theme available for investors to choose from. Investment and commercial banks have recognized that this is an opportunity where they can derive comparative advantage by being the first to launch new products across a whole range of asset classes. Table 5.3 provides a summary of climate change-related products that have been introduced by banks.

Observation 4: In 2007, climate change became a mega-trend for investors

The year 2007 may well go down as the year that climate change became a mega-trend for investors. A combination of high-profile events has contributed to this phenomenon, among which are the release of the Intergovernmental Panel on

Table 5.3 *Carbon market enables the development of new carbon-driven financial products across asset classes*

Carbon markets	Structured emission products, carbon funds, emission price indices, EUA/CER swaps, synthetic portfolios of carbon credits
Equities	Portfolio screening, SRI funds, low-carbon technology stocks, index products
Bonds	Portfolio screening, tropical forestry bonds
Private equity/venture capital	Carbon venture capital, carbon-driven principal investing
Real estate	Energy efficiency/green-building real estate investment trusts
Hedging instruments	Weather-derivative products, catastrophe bonds, insurance products

Source: Karmali (2007)

Climate Change's *Fourth Assessment Report* (IPCC, 2007); the dissemination of the *Stern Review Report on the Economics of Climate Change* (Stern, 2006); the commercial and mass-market success of former US Vice President Al Gore's *An Inconvenient Truth*; the apparent tectonic shift in how climate change is viewed by policy-makers in the US; the awarding of the Nobel Peace Prize to Al Gore and the IPCC; and the intensification of United Nations negotiations taking place to agree a global climate change policy framework by the end of 2009 for post-2012. At the climate change negotiations in Bali, Indonesia, the investment community represented by groups such as the Carbon Markets Association and the World Business Council for Sustainable Development called for clear market signals from the negotiations to help mobilize the estimated US$200 billion in incremental funding in 2030.

The implications for the investment community are clear. Investors, whether sovereign, institutional or individual, increasingly want their investment portfolios to be climate-proofed against climate change-related risks, including the physical impacts of climate change (temperature changes, precipitation changes and sea-level rises). This trend is one increasingly being recognized by global investment banks now aiming at enhancing their capacity to provide clients with these types of opportunities. In addition, they are increasingly looking for opportunities to obtain exposure to investments that will gain from a shift to a lower-carbon economy or exposure to the carbon markets.

In order to provide a fact base for investors, it is important for the financial community to seek greater disclosure about different companies' approaches to managing climate change. Some important grassroots mechanisms have emerged to provide an enabling environment to promote carbon finance. One good example is the Carbon Disclosure Project (CDP), which since 2002 has been gathering momentum by encouraging the FT Global 500 (the world's largest companies measured by market capitalization) to disclose their greenhouse gas emissions, their perceived risks and opportunities from climate change, and their strategies for addressing climate change. In 2007, the effort has now extended to the S&P 500 and other country-specific sets of publicly listed companies. Furthermore, the signatories to the CDP now represent investment managers with more than US$41 trillion of assets under management. In 2006, Merrill Lynch become the global lead sponsor for this initiative, recognizing that the responses by companies to the questionnaires sent by the CDP form part of an important dialogue between the investment community and the private sector about climate change and its financial implications. The resulting answers to CDP questionnaires represent a valuable data set in the public domain for all stakeholders to use for their own engagement efforts. In analysing longitudinal trends over the first five years of the CDP, some interesting insights come to the fore:

- Companies' response rates and the quality of those responses are steadily improving over time.
- The engagement by senior executives on the topic of climate change has increased over time but is still lower than should be expected for some carbon-intensive companies and is not widely reflected in capital allocation decisions.
- Companies are increasingly identifying new upstream and downstream carbon-related risks and opportunities from managing their supply chains.
- Companies are generally uncertain about how to analyse and report on the financial implications arising from the potential physical risks of climate change.

The CDP effort is one that will probably continue to provide important insights for the financial sector and other stakeholders about new risks and opportunities for carbon finance.

In order to gain from a shift to a lower-carbon economy, investors are increasingly looking for opportunities to receive exposure to the carbon markets. Carbon has emerged as a new asset class and investors can enter the market through specialized investment vehicles. Since 1999, 58 carbon funds with a total volume of US$11 billion under management purchase carbon credits or invest in emission reduction projects (Caisse des Dépôts, 2007). Their initial purpose was to assist governments and companies to comply with their obligations; however, the market has seen a substantial increase in funds that seek to provide a return on the investment capital instead of an efficient compliance strategy. Figure 5.2 shows that 30 per cent of the 58 carbon funds are capital gains-driven investment vehicles that manage 45 per cent of the total capital pool. This trend continues with several fund managers proposing new carbon vehicles to investors focusing on a certain region, technology or carbon asset class.

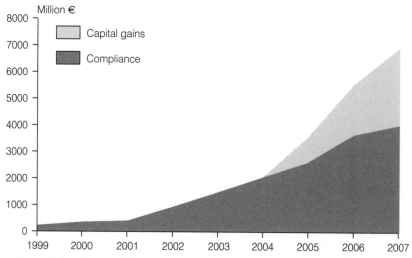

Note: Financial information available for 53 of 58 vehicles.
Source: Caisse des Dépôts (2007)

Figure 5.2 *Evolution of investment capital by vehicle strategy*

OBSERVATION 5: GLOBAL INVESTMENT BANKS ARE SCALING UP THEIR CARBON FINANCE ACTIVITIES, BUT NEED STRONG SIGNALS FROM POLICY-MAKERS

Notwithstanding the absence in the negotiating mandate agreed to in Bali in December 2007 of explicit quantitative emission-reduction targets, the signals coming from policy-makers increasingly indicate a future that will be characterized by constraints on greenhouse gas emissions. To take advantage of the new commercial opportunities presented, investment banks have been expanding their involvement in the carbon emissions markets and scaling up their carbon finance activity. Most banks now have emission trading desks and a few also have principal investment activities that include a focus on low-carbon technologies. For example, Merrill Lynch has established Merrill Lynch Commodity Partners (MLCP), a joint venture between its investment banking and commodities businesses that in 2007 invested in Californian geothermal company Vulcan Power and took an equity stake in Core Carbon Group, a Danish company undertaking greenhouse gas emission reduction projects in Russia. Merrill Lynch's Asian private equity and principal investment activities include equity stakes in Chinese and Indian companies in the solar and wind power sectors.

One of the challenges facing banks is a decision about how early in the technology life cycle to invest. Typically, investment banks do not invest in the development and demonstration phase (see Figure 5.2) but look for opportunities in the deployment phase where incentives such as carbon dioxide (CO_2) pricing can help to pull a technology to market and increase the commercial

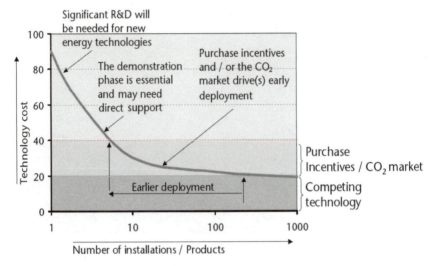

Source: WBCSD (2007)

Figure 5.3 *Development, demonstration and deployment cycle*

returns. A price for CO_2 is not so crucial for early stage technologies. Another challenge highlighted by the London Accord (2007) in its research paper *Making Investment Work for the Climate* is that policies to promote low-carbon technology typically have a short lifetime and this is at odds with the long-term nature of climate change.

Another key challenge for carbon finance is that new low-carbon technologies often face numerous technical and cost barriers, and require substantial time to progress from the initial research and development (R&D) stage to full commercial deployment. This significantly increases the risk to investors compared with investments in established technologies. Although large investments in the R&D phase of technology development are much needed, many technologies have seen some success and yet failed to overcome barriers in the demonstration phase. The track record tells us that in the absence of strong policy support mechanisms and incentives, and while fossil fuels are cheap and readily available, public and private funds are unlikely to deliver the necessary technologies at a cost and scale necessary to address climate change unless there are major changes in investment frameworks. Most low-carbon technologies will not be cost-competitive at scale without some combination of investment support mechanisms, technological advances or regulatory regime improvements. An abundance of potential projects, technologies or investment opportunities will not in itself necessarily translate into the mobilization of capital flows for implementation.

Observation 6: Carbon-related financial and technology flows will increasingly be South–South, South–North and North–South

It has been traditional, particularly in the United Nations climate change negotiations, to think in terms of financial and technology flows as only north–south. This paradigm is less relevant for carbon finance given the emergence of a new set of low-carbon technology companies in so-called emerging markets that have the ability to diffuse clean technology locally and perhaps even supply cutting-edge technology to meet northern countries' needs for reduced emissions. Investment banks are increasingly identifying these opportunities and helping to mobilize capital that will enable innovative companies to execute their business expansion plans. For example, in 2007, Merrill Lynch's private equity arm invested US$55 million into leading wind turbine developer Vestas's Indian operations and made principal investments of around US$400 million in a series of clean technology companies, including China-based solar companies Trina Solar and China Sunergy.

The shift from a north–south paradigm is, of course, not limited to carbon finance. For example, following the write-downs of sub-prime mortgage-related investments by major investment banks in 2007, capital infusions to shore up the banks' balance sheets came from investors in Singapore, the United Arab Emirates and China. What is more relevant is not so much the location of the investment opportunity or the investor, but the return expectations of the category of investors (see Figure 5.4), which often transcends geographic boundaries. Investment banks are uniquely placed to help mobilize the capital necessary for low-carbon technology given their ability to use their own balance sheets to make principal investments and to structure investment opportunities for different classes of investors who share risk–reward profiles and return expectations.

Concluding observation: The financial community must be an active participant in international policy efforts to ensure that financial mechanisms have the intended impacts

Hitherto, the financial community has not been extensively engaged in the policy debate surrounding climate change; but it is now critical for it to become an active participant. Financial institutions have a crucial part to play in the solution to climate change by mobilizing capital flows and are best placed to offer practical insights on how to ensure that carbon markets can function in as efficient a manner as possible. It is possible that some of the teething problems with the

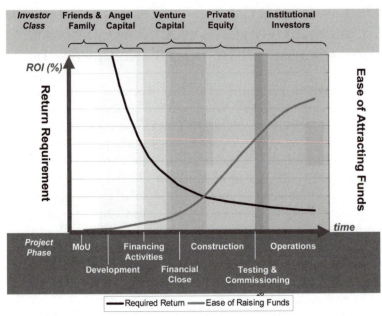

Figure 5.4 *Return expectations for different investors in clean technology*

CDM could have been avoided had there been earlier engagement from the financial sector. Some recommendations to promote the health of the carbon markets and to remove barriers to carbon finance include the following:

- Incorporate explicit short-, medium- and long-term quantitative emission-reduction targets in future climate change agreements to provide the necessary long-term signal to the market about the unambiguous direction of future climate change policy.
- Ensure that carbon markets are indirectly linked via common acceptance of the Kyoto-compliant carbon credits and provisions that allow companies to import international carbon credits to meet their domestic compliance obligations.
- Work towards a gradually more integrated global carbon market by ensuring that new national cap-and-trade schemes do not include price controls, recognize existing carbon instruments from other cap-and-trade schemes, and include banking and borrowing provisions broadly in line with existing schemes.
- Dismantle trade barriers that restrict diffusion of low-carbon technologies in order to encourage investment and business participation.
- Manage the intellectual property rights regime to balance the need to provide incentives for innovation in new low-carbon technologies and the dissemination of existing low-carbon technologies to developing countries.

- Influence public behaviour and acceptance of all low-carbon technologies through awareness-raising and education about their contribution to combating climate change to help ensure uptake and future demand. This is of particular relevance for technologies such as nuclear power that will face significant local opposition that could delay or even limit their implementation.

NOTE

1   The author would like to acknowledge the following colleagues at Merrill Lynch who have provided valuable input: Martin Berg, Ed Bratton, Tessa Brown and Matt Hale. The author would also like to reinforce that any opinions expressed herein are the author's own and not necessarily those of Merrill Lynch.

REFERENCES

ADB (Asian Development Bank) (2007) *Investing in Clean Energy and Low Carbon Alternatives in Asia*, Asian Development Bank, Philippines

Caisse des Dépôts (2007) *Mission Climat: Environmental Finance*

Ellerman, A. and Buchner, B. (2007) 'The European Union Emissions Trading, Scheme: Origins, allocation, and early results', *Review of Environmental Economics and Policy*, vol 1, no 1, Oxford Journals

ICF International (2008) *Outlook on the Voluntary Carbon Market*

IETA (International Emissions Trading Association) (2007) *Investment and Financial Flows to Address Climate Change*, United Nations, Geneva.

IETA/World Bank (2007) *State and Trends of the Carbon Market*, IETA, Washington, DC

IPCC (Intergovernmental Panel on Climate Change) (2007) *Fourth Assessment Report*, Cambridge University Press, Cambridge

Karmali, A. (2007) 'Carbon Finance 2.0', Presentation at IETA Annual General Meeting, Washington, DC, September 2007

London Accord (2007) *Making Investment Work for the Climate*, City of London Corporation, London

Stern, N. (2006) *Stern Review Report on the Economics of Climate Change*, Cambridge University Press, Cambridge

UNFCCC (2007) *Investment and Financial Flows to Address Climate Change*, UNFCCC Secretariat

WBCSD (World Business Council for Sustainable Development) (2007) *Investing in a Low-Carbon Energy Future in the Developing World*, WBCSD Publications, Switzerland

6

Carbon Exposure

Matthias Kopp and Björn Tore Urdal

THE CARBON ENVIRONMENT

The Stern Review (Stern, 2006) found that not properly factoring in climate change may turn out to be the widest-ranging market failure ever seen. Correcting for this will inevitably create substantial risks and opportunities for global companies and investors alike. In this chapter we provide one specific example of corporate value at risk from a carbon-constrained future using the framework established by the European Union Emissions Trading Scheme (EU ETS).

Electricity generation is one of the sectors most exposed to carbon risk. To date, power generation has largely been based on fossil fuel combustion, hence intrinsically linked to great quantities of greenhouse gas (GHG) emissions. As a legacy, power plants require replacing on a generational basis, and as demand continues to accelerate, this industry requires constant large-scale capital investment in new capacity. Often, new facilities will have a very long life, up to 50 years, and little flexibility in terms of efficiency improvements of deployed assets over their scheduled existence. Structurally, this industry is or was highly regulated, and often operates under a monopolistic structure, one not typically associated with innovation and deployment of new technologies. Yet, energy generation is the backbone of every economy and is dealt with very cautiously by the stakeholders involved. In a framework where it is clear that conventional means of operation – namely, deploying coal-fired power stations – will continue to accelerate climate change, these actors, not at all used to speeding up innovation and making entrepreneurial decisions under uncertainty, are now required to do exactly that.

Electric utilities are increasingly subject to market constraints globally regarding the availability of carbon dioxide (CO_2) emission certificates, both in terms of new and emerging cap-and-trade systems and tightening rules and possibilities, particularly for coal-based generation. Reversing the growth trend of carbon emissions globally by 2015 to 2020, as demanded by the Intergovernmental Panel on Climate Change's *Fourth Assessment Report* (IPCC, 2007) requires the most emission-intensive sector, power generation, to enter into a carbon-free mode soon thereafter. The findings of the aforementioned Noble Peace Prize winning 2007 IPCC report showed that to keep the world below 2° Celsius (C) incremental warming, compared with pre-industrial times, global emissions need to peak and decline well before 2020. If the scientific consensus leads to a political imperative to limit global warming to 2°C to 3°C above pre-industrial levels, this would then translate into, at a minimum, a 50 per cent decrease in global GHG emissions by 2050.

Since the establishment of the EU ETS on 1 January 2005, Europe's power sector has been subject to a cap on emissions, with the ability to trade allowances – through the European Union Allowance (EUA). In the first 'learning by doing' phase, the emission cap proved too loose, prompting a collapse in the carbon price in 2006. By January 2008, the European Commission had tabled its plans for the ETS in order to achieve the EU's goal of a 20 per cent cut in CO_2 by 2020, recommending 100 per cent auctioning of permits in the power sector, along with a steady reduction in the emission cap until 2020 and beyond. The EU has also indicated that it is willing to adopt a 30 per cent cut if an international agreement to succeed the Kyoto Protocol, which expires in 2012, is achieved. At Bali in December 2007, governments agreed a negotiating mandate for a 'global deal' to be finalized in Copenhagen two years later. Indicatively, industrialized regions such as the EU will need to make reductions of 25 to 40 per cent by 2020 if the global economy is to first peak and then halve emissions by mid century.

RWE: A SPECIFIC EXAMPLE OF CARBON IMPLICATIONS

Against this backdrop, we undertook a specific analysis on one company, RWE, the single biggest CO_2-emitting corporation in Europe. RWE is largely a coal-, lignite- and nuclear-based electric utility.

European utilities will need to replace significant portions of their electricity-generating capacities over the coming years. These investments will determine the carbon path of Europe for decades; but lack of a clear EU climate legislation framework post-2012 is a major uncertainty in these investment decisions.[1] Utilities have delayed capacity replacement decisions in the hope of more clarity and success in lobbying for less stringent CO_2 regulation, but nevertheless need to pursue replacement strategies in spite of this uncertainty. The ability to accurately build in future carbon constraints in these investment decisions will be a major driver of their competitive positions. The ability of investors to understand this link between replacement strategy and future climate change policy will be crucial for investment success. Sustainable Asset Management (SAM) and the WWF earlier developed a model to assess the financial impact of different replacement strategies under different carbon prices based on assumptions that seemed conservative and reasonable in early 2006. In a future with legislation in place to stabilize carbon emissions at sustainable levels, lower-carbon replacement strategies emerged as winners. Using RWE as an example, we calculated a potential value at risk of 17 per cent of the net equity value in a business-as-usual scenario.

A SUSTAINABLE CO_2 REDUCTION PATH

The concentration of CO_2 in the air has reached a level of around 380 parts per million (ppm) today, and some suggest it is higher than that already. The prospect of anything much above 500ppm makes scientists quite nervous indeed, and a sustainable carbon-stabilizing profile constrained at 450ppm in the atmosphere needs to be met by 2050, as recently re-emphasized by the IPCC (2007). For Europe, the *sustainable CO_2 reduction path* translates to lowering emissions in the order of 80 per cent by 2050 compared to a 1990 emissions baseline. For the German ETS sectors, responsible for about half of German CO_2 emissions, this would necessitate cutting emissions to 100 million metric tonnes CO_2 per year (mtCO_2/y) by 2050. This compares to a total allowance of around 500mtCO_2/y for the period 2005 to 2007 under the current German National Allocation Plan (NAP1). The NAP dictates the number and distribution of allowances per country under the European Union Emissions Trading Scheme (EU ETS), which is supposed to cut emissions from EU's most CO2-intensive industries.

On a global basis, the biggest contributor to CO_2 emissions is power generation (33 per cent). In Europe, Germany is the largest carbon polluter, with some 40 per cent of the country's CO_2 emissions coming from the power generation sector, while the lion's share (55 per cent) of power assets is fuelled by coal and lignite – the dirtiest means of electricity production.[2] Over the next 25 years, German generation capacity will decline by over two-thirds, which is a similar situation to many other European countries, as in the US. Until then, approximately 60 per cent of the lignite and 50 per cent of the coal plants will have reached the end of their operating lives and will be retired. Capacity replacement decisions clearly represent both a big opportunity, and a big risk, for the companies and investors involved.

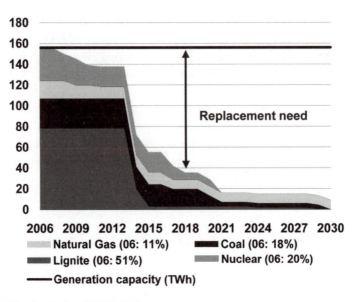

Source: RWE, estimates from WWF, SAM Group

Figure 6.1 *RWE's expiring lifetime curve*

MODELLING RWE'S POWER GENERATION ASSETS

In this study, we comprehensively model cash flows from a set of 26 of RWE's German power plants, representing 88.5 per cent of RWE's total net generation capacity. The portfolio generated 114 million tonnes of CO_2 emission in 2005, representing 95 per cent of RWE's total emissions, and received 116mtCO_2 emission allowances for 2005, representing 97 per cent of RWE's total CO_2 allowances under the first NAP period from 2005 to 2007.

We estimate that 76 per cent of the portfolio's total lifetime span is already over and, by 2020, 80 per cent of capacity will have to be replaced. The capacity is tailing off over time as depicted in Figure 6.1.

At the end of the economic cycle of each existing power-generating asset, we replace it by investing in new assets of the same capacity. We model a range of fuel technology replacement options: fuel-by-fuel replacement (business as usual, which has been the publicly stated strategy by RWE at the time) or replacement only by gas-fuelled stations.

The model includes the regulatory framework in place under the EU ETS system. Each individual asset's CO_2 allowance in 2005 is taken as the starting point for future cash-flow analysis. Future allowances are modelled based on coal and gas benchmarks. We calculate plant-by-plant discounted net asset values (NAVs) of RWE's power generation division, including the post-tax discounted carbon cash flow. The carbon cash flow is calculated as CO_2 emissions minus allowances for a range of carbon permit prices.

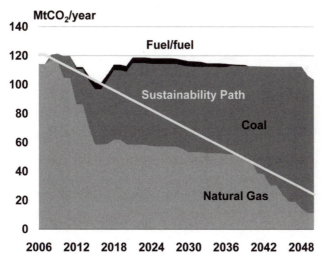

Source: WWF, SAM Group

Figure 6.2 *RWE's CO$_2$ emission trajectories (2006 to 2050)*

The model shows that at a long-term carbon price of 30 Euros per tonne of CO$_2$, RWE and its shareholders are, all else being equal, clearly better off replacing the entire generation capacity with coal. Of new plants currently under construction or planned in Germany for the period of 2006 to 2020, 70 per cent of new capacity is either coal or lignite. This, on the other hand, runs contrary to a strict application of a sustainability path in overall emissions reductions.

CALCULATING VALUE AT RISK

What if the concept of a sustainable reduction path is transferred to RWE (i.e. 80 per cent CO$_2$ emission reduction by 2050 compared to 2005)? We calculate a steady declining sustainable reduction path until 2050, depicted as the light-grey straight line in Figure 6.2. For RWE, we calculate that the accumulated emissions for the period of 2006 to 2050 will be 50 per cent beyond sustainable levels if the existing capacity is replaced by coal or under a fuel-by-fuel replacement scenario.

Clearly, the failure of incentivizing utilities to build low carbon-intensive capacity has to be corrected. Investors need to deeply reflect on the above situation as a material risk factor. The most likely correcting measures will be market based and, specifically in our view, an improvement of the system in place, such as terminating the grandfathering of permits and/or lowering the supply of permits altogether. Consequently, correcting measures could (and would) drive up the carbon commodity price significantly from our base case of 20 Euros per tonne of CO$_2$, which changes the picture entirely.

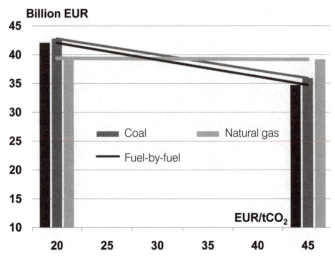

Source: WWF, SAM Group

Figure 6.3 *Carbon impact upon RWE's net equity value at different carbon prices*

CARBON IMPACT UPON RWE'S NET EQUITY VALUE

We ran the RWE model for a range of long-term carbon permit prices and replacement investment strategies, all else being equal, and calculated the net equity value impact upon RWE. The main findings are as follows (see also Figure 6.3 for illustration):

- At 20 Euros per tonne of CO_2, a *gas-only* replacement strategy carries a net equity value 6.3 per cent below a *fuel-by-fuel* replacement.
- At 45 Euros, a *gas-only* replacement carries a net equity value 13 per cent above that of a *fuel-by-fuel* replacement strategy.
- In our example, a long-term carbon price of 33 Euros per tonne of CO_2 is the breakpoint at which replacing the portfolio with gas only carries the highest net equity value.
- At 45 Euros per tonne of CO_2 versus 20 Euros per tonne of CO_2, we calculate a 17 per cent reduction of the equity value for *fuel by fuel*, compared to an insignificant loss of equity value of 1 per cent for *natural gas only*.

CONCLUSION: SIGNIFICANT RISK TO VALUATION

The valuation exercises in this study demonstrate the significance of carbon exposure in a future with stricter regulations. What is the probability of future legislation internalizing external carbon emission costs at a long-term price above 33 Euros per tonne of CO_2? Taken together with the relative volatility in value, balancing the fuel mix with respect to value maximization could well give a strong tilt towards gas.[3] In the case of RWE, we have demonstrated that, all else being equal, value at risk from carbon is significantly reduced by increasing gas exposure as an active replacement strategy. This clearly needs to be carefully undertaken as a fully fledged gas strategy entails different risks. Nevertheless, a much more balanced approach as to the fuel sources is a clear consideration for a corporate strategy interested in maximizing corporate value in a carbon constrained or even carbon-neutral world.

Utilities are increasingly finding themselves between a rock and a hard place with respect to generation replacement strategies and long-term value creation – and investors need to consider carefully the long-term risks and opportunities inherent in such future-looking decisions.

Since we have conducted this valuation exercise over a period of time of continuing uncertainty about regulatory decisions, it makes sense to match the assumptions taken originally along with more recent developments. All of the assumptions taken for the regulatory framework in Phase II of the EU ETS did, in the meantime, turn out to be surpassed by stricter actual decisions taken:

- The cap for Germany was set at 453 million tonnes per annum (compared to 480 million tonnes).
- Auctioning was introduced at 9 per cent.
- Special provisions for CO_2-intensive power plants, arguably particularly in favour of RWE, have been ended (the transfer rule).
- Existing benchmarks have been fixed at slightly lower rates as planned, and no special benchmark for lignite production was introduced.

Furthermore, at the time of penning this review, the European Commission (EC) has made its first public announcements of Phase III of the EU ETS for the period post-2012. First, the EC indicated that in Phase III, two-thirds of the EU-wide cap on carbon allowances will be auctioned, forcing through a more stringent working of the 'polluter pays' principle. Second, the EC indicated a burden of risk on the electric utility sector through a very high percentage of allowance auctioning planned for the power sector. A full auctioning of the allowances for the electric utility sector also works to curb potential windfall profits that have benefited utilities in the past, as prices of carbon allowances have been transferred to electricity prices charged to customers.

Furthermore, there is increasing evidence for the introduction of national carbon constraints in the US after the general election in 2008 and increasingly loud calls, particularly by business, for certainty arising from the establishment of a national emissions trading scheme. As one example of businesses' growing recognition of a carbon-constrained future, many US banks, including Citigroup, Morgan Stanley and JPMorgan Chase,[4] in the anticipation of national regulation on carbon, imposed policies on financing power stations upon themselves. By doing this, they could argue that they *de facto* put a moratorium on new build conventional coal power stations without CO_2 capture facilities. This decision was made on the basis of risks to the banks project finance and also is relevant for shareholders and other intangibles, such as showing internal employees that the issue is relevant to their company. In February 2008, the largest US banks also developed a framework for requiring carbon emissions transparency and for integrating this much more consistently by means of the Carbon Principles agreed by these same banks. The driving force behind these principles was increasing clarity that a cap-and-trade system will soon arrive in the US. Yet, on the side of investors, a firm signal of required strategic direction of utilities away from coal-based generation towards researching technology advancements in carbon capture and sequestration (CCS), etc. remains to be seen.

Finally, as demonstrated for utilities here, the EU ETS already extends to several industries (pulp and paper, glass and ceramics, metals, etc.), and clearer ideas for carbon regulation in other sectors are emerging (automotive with engine benchmarks, emissions trading for airlines, etc.). Integrating such future risk within corporate valuations is becoming increasingly important for many sectors going forward.

One more important aspect in assessing a company's carbon exposure can currently be seen occurring in Germany. At the time of writing, several power plant replacement projects have been put forward for governmental approval. Over two-thirds of the applications are for best available technology, but still using conventional and heavily CO_2-emitting technologies. Unexpectedly, local resistance by people or decisions by municipal councils have caused the rejection of 7 out of approximately 25 applications for coal plants, among them one by RWE, who is now forgoing a US\$3 billion hard-coal power plant project.[5] Investors and companies alike need be aware of the additional potential for local obstructions to CO_2-intensive investment decisions.

The role of investors is a crucial one. The whole scenario laid out above leading to a carbon-neutral system could be seriously jeopardized if investors do not act as long-term economic rationale would seem to dictate is required. If investors in Europe support the cause of electric utilities not investing in low-carbon assets at a time when significant replacement capacity is needed, and allow for the building of conventional coal plants, this will lock in a tremendous carbon commitment for the future, minimizing reduction options dramatically. This will come with all the negative economic consequences described by the Stern Review. Hence, a paradigm shift is required. Perhaps the only real question is: when will it occur?

NOTES

1 The EU is currently in the process of finalizing the rules and regulations for the EU Emissions Trading Scheme post-2012 – that is the level of free certificates, auctioning, additional industries (airlines, etc.), processes, etc.
2 This is by no means exceptional. For instance, the US, China, Australia and others also rely heavily on coal combustion for power generation.
3 At the time of writing, cost and technical details for carbon capture and sequestration (CCS) are too uncertain upon which to sensibly base a scenario. If and when this technology is demonstrated to work and be commercially viable, additional scenarios come into play.
4 Referenced in *The Wall Street Journal* (4 February 2008, pA6) and according to the Carbon Principles, released in February 2008 by Citigroup, Morgan Stanley and JPMorgan Chase.
5 Ensdorf was the most recent plant not to have been approved, but a few others have also been rejected. This increases the capacity constraints, the need to invest and, hence, should be of utmost importance to investors.

REFERENCES

IPCC (Intergovernmental Panel on Climate Change) (2007) *Fourth Assessment Report*, www.ipcc.ch/ipccreports/ar4-syr.htm
Stern, N. (2006) *Stern Review Report on the Economics of Climate Change*, Cambridge University Press, Cambridge, UK

7

Clean Energy Opportunities

Emma Hunt and Rachel Whittaker[1]

Concerns over climate change, increased interest in environmentally sensitive products and services, and high oil prices are creating opportunities for long-term investors. Environmental concerns are no longer seen merely as sources of risk that create an unnecessary legislative and cost burden for companies and their investors. They are now a catalyst for new technologies, new products and new services, and a driver for changing consumer preferences. Today's business practices are shifting to adapt to changing consumer preferences and national and international standards, and to establish a competitive edge in new and innovative markets. Tomorrow's business environment may be defined by efforts on the part of sectors and individual companies to recognize and capitalize on these evolving issues.

Institutional investors have an opportunity to benefit from these trends. The number and variety of investment strategies focused on addressing concerns over the impacts of climate change and approaches to mitigate those impacts are increasing.

CLEAN ENERGY AND CLEAN TECHNOLOGY: WHAT ARE THEY?

'Clean technology' or 'cleantech' or 'clean tech' are sometimes used as umbrella terms for all the investments discussed here. They can be broadly defined as a range of products, services and processes that reduce or eliminate ecological impacts and/or provide superior performance while requiring lower resource usage. More detailed academic definitions are available; but most investment funds define their own vision of cleantech along similar lines, including or excluding certain sectors. Typical areas are energy, environmental technology and controls, materials and resource efficiency, sustainable transportation (hybrid technology, batteries, etc.), agriculture, and water and waste management. The lack of a concrete definition makes it difficult to estimate the precise market size; however, for the energy sector alone, New Energy Finance (see www.newenergyfinance.com, accessed January 2008) estimates that total worldwide investment in all parts of the clean energy industry is currently between US$500 billion and US$600 billion per annum – that is, around 10 per cent of all total worldwide investment in energy is going into clean energy. In 2007 New Energy Finance estimated that the amount of new money invested in clean energy was US$117 billion, up 41 per cent from 2006, with the biggest portion going to asset financing, but the public markets showing the highest growth rate.

'Clean energy' is a term that covers a range of low carbon-emitting energy sources, including solar photovoltaics (PV), solar thermal, wind, biomass, marine, geothermal and small hydro. It does not normally include energy derived from large hydro projects or nuclear, though funds labelled as 'alternative' or 'renewable' energy may include these categories. Clean energy (or 'renewable energy') funds include all funds focused on investing in companies developing low-carbon energy technology and renewable energy projects. The market for clean energy is growing rapidly. Clean Edge (see www.cleanedge.com, accessed January 2008) estimates that the market for the four clean energy technologies it has designated as 'benchmark technologies' – solar photovoltaics, wind power, biofuels and fuel cells – grew 39 per cent, to US$55.4 billion, in 2006, and the company expects that to quadruple to more than US$226.5 billion within a decade. These energy technologies form the largest subset of the cleantech market.

INVESTMENT DRIVERS

The investment drivers for cleantech are compelling:

- *High and stable demand for energy.* The energy sector is set for a period of high growth. With the rapid industrialization of many developing countries and their heavy reliance on energy, demand is expected to grow significantly.
- *Rising fossil fuel prices.* We have seen a steep change from US$20 to US$30 per barrel of oil (in real terms) throughout the 1990s to more than US$90 per barrel more recently.
- *Concern over continuation and security of supply of fossil fuels.* Broadly speaking, geologists have already mapped out where oil is going to come from over the next century. There is general consensus that cheap easy-to-access oil is no longer available and we are now in the stage of expensive hard-to-get oil.

- *The global threat of climate change and support for renewable energy.* This is resulting in government legislation and intervention, including regulation, subsidies, tax relief and procurement strategies. Worldwide, 45 countries have enacted new laws, with commitments to increase renewable energy as part of the energy mix. For example, in China, 15 per cent of the energy mix is to come from renewable energy by 2020 (Goldman Sachs Global Investment Research, 2006) and in Europe, 21 per cent by 2010 (Martinot, 2005). While there is no federal figure for the US, individual states such as California and New York have set themselves targets of 20 per cent by 2017 and 25 per cent by 2013, respectively (Evolution Markets Inc, undated). In addition, eight mid-Atlantic and northeast US states have joined the Regional Greenhouse Gas Initiative to discuss a regional emissions trading system. Even where fossil fuels such as oil and coal are still widely used, there is significant effort being made to minimize the negative environmental impacts of those energy sources through technology.
- *The impact of a changing climate on the supply and reliability of raw materials.*
- *The shortage of clean, safe water.*
- *Changing consumer preferences.* While slow to start, there is now a growing movement towards more resource-efficient products among commercial, industrial and retail consumers.

While there are numerous drivers underpinning the investment case for this investment area, risks are also prevalent. These typically include technology risk, regulatory uncertainty, a perceived dependence upon high oil prices for the success of renewables and the survival rate of new companies.

INVESTMENT VEHICLES AVAILABLE TO POTENTIAL INVESTORS

A variety of funds are now available to institutional investors who want to capitalize on the cleantech opportunity. Broadly, these funds include private equity and venture capital, public equity, project finance (including infrastructure), or a combination of these. Funds can be sector or theme specific, ranging from broad cleantech funds to narrower alternative energy funds, or even narrower 'niche' funds, such as methane recovery and water funds. Most funds are actively managed, although a number of public equity index funds have recently been introduced, as have exchange-traded funds.

GENERAL INVESTMENT CHARACTERISTICS

With many hundreds of funds available to investors, we focused our research on a selection across a number of asset classes, geographic regions, sector specializations, sizes and business structures. In this section we explore some of the common investment characteristics that we encountered and share some of the early insights from our research:

- Investment horizons tend to be long term, allowing for the maturation of markets, managers and investment opportunities.
- Risk-and-return profiles are hard to establish given the relative immaturity of these sectors, associated uncertainties and the private equity nature of many of the opportunities. Risk-and-return profiles are driven by the underlying investments, which tend to have high idiosyncratic risk and characteristics of sector concentration. Many funds aim to achieve comparable risk-and-return profiles to their counterparts in mainstream private or public equity markets, or project finance and infrastructure, although this varies on a fund-by-fund basis. Most funds do not yet have a meaningful track record. Where track records exist, these may not be helpful when trying to forecast future risk-and-return profiles due to the rapidly evolving investment environment in which they are operating. The business environment in this area five years ago was vastly different from the operating environment today. To increase the chances of a favourable risk-and -return profile, investors should consider diversification, which is possible even within this relatively narrow sector.
- Managerial skill is likely to be a deciding factor. As identified earlier, funds can have broad definitions of clean energy and cleantech, or they can be single-sector or single technology funds. The clean energy and cleantech sectors are still young and rapidly evolving, and it is very difficult for even experienced technicians and investors to keep up to date with emerging new technologies and opportunities across these sectors all over the world. 'Niche' funds that track a single sub-sector allow fund managers to become experts in a particular area and develop a strong network of contacts, and enable superior access to investment opportunities. The funds with the best chances of success are likely to be those that have a clearly articulated focus designed to suit the experience and skill set of the manager or team and the resources at their disposal. In such a dynamic field, one so dependent upon a mix of technology, politics and economics, a team that can demonstrate an ability to correctly forecast and stay ahead of current trends will be most desirable.
- Funds are being launched by both boutique organizations and large well-established financial organizations, either directly or through affiliations. Each organizational structure can have its advantages. For example, the backing of a large organization can be positive as it can bring business management benefits and access to resources and investment opportunities. Boutique organizations, on the other hand, may be able to move more quickly, have greater freedom and be less hindered by bureaucratic

processes. In assessing manager ability, it is more difficult to get a true sense of how well run and controlled these smaller players are; therefore, investors looking to invest with a smaller organization must be prepared to subject them to a more demanding level of due diligence.

- Idea generation and implementation are crucial to the overall success of the fund. Given the rapid increase in capital being allocated to this sector, if there is too much money chasing too few investments, the danger arises of a bubble being created where companies are overvalued due to immediate market conditions as opposed to long-term value creation prospects. In addition, shifts in government programmes and public sentiment may cause changes in valuations. Investors should pay particular attention to the stage of technology being targeted for investment. A later-stage strategy focused on mature and price-competitive technologies may be less susceptible to changing government priorities. However, valuations also vary by sector. At any given time, certain sectors may appear over- or undervalued relative to other cleantech industries. Hence, it is important to understand the value drivers of the particular sector or sub-sector being examined, as well as where that sector is geographically located. In our research, we found a variety of approaches to idea generation and implementation, and we concluded that funds that actively research the sector, source their own deals and use their networks to find leads are more likely to have better access to good investments and are therefore better placed to perform in the long term.

- In portfolio construction, diversification is a key issue for investors who want to reduce their portfolio risk. This can be done by considering a mix of fund characteristics, such as geographic distribution, asset class, sub-sectors and technological stages. For example, a broader strategy with a particular cleantech fund will include a range of sectors from energy to information technology, whereas niche funds will obviously offer less diversification. In addition, the variety of asset classes discussed previously offers a way of addressing diversification. Investors may also consider one of a few cleantech/clean energy funds. In summary, the risks here are similar to those of other investment strategies, requiring investors to view cleantech in the context of their overall portfolio.

SPECIFIC INVESTMENT CHARACTERISTICS
BY ASSET CLASS

Private equity

There has been a strong rise in the number of clean energy or cleantech private equity funds coming on to the market. Cleantech Venture Network (see www.cleantech.com, accessed January 2008) estimates that total US and European venture capital investment in cleantech reached a record US$3.6

billion in 2006, representing a 45 per cent increase over 2005. Approximately 72 per cent of this investment was in energy-related cleantech. The majority of private equity vehicles currently available are direct investment vehicles (e.g. BankInvest's New Energy Solutions, Climate Change Capital's Cleantech Private Equity Fund, and London Asia's Energy and Environment Fund). There are a growing number of cleantech private equity fund of funds, though, offered by institutions such as Robeco, Macquarie and Piper Jaffray.[2]

As is generally the case with private equity, the market covers different stages of investment, from early stage/start-up through development capital and expansion financing, to funding management buyouts from larger, often-listed companies. Diversified investments in private equity are expected to achieve returns above those available from the quoted market over extended time periods. This expectation is based on two factors: the existence of a premium for illiquidity and the enhanced ability to capture returns that arise from companies entering a phase of rapid growth. The success of private equity investment is extremely sensitive to the choice of investment managers and the timing of the commitment. This is no different for clean energy or cleantech private equity choices. This risk may be slightly higher due to the technological and regulatory risks, as well as the relative newness of these sectors.

Arguably, the very long-term, highly illiquid nature of these investments makes private equity inappropriate for poorly funded or very mature liability funds. Investment tends to be via pooled funds structured as closed-end vehicles. In the area of clean energy and cleantech, demand for these funds is proving to be high, with investors such as investment banks, entrepreneurs, family offices and a handful of public funds tending to lead the way. Investors need to be swift, though, as funds are tending to reach their close on time and sometimes well beforehand.

Public equity

There are a growing number of actively managed funds and indices in the public equity markets. Some clean energy and cleantech funds are offered by large institutions as part of their wider product offering (e.g. Blackrock's New Energy Fund, F&C's Global Climate Opportunities, and UBS's New Power Fund), while others are offered by institutions specializing in clean energy or eco-related sectors (e.g. Impax Environmental Markets Fund).[3] Exchange-traded funds are also becoming available based on, for example, the Ardour Global Index, the Wilderhill Clean Energy Index and the Cleantech Venture Network's Cleantech Index. Some of these funds may include industrial conglomerates or other (arguably) non-pure-play holdings. Thus, there is reasonable liquidity in public equity markets, with many funds offering daily liquidity. However, due to the smaller number of underlying companies available and the smaller capitalization of most pure-play clean companies, clean energy or cleantech funds may not be as liquid as their non-clean energy or cleantech counterparts. Risk-and-return profiles appear comparable to those of private equity investments in other sectors, although given the relative immaturity of the cleantech sector, track records, where available, should be considered along with other factors.

Due to easier accessibility and greater liquidity compared to private equity, public equity investment vehicles may make exposure to the clean energy and cleantech markets more appealing to a wider group of investors. There are also sector-specific funds focusing on themes such as water or energy that invest in both cleantech and traditional industries around the theme, helping to get around the issue of there being few listed equity clean energy investments.

How to invest

For investors considering an investment in private equity or public equity funds that focus on clean energy or cleantech, either a satellite investment or part of the normal asset allocation (e.g. private equity allocation, public equity allocation, alternative assets allocation, etc.) may be appropriate. Either way, while only a small portion of the assets is likely to be invested, active oversight should be performed.

Benchmarking is notoriously difficult to undertake in this area, whatever the asset class. This is due, in part, to the variety of definitions being used by fund managers. For example, one clean energy or cleantech fund may be defined very differently from another, making it difficult to compare like with like. Similarly, clean energy or cleantech public equity funds have severely restricted universes and different capitalization exposures in comparison with mainstream global equity indices such as FTSE Global or Morgan Stanley Capital International (MSCI) World. As these sectors mature, benchmarking may become easier. In the meantime, a cautious and developed understanding of the expectations of the funds and how the allocation fits into the overall portfolio are recommended, together with close monitoring and oversight.

CONCLUSION

Clean and renewable energy investments could play an important (and multidimensional) role in a long-term investor's broader investment strategy. Generally, they are likely to have a relatively small but meaningful allocation within a diversified portfolio. Given the secular trends in place and the idiosyncratic nature of investments, we expect a low correlation with other assets. Hence, a diversified 'clean' portfolio can, in turn, offer diversification benefits by lowering the overall investment risk. For investors pursuing responsible investment strategies, cleantech may offer the benefit of allocating resources to resolve environmental issues.

Long-term investors are beginning to direct their money into these funds. In the US, five state-sponsored funds have invested a total of more than US$1 billion in cleantech strategies.[4] The Oslo Pensjonsforsikring (Norway's largest municipal pension plan), ABP (the Dutch government and education sector retirement fund) and several local authorities in the UK have made commitments to these funds as well (Hernandez, 2006). Investment has come from corporate pension funds including that of British Airways (Hernandez, 2006). Many major corporations, such as GE, Siemens, Shell, BP, Sanyo and Sharp, have also made considerable renewable energy investments and acquisitions (Martinot, 2005).

Finally, we note that 'clean' energy does not necessarily mean 'responsible' or 'environmentally friendly'. The growth potential of the clean energy and cleantech sectors has led to many funds branding themselves 'cleantech' in order to ride the wave of popularity; but many do not consider the true social or environmental impact of their investments alongside the financial returns. Hence, investors looking to this sector as part of a responsible investment strategy need to ensure that they identify funds that have a philosophy aligned with their own.

ADDENDUM: RENEWABLE ENERGY AND OTHER CLEANTECH SECTORS[5]

Renewable energy sources capture their energy from existing energy flows (e.g. ongoing natural processes and geothermal heat flows). Key features of some of the most important sources of renewable energy are outlined below. In addition to investing directly in the generation plants or farms, there is also a huge industry in the manufacturing, infrastructure and supporting technologies of renewable energy, particularly generation efficiency, distribution and energy storage. We have given some examples of companies that are currently operating in these sectors:[6]

- *Solar* technology covers all applications that capture energy directly from the sun, either using a photovoltaic (PV) material or via passive technologies, such as concentrating systems that use curved reflectors to focus sunlight. Solar energy became popular during the 1970s when oil prices were high, but lost momentum when oil prices dropped in the 1980s. Solar power currently costs around ten times higher (in broad terms) than electricity from a traditional coal-fired power plant and costs have been increasing in recent years due to the high price of silicon used in PV materials. Nevertheless, solar has niche applications and is a substantial sector worth US$15.6 billion globally in 2006. The drivers of growth in the future are likely to be cost reductions through new technology or through increased manufacturing scale. Germany and Japan are notably strong players in the solar market, with strong research bases, and driven by government support through subsidies and targets. Companies operating in the solar sector include Solarworld, QCells, and Everlight.

- *Wind* technology has had the biggest impact upon renewable energy usage patterns over the past decade, providing more energy output today than solar. The global sector was worth US$17.9 billion in 2006. Wind is a completely free source of renewable energy and wind turbines emit no greenhouse gases when operational, while taking up minimal amounts of land to install. However, the unpredictability of wind patterns means that back-up generators are usually necessary to ensure stable power generation. Also, wind farms are frequently regarded as a threat to local amenity and location decisions can be controversial. Opportunities for investment in the wind sector are varied, including the wind farms directly, or a fund that invests in a portfolio of wind farms, or the supporting industry (e.g. components for, and manufacturers of, wind turbines). Europe leads the world in wind technology development and has about four times as much installed wind energy capacity as the US. The next decade is likely to see continued activity, particularly in developing countries and offshore, and growth will come from technologies and services that improve energy storage, wind predictability and power stability. Companies operating in the wind sector include Clipper Windpower, Vestas and Gamesa.

- *Small hydropower* is power generated from the flowing water of rivers and streams, typically generating up to 10 megawatts (MW) of electricity and with minimal environmental impact. It differs from large hydropower, which uses dams to channel water through electricity-generating turbines. Large-scale projects can have a serious environmental and human impact by flooding residential land and damaging river ecosystems. Hydropower currently provides more than 15 per cent of global electricity capacity, of which 1 to 2 per cent comes from small-scale hydro. The small hydro projects use different technology than large-scale hydro (i.e. they are not just smaller versions of larger projects). Along with tidal (*marine*) generation projects, small hydro is likely to be a growth area for the future. During recent years, European companies have pioneered much of the technical development and dominated international contracts for small hydropower equipment and installations.

- *Geothermal* power is drawn from the hot water and steam produced by underground volcanic activity. Iceland and Japan benefit from natural sources of geothermal power, as do Italy, Turkey and France. Carbon dioxide emissions from harnessing geothermal energy are about 10 per cent of the amount emitted by coal-fired power plants for the same capacity; but recent advances in binary geothermal plants (all underground) may reduce this even further. New drilling techniques also allow energy generation from resources that have previously been too deep or expensive to access. There are a handful of investment funds focusing on this area; but geothermal tends to get less attention than solar or wind. Companies operating in this sector include Enex China, Western Geopower and Magma Power Company.

- *Bioenergy* is the energy derived from biomass for heat, electricity and transport fuel (biofuels). There is a range of biomass sources, including conventional starch, oil and sugar crops; biodegradable industrial and municipal waste; food, agricultural and forestry residues; short rotation forestry and grasses, and marine biomass. *Biofuels* such as bioethanol can be derived from a range of biomass sources, including sugar cane, rape seed (canola), soybean oil or cellulose. The explanation for their classification as carbon neutral is that the carbon dioxide released into the atmosphere on burning is equivalent to the carbon dioxide that plants absorb during the growing cycle. Biofuels are currently the subject of much debate over their suitability as a replacement for fossil fuels as the plants used to generate ethanol may be intensively farmed and require substantial areas of land to grow sufficient supply, thereby displacing food crops. The bioenergy sector encompasses producers of base biomass, suppliers of processing technologies and equipment, logistics and distribution, and the manufacturers of energy systems that are specially adapted for the use of biofuels and products, and the services upon which they depend. Growth in this sector is likely to come from next-generation biofuels and supporting technologies (e.g. refining techniques), in part driven by government backing such as that outlined in President Bush's 2007 'State of the Union' speech in which he called for 35 billion gallons a year of biofuels by 2017. Companies operating in this sector include Nova Biofuels and Abengoa.

The key focus for clean technology is innovations that minimize environmental impacts through reducing usage and demand, improving efficiencies, and mitigating environmental damage already caused, for example, by improving air quality with air purification products and air filtration systems, pollutant controls, and fuel additives to increase efficiency and reduce toxic emissions. As a concept, clean technology is wide-reaching as cleaner, more efficient practices are sought in many traditional sectors such as transportation (e.g. developing hybrid vehicle technology; lighter materials for manufacturing cars; smart logistics software to reduce distances covered; temperature and pressure sensors to improve transportation fuel efficiency; and telecommuting technology) and agriculture (e.g. micro-irrigation systems; bioremediation; non-toxic cleaners; and natural pesticides). We highlight, here, the water sector, as the importance of access to clean water is greater than energy security. Although it tends to be eclipsed by the current popularity of clean energy, the number and variety of investment opportunities focused on the water sector are growing.

The *water* industry, globally, is huge, fragmented and mostly publicly owned. Over time, there has been little investment in the improvements needed to conserve water. With global populations expanding annually, particularly in some of the driest regions of the world, water is becoming an increasingly scarce resource. Technological innovations driving growth in the water sector include water recycling and ultra-filtration systems; water utility sensors and automation systems; metering; and desalination equipment. Substantial problems face the sector, however. Large-scale projects are required to make significant change; but such projects entail major capital investment. Water is currently priced cheaply in most developed markets and attempts to adopt more rational pricing regimes generate resistance. As a result, the motivation to risk capital on new technology is reduced. Over the next century, declining access to clean water will become increasingly critical and climate change will alter the geographical distribution of water. Despite the problems identified above, an increasing amount of investment is being made in the water sector with a corresponding increase in investment opportunities in new companies, venture capital, indices and funds. Companies operating in the water sector include Veolia, ITT Industries and Waste Management.

NOTES

1 The authors would like to acknowledge the significant contributions of Craig Metrick and Kelly Gauthier.
2 Fund names are given for illustrative purposes only and should not be interpreted as an endorsement of their strategy or an investment recommendation.
3 Fund names are given for illustrative purposes only and should not be interpreted as an endorsement of their strategy or an investment recommendation.
4 The five funds are the California Public Employees' Retirement System; the California State Teachers' Retirement System; the New York State Retirement Fund; and the treasurer's offices of Oregon and Pennsylvania. All are members of the Investor Network on Climate Risk (see www.incr.com, accessed January 2008).
5 Sources used for this section include the European Renewable Energy Council (see www.erec.org, accessed January 2008) and New Energy Finance.
6 Company names are given for illustrative purposes only and should not be interpreted as an endorsement of their strategy or an investment recommendation.

REFERENCES

Evolution Markets Inc (undated) *Renewable Energy: State and Regional Compliance Markets,* www.evomarkets.com/rec/index.php?xp1=3&mk=4, accessed January 2008
Goldman Sachs Global Investment Research (2006) *Alternative Energy,* Goldman Sachs, London, 27 April, p5
Hernandez, S. (2006) 'Pensions tack with the wind: Funds pursue low risk, high yields in power from the skies', *Wall Street Journal,* 31 July
Martinot, E. (2005) *Renewables 2005 Global Status Report,* Worldwatch Institute and Tsinghua University, Washington, DC, p5, www.martinot.info/RE2005_Global_Status_Report.pdf

8

Water

Katherine Miles Hill and Sean Gilbert

A global water crisis is apparent. Put simply, dwindling supplies are not enough to meet the explosive demand in many regions. Population growth, climate change, inefficient use of water, rapid industrialization in developing countries, and urbanization are among the broad global trends all influencing the quantity and quality of water supplies. It is not just scarcity of supplies, though; unequal access to water supplies is also part of the problem. Governments will have to find ways of delivering more water to growing populations and arbitrate allocation among different users. For business, this means preparing for the risk of having less water for operations at greater cost. As well as challenges, there may be opportunities that emerge from this crisis and many scenarios for how it may evolve; however, the only certainty is that business and investors will have to adjust to this new reality.

Climate change has captured the attention of the world and investors as a global environmental challenge that threatens to bring fundamental changes to living conditions with consequences to be felt by all. However, the climate is not the only ecological system that touches many aspects of our social and economic life where changes can have long-term impacts upon business – water is another.

The most obvious trend is a growing pressure on the availability of sufficient freshwater supplies in many regions of the world with little sign of respite. Human pressure is directly affecting water systems. Industrial development – namely, wastewater from manufacturing – has led to contamination of vital supplies (see www.unep.org/geo/geo4/report/04_Water.pdf, accessed December 2007). Alongside the relatively predictable factors of human intervention, further changes will be driven as a consequence of climate change, but with impacts that are harder to predict. The consequence is that regions such as China and South

Asia that are key engines for global economic growth and critical to the supply chains for many companies are facing growing stress on water supplies and rapid groundwater depletion. These pressures have the potential to influence the stability of existing agricultural and industrial investments and to limit opportunities for further growth in some parts of the world.

Even as supplies dwindle in many regions, there remains a lack of access to this essential resource and growing political pressure to increase the number of people with access to water. At just over the halfway point to the 2015 deadline to the United Nations Millennium Development Goals (MDGs), the goal for half the proportion of people without sustainable access to safe drinking water is far from being met. Some 1.1 billion people in developing countries still have inadequate access to water (UNDP, 2006, p2).

As pressure on water systems increases, governments will be challenged to manage this elixir for life effectively and equitably. The water crisis will affect government policy and the situation is already forcing difficult policy decisions about allocating limited resources among households, agriculture and industry. As it stands, 70 per cent of the world's fresh water is used for agriculture, 22 per cent is used for industry and the remaining 8 per cent is for domestic use (WBCSD, 2005). Even as governments press to improve access for rural and urban populations, industrial and agriculture pollution is making the goal more elusive. In China, over 40 per cent of river stretches have been classified as severely polluted (Browder, 2007).

Disputes over water threaten to become more commonplace as a source of regional disputes, increasing the political risk and even operational risk for companies and their investors. Consequently, the global rise in demand for water is predicted to be a cause of competition and conflict between countries in the future (Garamone, 2007). It will also be a cause of friction between other sectors and businesses.

EMERGING INVESTMENT RISKS

For investors and markets, the global water crisis brings several core messages. First, water can no longer be taken for granted as a readily available resource and therefore in this context deserves attention as an operating risk. Whether it is a consequence of industrial pollution, climate change or growing household demand, companies in water-intensive industries, such as steel, pulp and paper, among others, will have to plan how to ensure a dependable supply of this vital resource and be prepared for price changes. Industries such as tourism, fishing and others that depend upon healthy rivers and coastal areas may find their business literally disappear, as has occurred in salmon runs in the US Pacific Northwest. This could have implications for the financial performance of companies.

Second, business and investment decisions will have to take into account a new policy environment as part of its operational context. Water supplies do not recognize national boundaries, and so governments have to work together regionally to create multilateral or bilateral treaties as protection mechanisms to guarantee the right to water for all individuals. For example, the governments of Cambodia, Laos, Thailand and Vietnam together signed an agreement on cooperation for the sustainable development of the Mekong River Basin (see www.waterlaw.org/regionaldocs/mekong.html, accessed December 2007). This means that businesses' and investors' decisions may be influenced by governments differently than before, and securing water supplies for activities will become more complex, rather than less difficult.

Third, the pressures around water will create the need for new investment by both governments and business in the water sector in order to improve the efficiency of water use and to bring it to more individuals and entities. This will require investment in new technologies for manufacturing, irrigation and industrial operations, as well as new infrastructure to improve water-supply capacities. This need for infrastructure investment will be a financial risk for some businesses; but, for others, it will signal new commercial opportunities.

INVESTMENT OPPORTUNITIES

As the water crisis deepens, there will doubtless be more demand for products and services that offer creative solutions to water supply and use, which represents an area of opportunity for investors. Just as climate change has driven the emergence of renewable energy, water limitations have the same potential to drive a host of regulatory changes, new fiscal incentives, and demand for new technologies and services. Just as they have done for climate change, businesses are beginning to state in their non-financial reports how they will capitalize on new market opportunities afforded by water shortages – such as introducing new products and services that require less water consumption or improve water access to the world's poorest citizens.[1]

Water points towards two broad areas as an investment theme. The first is opportunities to invest in companies offering new technologies to improve the efficiency of how water is used by businesses, in general. Asset managers such as those at Sustainable Asset Management (SAM) have already moved to create funds to identify suitable investment targets, while also selecting companies that are instigating change in the water sector – companies not just creating water-friendly products, but also those reducing the impact of their production process on water resources (SAM, 2003). For example, SAM has a Sustainable Water Fund for investment, launched in 2001, which invests in four areas: water management and distribution, water purification, demand-side water efficiency, and water and food (SAM, 2003).

The second area lies in products and services to enhance the supply of water, particularly to those who still have inadequate access to water (UNDP, 2006). These opportunities come in a range of forms. At one end of the spectrum lie opportunities associated with meeting the demand for water from cities that are bursting at the seams with population growth. In 2008, for the first time in history, half of the global human population will be living in urban areas (UNFPA, 2007). However, many of the cities facing rapid growth have not been able to develop the necessary infrastructure and will require massive investment in municipal systems. This point is emphasized with the prediction by the United Nations Population Fund (UNFPA) that 81 per cent of the urbanized world will be made up of towns and cities from the developing world by 2030 (UNFPA, 2007).

At the other end of the spectrum are the 1.1 billion people in developing countries who still have inadequate access to water and who are targets of the Millennium Development Goals (UNDP, 2006).[2] In the face of limited growth in developed markets, many companies are looking at *bottom of the pyramid* strategies where many basic needs such as water sit. For example, Philips has created an affordable ultraviolet (UV) light that doubles as a water purifier because UV light kills bacteria.

CONSIDERATIONS FOR INVESTORS

Mainstream individual and institutional investors are beginning to recognize that water is a new factor, both as a risk and opportunity, to consider in their investment decisions. It is relevant to all investors as a generic risk requiring due diligence in the investment process and has the potential to serve as an investment theme for an alternative investment strategy. It is also having emergent implications for where to put ones money and for generating long-term financial value from investment. From ABN AMRO to S&P, it is no longer just the socially responsible investment community driven by moral imperative and the social values of their clients, but also the wider investment community who is now paying attention to the issue of water. A diverse array of investment vehicles has emerged from water-themed exchange-traded funds to structured notes, and water infrastructure projects are being identified as good investment targets.

BOX 8.1 S&P GLOBAL WATER INDEX

The S&P Global Water Index belongs to the S&P Global Thematic Indices, and it provides liquid exposure to companies in the emerging investment theme of water. The index contains 50 companies that are drawn from two clusters of water-related businesses: water utilities and infrastructure, and water equipment and materials. The returns (percentage per annum) of this index after five years were 23.44 per cent, as opposed to 14.62 per cent for the same period of the S&P Global 1200, which is an index of global stocks covering 31 countries and 70 per cent of global market capitalization.

BOX 8.2 SUSTAINABLE ASSET MANAGEMENT (SAM) SUSTAINABLE WATER FUND

As part of its Water Fund, Sustainable Asset Management (SAM) has identified four investment clusters as part of its water fund: distribution and management of water; advanced water treatment; demand-side efficiency; and water and nutrition. The percentage return of the water fund was 108.85 per cent after five years, while the benchmark, Morgan Stanley Capital International (MSCI) World, had a return of 57.10 per cent for the same period.

Another sign of momentum around the theme of water and investment is that the United Nations Environment Programme's Finance Initiative (UNEP FI) has worked with their advisory board on water and finance to develop a voluntary framework to guide investors with their decision-making with regard to water. These guidelines are called *Half Full or Half Empty? A Set of Indicative Guidelines for Water Related Risks and an Overview of Emerging Opportunities for Financial Institutions* (see www.unepfi.org/fileadmin/documents/half_full_half_empty.pdf, accessed December 2007).

Investors need hard quantitative data produced on a common and comparable basis if they are to be able to fully assess the risks and opportunities posed by rising water stress. The *G3 Guidelines* of the Global Reporting Initiative (GRI), the world's most widely used sustainability reporting framework, has a number of water-related metrics that companies can and do use to manage their associated impacts. Within the environmental indicators, there are four water-related metrics: EN8 total water withdrawn by source; EN9 water sources significantly affected by the withdrawal of water; EN10 percentage and total volume of water recycled and reused; and EN21 total water discharge by quality and destination. EN8, EN10 and EN21 have been integrated within the World Business Council for Sustainable Development (WBCSD) Global Water Tool.

Most manufacturing operations require water as an input and it is a critical input for a range of sectors, from agriculture to semi-conductor chips. The absence of a reliable source of sufficiently clean water can literally be a show stopper to operations. Virtually all manufacturing processes will use water to some degree. However, the volume and purposes will vary widely; therefore, changes in the availability of water will have differing impacts.

The most basic building block is to understand how much water the company consumes on a regular basis (indicator EN8 in the GRI *G3 Guidelines*) and to consider this in the context of overall supply. Similarly, for some sectors and regions, it can also be important to look at the degree of water recycling used. Certain industries such as pulp and paper have developed systems with extremely high levels of water recycling (EN10). The level of recycling in a given company can offer insights into both the process sophistication of a company and its exposure to supply disruptions. In industries with very tight margins, this can also offer key advantages in cost savings. Some companies are using the GRI *G3 Guidelines* metrics and the WBCSD Global Water Tool, which incorporates these, to assist with companies' own internal management of water.

While the internal operations of a company are important, it is equally crucial to consider what happens *beyond the fence line* and whether a company is perceived as a good neighbour and industry leader on the issue. A company that is perceived as consuming an unfair share of water resources or discharging wastewater into local supplies can rapidly find itself in conflict with local communities and regulators.

To this end, it is important for investors to consider water inputs (EN8 and EN9) and water outputs (EN21). Which water sources are used by companies and what are their relative impacts upon other users? Is a company drawing down groundwater supplies in a water-stressed region or a river that is already taxed for multiple uses? What types of pollutants are released into their waste-water and what is the impact?

BHP Billiton and Watercare Services Ltd are just two companies that have reported on water indicators according to the GRI *G3 Guidelines* in their 2007 sustainability and annual reports.

The objective information about water use needs to be placed in the context of where a company operates and common practices within its sector. For example, if the company's disclosure shows that it is a water-intensive industry, one should ask whether its operations are placed in water-stressed areas or regions that are susceptible to the impact of climate change. If a company reports a low level of water recycling, how does this compare with its peers in the industry? What does this suggest about their technology and production processes? Equally important, how does the company see water as part of its operational or forward-looking strategy?

Companies that do not manage water well become a greater investment risk because they face a greater chance of disruption to their operations or financial impacts if pricing of water changes. Companies that do manage water well have the opportunity to realize cost savings due to increased efficiency through reduced water consumption. They also remain one step ahead of regulation, and demonstrate organizational commitment to sustainable development and differentiate themselves in the marketplace by showing accountability and responsibility towards the environment, which protects brand value and can generate more customers and greater acceptance of their operations by communities.

All of this means that companies cannot afford to ignore their own impacts and must report on them in order to help shape a more sustainable global future.

THE TOOLS FOR THE JOB

Investors require disclosure in order to analyse sustainability factors such as water and to incorporate this information within their investment decisions. The current trends in water point towards two types of needs.

At an operational level, there is a need for disclosure of core information around water use, covering topics such as consumption, water sources and their stability, discharges and community impacts. The GRI metrics on water provide companies with an effective management tool that can be used to respond to the global water crisis and to assist with companies' own internal management of this essential resource by embedding water conservation within the production process. By disclosing information on these metrics as well as other indicators in the GRI framework, companies can benchmark their organizational performance with respect to laws, norms, codes, performance standards and voluntary initiatives; demonstrate organizational commitment to sustainable development; and compare their organizational performance over time. The comparability of organizational performance with other companies is particularly useful for financial analysts who want to assess the impact that specific companies have for their consideration in water investment funds.

At a more strategic level, there is a need for disclosure that can help investors identify organizations who offer products and services that can contribute to resolving the water crisis. Equally important is the company's vision for how trends will unfold and the role that its products and services will play in the emerging markets.

Much of this type of disclosure is currently not found in annual accounts, but can be derived from sustainability reports. However, at present, the sustainability performance information provided by companies is not always sufficient for investors to incorporate it satisfactorily within their decision-making process. A report entitled *GRI Reporting: Aiming to Uncover True Performance* was published on the theme of sustainability reporting and investors in November 2007 by WestLB AG, a German commercial bank, with the input of Walden Asset Management and Trillium Asset Management.[3,4] The study concluded that more progress is needed before the information provided in sustainability reports provides investors with sufficiently comparable information to support broad-based analysis. The biggest problem they identified was that many companies still do not sufficiently use common standards, such as GRI.

As a result, in the context of the international water crisis, water has become an increasingly relevant theme for investors and businesses. The lack of water quality and availability poses an operating risk and a new influencing factor in the policy environment. At the same time, the demand for investment in the sector has opened up new commercial opportunities twofold. These include both companies offering new technologies to improve efficiency of how water is used by businesses and also those that improve the infrastructure and supply of water. Consequently, there are a number of considerations that investors need to make as part of their investment decision to assess the risks and opportunities of water-related factors, such as the quantity of water used and the sources from where it is drawn, the extent of water recycling and wastewater.

Disclosure of this information is needed by investors to integrate sustainability criteria within their investment decisions. Reporting on water indicators and using a global comparable framework for disclosing such information is vital to this. Looking to the future – with the increased need for sustainability information regarding water indicators – it will not just be the water context that is crucial, but the use of sustainability information by investors as part of their decision-making process.

NOTES

1 The GRI *G3 Guidelines* recommends that, as a standard disclosure in their sustainability report, companies include a statement from the most senior decision-maker of the organization about the relevance of sustainability to the organization and its strategy. In this statement companies should present their overall vision and strategy for the short term, medium term and long term, particularly with regard to managing the key challenges associated with economic, environmental and social performance. Given the emerging water crisis, companies can use this disclosure to explain how they intend to manage their future water impacts.

2 Goal 7: ensure environmental sustainability. Target 10: halve, by 2015, the proportion of people without sustainable access to safe drinking water and basic sanitation (see www.mdgmonitor.org/goal7.cfm, accessed December 2007).

3 The comprehensive study of corporate sustainability reporting among the Dow Jones STOXX Global 1800 Index found that 45 per cent (785 companies) issued sustainability reports and out of the 785 companies that produced such reports, 38 per cent based their reports on external standards based on the GRI *G3 Guidelines*.

4 Members of the Sustainable Investment Research Analyst Network (SIRAN).

REFERENCES

Browder, G. J. (2007) *Stepping Up: Improving the Performance of China's Urban Water Utilities*, World Bank, Washington, DC

Garamone, J. (2007) *Army Must Adapt to Changing Threats*, 15 November, www.defenselink.mil/news/newsarticle.aspx?id=48156, accessed December 2007

SAM (Sustainable Asset Management) (2003) *SAM Insight: Water Crisis and Opportunity*, SAM, Zurich

UNDP (United Nations Development Programme) (2006) *UNDP Human Development Report*, UNDP, New York, p2

UNFPA (United Nations Population Fund) (2007) *State of the World Population 2007*, www.unfpa.org/swp/2007/english/introduction.html, accessed December 2007

WBCSD (World Business Council on Sustainable Development) (2005) *Water Facts and Trends*, 23 August, www.wbcsd.org/web/publications/Water_facts_and_trends.pdf, accessed December 2007

WestLB AG (2007) *GRI Reporting Aiming to Uncover True Performance*, WestLB AG, Walden Asset Management and Trillium Asset Management, Boston, MA, November

Part III

Sustainability across the Other Asset Classes

9

Fixed Income and Microfinance

Ivo Knoepfel and Gordon Hagart

Investments in fixed-income securities such as sovereign and corporate bonds play an important role in the asset allocation of both private and institutional investors. The demand for fixed-income investments is particularly strong from investors with long-term liabilities, such as insurance companies and defined-benefit pension schemes.[1]

A combination of regulatory, demographic and market developments seems to be reinforcing this demand. For example, requirements for defined-benefit corporate pension funds to close their funding gaps have driven many large schemes to adopt 'liability-driven' investment (LDI) strategies[2] for managing their members' assets, which can involve switching a considerable part of their assets into fixed-income investments. In 2006, one survey suggested that 42 per cent of UK-based institutional investors plan to increase their bond allocations in 2007 (*Financial Times*, 2006). Similarly, a 2006 survey of UK asset managers showed that the major asset class undergoing most rapid growth is fixed income.

Despite the substantial exposure of investors to this asset class, fixed-income investments that include a sustainable investment approach have traditionally received substantially less attention than equities. Indeed, even as institutional investors such as the signatories of the United Nations Principles for Responsible Investment turn their attention to the effect of environmental, social and governance issues (ESG) on asset classes such as commodities and real estate, discussions of fixed income remain conspicuous by their relative absence.

Nonetheless, a small but growing range of sustainable fixed-income strategies is available on the market today (see Novethic, 2007). These strategies invest in securities issued by both public entities (such as municipalities, nations and supranational agencies) and companies. Their inclusion of sustainability

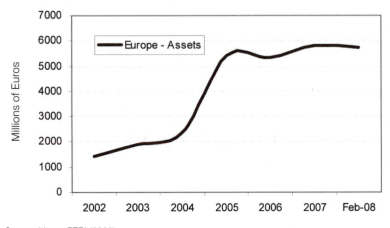

Source: Lipper FERI (2008)

Figure 9.1 *Growth of SRI fixed income in Europe*

issues in the investment process is driven either by the desire to improve the financial return of the investment or to provide products that are suitable for investors with a socially responsible or ethical investment strategy (i.e. investors with objectives that go beyond financial returns). Such vehicles experienced rapid growth over the earlier part of this decade (see Figure 9.1).

COMPARISONS WITH THE EQUITY PARADIGM

While both equity and fixed-income investors are concerned with any factor, including sustainability issues, which may affect the value of the enterprise as a whole, the two investor types may interpret and prioritize such issues differently.

In terms of security selection, the financially focused equity investor is interested in how the integration of ESG issues within the investment process can help him to identify either:

- opportunities for an issuer to which the market has not yet ascribed fair value (i.e. a chance to own assets and participate in future cash flows 'on the cheap'); or
- risks to an issuer that have been insufficiently priced in by the market (i.e. where the market value is higher than the fair value).

In contrast, the key concern of the fixed-income investor is the ability of the issuer (whether it be a company or a public body) to meet its contractual obligations to its creditors – namely, making periodic interest payments and repaying the principal sum at the end of the security's lifetime. The cases of Parmalat, WorldCom and the US airline industry are recent reminders of the risks of investing in the bonds of even the largest companies. Accordingly, the fixed-income investor's interest in ESG issues focuses on the downside: where the integration of such issues can reveal risks to the timing and magnitude of the company's cash flows.

Fixed-income investors therefore usually analyse ESG issues in relation to interest cover, solvency and other indicators of credit quality in the lifetime of the security. Of particular interest are potential disruptions to cash flows around the time when the debt is due to be repaid.

However, in certain circumstances, the ESG interests of equity and fixed-income investors can become closely aligned. Examples include investors in very long-term debt issues (or 'rolling' investments in an issuer's shorter-term debt over a long period of time), and situations where the issuer has become financially distressed. The latter situation is interesting from an ESG perspective because fixed-income investors are often allocated the equity of restructured companies and because such situations can catalyse major changes in the issuer's strategy and governance.

WHAT STRATEGIES ARE FIXED-INCOME MANAGERS USING?

The current landscape for sustainable fixed-income investments is dominated by two-step approaches to including ESG issues in the investment process. The asset manager generally uses ESG analysis to construct a universe of investable issuers that does not substantially differ from the benchmark portfolio in terms of risk and return.[3] The manager then attempts to add value by making active bets within the reduced universe on traditional factors such as duration, yield curve position, sector allocations, market timing, etc.

Where the issuers in the portfolio are companies, most asset managers initially use the same ESG issues and methodologies as are employed to assess equities.

In the case of public fixed-income securities (e.g. municipal, sovereign and supranational bonds), the discussions of ESG issues have tended to concentrate on ethical and normative approaches to environmental and social issues. That is to say, the discussions of the sustainability of cities and nations have been somewhat detached from the direct financial impact of ESG issues upon the debt sold by those entities. Although it is difficult to imagine a developed country defaulting due to environmental and social issues, one should not underestimate long-term scenarios that could affect the credit quality of whole nations or regions – for example:

- physical impacts of climate change leading to massive burdens on public finances;
- local or geopolitical tensions around natural resources leading to conflict;
- a collapse of social security systems due to demographics and political inertia.

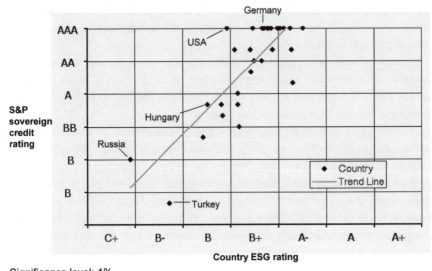

Significance level: 1%
Correlation coefficient (Pearson) > 0.8

Source: oekom Research

Figure 9.2 *Correlation between ESG performance and country credit ratings*

In the case of developing and emerging countries, these risks may be ampli-
fied, and it is possible to observe how environmental degradation and resource
depletion (as measured through the 'ecological footprint' concept) has led to
negative macro-economic effects in some countries. Social issues and corruption, through a complex chain of mechanisms, can also hamper the long-term
growth, economic productivity and, therefore, the credit quality of a country.
Empirical research seems to suggest that there is a positive link between the
ESG performance of a country and its credit rating (see Figure 9.2). Some
specialist research providers have in the past developed ESG ratings for
countries that include criteria such as political stability; corruption levels;
public health; education levels; human and labour rights policies; environmental capacity compared to environmental stress; and quality of public
infrastructure.

It is also important to mention the decisive role played by credit rating
agencies, such as Fitch Ratings, Moody's and S&P, in the area of fixed-income
investments. Most investors make wide use of the ratings provided by these
agencies in selecting issuers and securities. If the goal is to mainstream ESG
issues in fixed-income investments, credit rating agencies will have to play a
major role. This is not yet the case today, although most rating agencies take
corporate governance into account to a certain extent. An investor interested in
sustainable fixed-income strategies is therefore forced to rely on the knowledge
of specialist asset managers and research providers.

BNP Paribas Asset Management, Dexia Asset Management, HSBC Investments and Sarasin Asset Management are among those who have been active in launching ESG-inclusive fixed-income strategies for institutional investors. The strategies, many of which now have strong three-year-plus track records, use ESG issues either as a source of additional financial return or in order to satisfy the requirements of investors with environmental or social objectives.

OPPORTUNITIES AND RISKS FOR ESG-INCLUSIVE FIXED-INCOME INVESTMENTS

The combination of the growth in demand for all fixed-income investments and the surge in institutional investors applying ESG-inclusive strategies to the entirety of their investments would seem to bode well for managers of ESG-inclusive fixed-income investments. The immediate challenge will be to offer strategies that cover a wide range of issuer types, regions and currencies at fee levels that are attractive to institutional investors.

For financially focused fixed-income investors, there are risks that the asset manager overstates the materiality of ESG-inclusive issuer selection in the investment process, given that macro-driven factors such as position on the yield curve (where ESG analysis is not an explicit part of the investment decision-making) often have the biggest impact upon relative performance. Similarly, if managers attempt to 'retrofit' strategies that were designed for ethical investors to those who are interested in the financial value to be added by ESG analysis, the result is unlikely to be satisfactory over the long term.

Access to high-quality comparable data on different types of issuers (e.g. companies, municipal, national and supranational issuers) is an important challenge for both financially focused and ethically motivated investors.

From the point of view of ethical investors or those looking for an environmental or social return to their investment, a further risk exists if the manager screens out issuers based on an overly simple approach to ESG issues. The reality is that many companies (and, indeed, nations) outsource problematic ESG issues to other companies and countries. Failure to acknowledge the 'systems' nature of many ESG issues may result in inappropriate investment decisions. It is also possible that engagement with the issuer, as opposed to simple screening, may also be an effective way to achieve the investor's objectives in the fixed-income space.

As demonstrated in Chapter 2 on sustainable equity, ethically focused funds dominate socially responsible fixed-income portfolio options. It is suspected that fixed-income funds will move more towards a greater financial focus as time progresses; but that has largely not occurred to date. Some of the larger examples of funds that already have moved in this direction are based in continental Europe, and include Sarasin Sustainable Bond EUR. Based in Switzerland, this fund only invests in perceived top-quality bonds whose issuers, whether governmental or corporate, are thought to make a positive contribution towards sustainability. Suitable countries are isolated based on their overall low and efficient consumption of environmental and social resources, and companies are selected based on their adoption of sustainable goals and efficient use of resources.

One of the very few current US-based fixed-income funds that is sustainability minded is Pax World's High-Yield Bond Fund. This fund seeks to invest in forward-thinking companies with perceived sustainable business models that, at the same time, meet high ESG standards as well. A similarly minded fund in the UK using a similar methodology would be Norwich Sustainable Future Corporate Bond. Although many of the funds listed above have not outperformed their benchmarks, going forward, they aim to provide maximum risk protection with steady income for their investors.

The largest fixed-income fund with a sustainable angle has been ABN AMRO Groen Fonds, whose chief aim has been to finance green projects, which to date, have included biological agriculture, green warehouses and new clean technology projects. ABN AMRO also sponsors the Sustainable Global Credit Fund: a fund that invests in global debt securities that comply with sustainable criteria.

MICROFINANCE INVESTMENTS

The past years have seen the emergence of a new class of fixed-income investments: investment in microfinance debt. A market that was until recently only accessible to large donors and development banks, today microfinance is also available to private investors thanks to the emergence of investment funds and structured finance products open to a wider public.

The rapidly expanding microfinance industry provides financial services to the economically active poor, mainly in emerging and developing countries. Over the past 20 years, so-called microfinance institutions (MFIs) operating in developing countries have proved that it is possible to provide financial services (including loans, saving and transfer services, insurance, etc.) to micro-entrepreneurs in a financially sustainable way. Because of the huge productivity gains that are made possible through access to finance, micro-entrepreneurs have both the willingness and capability to repay the loans provided to them. Indeed, well-managed MFIs achieve loan repayment rates of over 98 per cent.

The potential of microfinance – both in terms of its positive social impact and its market volume – is huge, given the estimated 500 million potential clients and the fact that only a small part of demand is covered. MFIs finance a part of their growth through the saving deposits of their clients and turn to local and international capital markets for additional financing sources. According to the Consultative Group to Assist the Poorest (CGAP), the 2004 combined portfolio

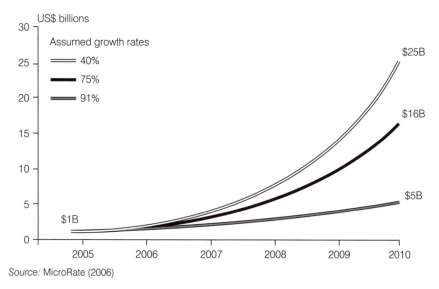

Figure 9.3 *The growth of microfinance*

of MFIs worldwide was approximately US$15 billion, with annual growth rates between 15 and 30 per cent, translating into a demand of between US$2.5 billion and US$5.0 billion of debt capital each year (USAID, 2004). The lion's share of debt capital is currently provided by large donors and development banks; but the share of private-sector investments has rapidly increased to over US$1.5 billion and is expected to become the main source of debt capital for commercially viable MFIs in the years to come. MicroRate, a research and rating institution, estimates that the combined portfolios of private-sector microfinance investment vehicles could reach US$16 billion to US$25 billion by the year 2010 (see Figure 9.3) (MicroRate, 2006).

In addition to private investors, institutional investors have recently stepped up their investments in microfinance. ABP, the US$300 billion Dutch civil service pension fund, started to invest in microfinance in 2005. According to ABP, the attraction of these investments is that 'their returns have little correlation with returns on equity and fixed income. Moreover, they are hardly susceptible to macro-economic developments, such as interest and inflation' (Investments and Pensions Europe Netherlands, 2007). A recently launched Dutch microfinance fund has attracted investments from a dozen large pension funds, including the railways pension fund SPF and the printing industry fund GBF.

CONCLUSION

In summary, the main characteristics that make microfinance debt a potentially interesting investment opportunity for sustainable investors are as follows:

- Given the emergence of globally diversified public funds, investments in microfinance debt have become easily accessible and are relatively low risk (MFIs have historically displayed very low default rates even during major emerging-markets crises).
- Microfinance investments represent an interesting source of diversification for investors. Given that the micro-entrepreneurs who are at the basis of microfinance operate in the informal sector and fulfil very basic needs of low-income populations, such as food and clothing, the correlation to other asset classes is almost negligible.
- If one acknowledges that risk levels are relatively low, microfinance debt investments provide acceptable risk-adjusted returns (the returns of commercial debt funds are in the range of 5 to 6 per cent annually at current rates).
- For those investors interested in a 'social return', microfinance provides very tangible outcomes in terms of improved livelihoods, creation of income and jobs for the poor. Innovative funds are today capable of quantifying the 'social return' of every dollar invested in microfinance.

As Deutsche Bank concluded in a research note in December 2007, 'microfinance can be characterized as an emerging investment opportunity that – if added as a supplement – seems to be conducive to enhancing the efficient diversification of portfolios. Ultimately, there is some evidence that it might even evolve into an asset class of its own over the long run' (Deutsche Bank Research, 2007).

NOTES

1 Indeed, fixed-income investments often account for more than 50 per cent of the asset allocation for pensions in countries such as Austria, Denmark, Germany, Norway and Singapore according to the Organisation for Economic Co-operation and Development (OECD).
2 LDI strategies typically involve combining prime long-term fixed-income securities with derivatives to minimize inflation and interest rate risks.
3 It should be noted, however, that the reduced number of issuers and issues relative to the public equity space may pose problems in terms of portfolio efficiency if strong negative screens are used to construct the investable universe.

REFERENCES

Deutsche Bank Research (2007) *Microfinance: An Emerging Investment Opportunity*, Deutsche Bank Research, Frankfurt, Germany, 19 December
Financial Times (2006) 'Bond allocations are likely to rise', *Financial Times*, 24 April, www.ft.com/cms/s/36a7f8fa-d32e-11da-828e-0000779e2340,Authorised=false.html?_i_location=http%3A%2F%2Fwww.ft.com%2Fcms%2Fs%2F36a7f8fa-d32e-11da-828e-0000779e2340.html&_i_referer=

Investments and Pensions Europe Netherlands (2007) *Microfinance Joins Pensions Portfolio*, IPE, London, November, p14

MicroRate (2006) *Microfinance Investment Vehicles (MIV): An Emerging Asset Class*, MicroRate, Arlington, VA, November

Novethic (2007) *The New Frontiers of SRI: Mapping a Viable Approach to Fixed-Income SRI*, Novethic, Paris, France, February

USAID (United States Agency for International Development) (2004) *Financing Microfinance Institutions: The Context for Transitions to Private Capital*, USAID, Washington, DC

10

Sustainable and Responsible Property Investing[1]

Gary Pivo and Paul McNamara

INTRODUCTION

A new view is emerging, based on a growing awareness among real estate professionals, that social and environmental issues can have significant material consequences for their portfolios. Worsening environmental hazards, tougher government regulations, expanding legal liabilities, increasingly expensive resource and material inputs, shifting consumer behaviour and greater pressure from affected stakeholders are converging to make it financially risky to ignore social, environmental and governance concerns. Likewise, it has become more and more beneficial to address such issues up front when funding new projects.

This chapter discusses sustainable and responsible property investing (RPI) as a positive way of responding to this emerging view. RPI allows for maximizing the positive effects, and minimizing the negative, of property ownership, management and development upon society and the natural environment in a way that is consistent with investor goals and fiduciary responsibilities. It requires both an understanding of how cities and buildings relate to these larger issues and knowing how to address them in a financially prudent manner.

WHAT ARE THE ISSUES?

Our understanding of how cities and buildings impact upon society and the natural environment has progressed a good deal over the past few decades. This understanding provides us with a solid foundation on which to build principles for RPI. The United Nations has focused on cities and buildings at least since the 1972 Toronto Declaration of the United Nations Conference on the Human Environment and the 1976 Vancouver Declaration on Human Settlements (Habitat I). These groundbreaking declarations framed both the constructive and destructive roles that urban areas can play in human health, poverty, housing, governance and our natural environment:

> *Planning must be applied to human settlements and urbanization with a view to avoiding adverse effects on the environment and obtaining maximum social, economic and environmental benefits for all.* (Declaration of the United Nations Conference on the Human Environment, Stockholm, 1972)

> *The improvement of the quality of life of human beings is the first and most important objective of every human settlement policy. These policies must facilitate the rapid and continuous improvement in the quality of life of all people, beginning with the satisfaction of the basic needs of food, shelter, clean water, employment, health, education, training, (and) social security.* (Vancouver Declaration on Human Settlements, 1976)

THE IMPORTANT ROLE OF NEW AND EXISTING PROPERTIES

The global environment and real estate markets are inextricably linked. For example, according to the United Nations' Intergovernmental Panel on Climate Change (IPCC), residential and commercial buildings account for 21 and 11 per cent, respectively, of global carbon dioxide (CO_2) emissions, with transportation adding a further 22 per cent (IPCC, 2001). Therefore, the decisions and choices made by those involved in the real property market (developers, owners, managers and tenants) are central to the potential mitigation or exacerbation of many critical urban issues.[2]

At any given time, there will be an existing stock of real properties with associated infrastructure and open spaces; depending upon demand pressures at any given time, there will probably be new development, redevelopment and property refurbishment works occurring, with the former typically adding 2 to 4 per cent to existing stock per annum in developed countries; a greater percentage in emerging economies. Commentators commonly focus on showing how the environmental and social impact of new additions to the built stock can be minimized. This work is clearly of great importance. However, any set of principles for RPI must also consider what can be done to reduce continuing impacts from the much larger stock of buildings that are already in place. In aggregate, small improvements to the social and environmental performance of existing properties could more than match the impact of significantly improving the quality of incremental new stock. Both new and existing properties need to be addressed.

DOING WELL WHILE DOING GOOD

RPI can add value and improve returns in several different ways (WWF, undated). First, legislation is more frequently holding companies responsible or accountable and subject to fines if they ignore various social or environmental issues. Second, development that addresses local concerns is often more quickly permitted or given subsidies by local government officials. Third, there are opportunities to improve operational efficiencies and increase competitiveness when costly resource consumption is reduced. Fourth, strong reputational benefits can be achieved. And fifth, responsible producers can increase market differentiation for their products, giving them an edge, especially with the growing number of consumers who are interested in socially and environmentally responsible products. The most fully documented case of RPI benefiting investment returns is energy conservation. Energy conservation generates a variety of societal benefits, including lower greenhouse gas (GHG) emissions, less air pollution and better public health. Meanwhile, it lowers operating costs, improves net operating incomes and raises valuations, resulting in higher returns from both operations and appreciation. According to research by the US Environmental Protection Agency (EPA), drawing on experience from real estate investment companies that participate in its Energy Star programme, a recommended sequence of upgrades designed to save energy costs an average of US$2.30 per square foot, reduces energy use by 40 per cent, produces an annual savings of US$0.90 per square foot, and is paid back in 2.5 years (see Table 10.1). If this sequence of costs and returns is analysed for a ten-year period, with the energy savings being capitalized into building valuation and returned at the end of ten years, the internal rate of return for the investment comes to 41 per cent. In separate research, cost estimators are finding that energy-efficient buildings are being built at the same cost per square foot as conventional buildings by developers making careful choices early in the design process. Any conservation premiums that do exist, however, typically fall below both the accuracy normally expected of early cost estimates and the contingencies carried on most project budgets at the conceptual stage (see Langdon and Steven Winter Associates, 2004; Matthiessen and Morris, 2004).

Investments in energy conservation can also moderate a variety of property investment risks, which when accounted for in a discounted cash-flow model, increase property values. These risks include financial risks (such as exposure to energy price shocks), policy risks (such as exposure to new energy conservation requirements),[3] and physical risks (such as exposure to more frequent or severe flooding, landslides and hurricanes produced by climate change).

Table 10.1 *Investments in energy efficiency have high returns*

	Investment per square foot (US$)	Rate of energy savings	Annual savings per square foot (US$)	Savings per 100,000 square feet of office building (US$)	Asset value increase at a 10% capitalization rate (US$)	Simple payback
Janitorial services	0.01	5%	0.14	13,500	135,000	Immediate
Operations and maintenance	0.05	9%	0.20	19,800	198,000	4 months
Lighting	1.04	16%	0.36	36,000	360,000	3 years
Heating, ventilation and cooling	1.21	9%	0.21	20,700	207,000	6 years
All combined	2.30	40%	0.90	90,000	900,000	2.5 years

Note: Calculations are based on national averages and US$0.09 per kilowatt hour (kWh) blended rate for office properties.
Source: US Environmental Protection Agency, Energy Star Program

There is scientific evidence that other types of RPI can be financially prudent as well. Opportunities include water conservation; hazard mitigation (asbestos, toxic chemicals, landslide exposure, etc.); tree planting and green-belt protection; construction and demolition waste recycling; flexible building systems; urban revitalization; transit-oriented housing; 'walkable' mixed-use infill development; and citizen engagement in project planning. Investments in all of these activities have been found to produce favourable returns, improved valuations or short payback periods, offering the potential for increased performance and reduced risk.

In one example, the Sustainable Property Appraisal Project, carried out by a team of researchers at Kingston University, London, UK, and by real property industry practitioners in the UK, analysed the extent to which the current value of existing property assets is potentially affected by the existence or absence of 'sustainable' features. Although the work remains preliminary in nature, their case studies suggest that such features, in a British context at least, could already be adding or subtracting up to 5 per cent to the current worth of the asset.

EMERGING INDUSTRY LEADERSHIP

Leaders have emerged among both investors and investment management companies, demonstrating that it is feasible to implement RPI practices.

In California, the state's two large public retirement funds – the California Public Employees' Retirement System (CalPERS) and California State Teachers' Retirement System (CalSTRS) – hold over 200 million square feet of property. In a move they explicitly recognize as both socially and financially responsible, both funds have set goals to reduce the energy use in their real

---

BOX 10.1 TEN DIMENSIONS OF RPI

The ten dimensions of RPI are as follows:

1 *energy conservation* (e.g. conservation retrofitting, green power generation and purchasing, energy-efficient design);
2 *public transport-oriented development* (e.g., transit-oriented development, walkable communities, mixed-use development);
3 *urban revitalization and adaptability* (e.g. infill development, flexible interiors, brownfield redevelopment);
4 *corporate citizenship* (e.g. regulatory compliance, sustainability disclosure and reporting, independent boards, adoption of voluntary codes of ethical conduct, stakeholder engagement);
5 *environmental protection* (e.g. water conservation, solid waste recycling and habitat protection);
6 *local citizenship* (e.g. quality design, minimum neighbourhood impacts, considerate construction, community outreach, historic preservation, no undue influence on local governments);
7 *social equity and community development* (e.g. affordable/social housing, community hiring and training, fair labour practices);
8 *voluntary certifications* (e.g. green building certification and certified sustainable wood finishes);
9 *health and safety* (e.g. site security, avoidance of natural hazards, first aid readiness);
10 *worker well-being* (e.g. plazas, childcare on premises, indoor environmental quality, barrier-free design).

---

estate holdings by 20 per cent over the next five years. They have also increased their investment in urban inner-city real estate to over US$2 billion, including US$300 million for affordable housing. CalSTRS has engaged its investment stream on energy conservation by adopting a set of conservation measures for the managers of their separate (i.e. not co-mingled) accounts to follow. CalPERS has adopted specific policies for urban investments that include a focus on low-income housing, redevelopment and 'smart growth' alternatives to suburban sprawl.

There are also publicly traded real estate investment companies and trusts around the world that have made significant commitments to corporate social responsibility (CSR) and sustainable development. Several have been listed in the Dow Jones Sustainability World Index and similar indices. Examples include British Land Plc (UK), Investa Property Group (Australia), Land Securities Plc (UK), Commonwealth Property Office Fund (Australia), Swire Pacific Ltd (China), Wereldhave (The Netherlands), Mitsubishi Estate Co, Ltd (Japan) and Klepierre (France). In addition, a 2004 survey of the UK's 13 largest home builders, produced for the World Wide Fund for Nature (WWF) One Million Sustainable Homes Campaign, found Countryside Properties and the Berkeley Group to be leaders in incorporating sustainability within mainstream business practices.

Closer study of the policies and practices of leading funds and companies generates a list of best practice guidelines for investors to consider. Of course, even the best may have room to improve; but the innovations they have achieved so far may well be feasible for others to consider.

BEST PRACTICE EXAMPLES

Green buildings

Green buildings are designed to conserve natural resources and improve human health. Several voluntary certification programmes, such as Leadership in Energy and Environmental Design (LEED) and Building Research Establishment Environmental Assessment Method (BREEAM), have established green building standards. Green buildings can deliver a variety of public benefits related to global warming, air pollution, resource conservation and indoor air quality. Systematic research is tending to show that green buildings can be built at the same cost as conventional properties. Survey research is also finding that occupiers may be willing to pay marginally higher rents to obtain the benefits of green buildings. Although studies are still inconclusive, evidence is mounting that green buildings increase worker productivity and lower running costs. If this is confirmed, green buildings could become more valuable relative to conventional properties over the coming years.

What investors are doing

ICADE/EMPG (France) developed a 10,000 square metre property in Aubervilliers that was certified under France's High Environmental Quality Office programme. To date, it has achieved a 20 per cent lower-than-average running cost and required no additional budget for its green features. *IL & FS Investment Managers* (India) financed Chennai-One, a 1.2 million square foot office space for information technology businesses. The aim is to achieve a 30 per cent energy saving. Environmental features added 3 per cent to the project cost, but rents have been higher than for conventional properties.

Morley Fund Management (UK) completed the City of Edinburgh Council Headquarters, incorporating a variety of sustainability measures. It achieved a BREEAM rating of 'very good' and has attained particularly efficient energy performance, allowing its tenant to reduce its carbon footprint.

Energy conservation

Saving energy can lower operating expenses and guard against future price spikes while simultaneously reducing CO_2 emissions. Systematic studies from around the world show that energy-related capital expenditures that improve lighting, boilers, air conditioning and office equipment are nearly always cost-effective for private investors. It is also cost-effective to check the performance of existing building energy systems, making sure that they are performing at expected levels.

What investors are doing

Investa Property Group (Australia) audits the energy use in its office buildings, diagnoses inefficiencies and identifies cost-effective ways of saving energy. In one building alone, it is saving US$27,000 and 363 tonnes of CO_2 per year, all with minimal or no-cost conservation strategies.

AXA Real Estate Investment Managers (France) is refurbishing the energy systems in its buildings. In one of its properties, updated heating and cooling units and a change from fuel oil to natural gas is saving more than 20,000 Euros and 107 tonnes of CO_2 per year.

PRUPIM (UK) cut the energy used by its mall at Cribbs Causeway by 14 per cent in just one year by switching off unessential lighting in the car park at night. Some electrical work was needed to make this possible; but with the energy savings, the capital expenditure will generate a rate of return of nearly 40 per cent per annum over its first ten years.

Green power purchasing

Green power is electricity generated from renewable sources and is offered by utilities worldwide. It is produced with fewer environmental impacts, particularly related to air pollution and global warming. There is generally a modest price premium for green power; however, it can be avoided through bulk purchasing or offset with cost-effective energy efficiency measures. Research also shows that customers are willing to pay a premium for green power to obtain the environmental benefits. Therefore, tenants, especially those with corporate environmental programmes, may be comfortable absorbing any remaining premiums.

What investors are doing

PRUPIM (UK) has worked with an energy procurement service provider to contract for green power for 240 of its properties, avoiding 21,000 tonnes of CO_2 emissions per annum. The US$112 million contract provides the properties with green power at a significant discount to the current market rate. Because the power is generated from combined-heat-and-power plants, it is also exempt from the UK Climate Change Levy, making the price even more competitive.

Parks, plazas, atriums and natural areas

Open spaces of all kinds, from urban to rural, provide important recreational amenities along with wildlife habitat, storm water management, energy conservation and other public benefits. Fortunately, they also increase property values, especially for residential properties, by anywhere from 10 to 30 per cent or more.

In fact, the added value produced by parks and open spaces is generally more than enough to offset the expense of providing them.

What investors are doing

Hermes/MEPC (UK) is developing a series of unique public squares and spaces culminating at a major new riverfront beach park as part of its 14 acre (5.7 hectare), 2.7 million square foot Wellington Place development. The creation of a high-quality public realm will add to the success of the project by creating a strong identity for the district. The pedestrian spine will be activated by a linear water feature running along its length and the riverfront will be planted and managed to support otters and other wild creatures.

PRUPIM (UK) supports the award-winning Prudential Grass Roots programme, which helps communities to improve their local environment. The projects bring lasting environmental benefits to neighbourhoods, while also removing blighted wastelands near Prudential-owned shopping centres.

Transportation-demand management and transit-oriented development

Transportation demand management (TDM) includes efforts such as car-pool services aimed at reducing or redistributing peak period travel. Transit-oriented development (TOD) includes property ownership and developments within walking distance of transit stops and stations. Together, these strategies can reduce energy consumption, air pollution, urban sprawl, traffic deaths and dependence upon foreign oil. They can also increase transit system ridership, improve housing choices and boost access to jobs and housing for the young, old, poor and handicapped. Economically, TODs are more valuable and outperform as investments. In Dallas, Texas, for example, office properties near transit appreciated more than 50 per cent faster than elsewhere. Future demand in these locations is expected to be strong as both older and younger householders seek housing near public transportation.

What investors are doing

KOAR Development Group and Shamrock Capital Advisors (US) are currently developing Solair Wilshire, a 22-storey mixed-use transit-oriented high rise in the Wilshire Entertainment Corridor of Los Angeles. Solair is projected to be consistent with KOAR's mission to develop projects that generally meet three economic thresholds: 20 per cent margin on project development costs; 20 per cent return on equity; and 20 per cent internal rate of return (IRR), assuming land assemblage, entitlement, construction and market risks.

Hermes/MEPC (UK) established the Birchwood Park Express Bus and Shuttle Bus to help the 4200 workers at its 123 acre (50 hectare) Birchwood business park become less reliant on car-based commuting. A service charge is added to the price for car parking to help pay for a free peak-time express bus between Birchwood Park and Warrington Town Centre where commuters can connect to train services.

Hughes Development (US) created Mockingbird Station, a transit-oriented project adjacent to a major Dallas Area Rapid Transit rail line station. It contains over 500,000 square feet of retail, restaurant, residential, office and other uses on 10 acres (4 hectares). The project has been very successful, with rents commanding a 40 per cent above-market premium.

Urban regeneration

Investments to revitalize and regenerate urban places can advance urban vitality, economic development, infrastructure efficiency and physical accessibility. It can also reduce urban sprawl, conserve natural resources and lessen auto use and related carbon emissions. Economic evidence suggests that such investments can also be financially competitive. A UK study found that property investment performance in regeneration areas matched or exceeded national and local city benchmarks, had a lower level of risk per unit of return, and added diversification to property portfolios.

What investors are doing

Morley Fund Management (UK) has created the UK's first urban regeneration fund, called the Morley Igloo Fund. It invests in mixed-use urban regeneration projects in major towns and cities in the UK. The fund was designed to take advantage of underpriced opportunities created by the regeneration market being erroneously perceived as high risk and low return. It is expected to outperform its benchmarks.

The *California Public Employees' Retirement System (CalPERS)* (US) created the California Urban Real Estate (CURE) programme as part of its overall property portfolio. It invests in low- to moderate-income housing, urban infill, community redevelopment and similar projects where the risk is no greater than in other property investments made by the system. Since CURE's inception, CalPERS's average annual return has been 16.5 per cent after fees, to 31 December 2006. This compares to the benchmark industry returns of 8.1 per cent.

Shamrock Capital Advisors and DECOMA Developers (US) are developing Pas Town Square – six mixed-use buildings on three blocks in south Pasadena's historic downtown core in the Los Angeles metro area. The certified green project is expected to produce an internal rate of return of over 25 per cent over four years.

Cherokee Funds (US) specializes in the sustainable redevelopment of brownfield sites, or properties affected by environmental contamination. Since 1993, they have acquired more than 520 properties.

Water conservation

Water in commercial properties is used for restrooms, cooling, heating and landscaping. Property owners can conserve water by reducing losses (e.g. fixing leaks), reducing uses (e.g. installing low-flush toilets) and reusing otherwise discarded water (e.g. catching run-off for irrigation). Water conservation benefits water quality, fish and wildlife, forests, groundwater reserves and other environmental systems. Studies indicate that cost-effective measures with acceptable simple payback periods can produce an average water savings of 28 per cent in offices and 22 per cent in hotels.

What investors are doing

CNP (France) is undertaking a programme to analyse and control water consumption for all of its apartment and office buildings throughout France. It focuses on invoices in order to identify opportunities for improvement.

PRUPIM (UK) reduced water consumption by 17 per cent in one year at its mall shopping centre at Cribbs Causeway. It was achieved through more prudent use of the external water feature and the installation of presence-sensing urinals and passive infrared sensors in the urinals. Meanwhile, at the PRUPIM headquarters, water-displacing 'hippos' were placed in all their toilet tanks, resulting in a 25 per cent savings.

Investa (Australia) cut water use by 27 per cent at one of its 34-year-old mixed-use properties. The savings came from adding flow restrictors to tap ware and installing urinal sensors and waterless urinals.

Hermes (UK) upgraded the urinals in Tower 42, the tallest building in the City of London, to a waterless system. This has significantly reduced the amount of water used from 8500 units in September 2005 to just 2600 units in 2006. Installation cost US$7000; but the programme is saving US$18,500 per year.

CONCLUSION

In effect, there are two types of financially sound RPI strategies: no-cost and value-added approaches. With the no-cost approach, managers find ways of improving the social or environmental performance of their properties at zero added expense. Turning out the lights in unoccupied areas, for example, is a no-cost strategy that fights global warming. Value-added strategies, on the other hand, require some initial financial outlays, but pay for themselves by either increasing net incomes (via higher rents or lower costs) or reducing risk premiums (via lower environmental risks, less depreciation, less marketability risk, etc.). For example, higher-quality design, which beautifies our cities, may cost more for finer materials and architectural services; but the added costs are offset by higher rents. RPI will continue to evolve, potentially also factoring in strategies not discussed here, such as flexible interiors, barrier-free design, stakeholder engagement and advanced sustainability reporting. Lenders, owners, fund managers, asset and property managers, and developers can all incorporate RPI strategies within their existing activities today.

NOTES

1   This chapter was largely derived from articles that previously appeared in Cal State Fullerton's *International Real Estate Review*, as well as from the United Nations Environment Programme's (UNEP's) Property Working Group.
2   There are different types of participants and different types of properties in the market. The opportunities that exist for addressing social and environmental issues may vary depending upon whether the investors are governmental or private entities, whether the investments are in direct ownership, joint ventures or co-mingled funds, and what types of properties are considered. These complexities will not be elaborated upon here; but readers should be aware of their existence.
3   *To halt global warming, a growing number of local planning authorities are implementing the (UK) Office of the Deputy Prime Minister's revised planning policy statement (PPS22), requiring a percentage of energy to be used in new residential, commercial or industrial developments, to come from on site renewable energy. At least 15 local authorities have written policies into their draft development plans, which demand that large new commercial buildings generate 10 per cent of their energy on site from renewable sources. A case in point is the London Borough of Merton, which in July granted planning permission for a 10,500 square metre development by DIY retailer B&Q in New Malden. B&Q will generate 10 per cent of its energy needs on site from renewable sources. A wind turbine and photovoltaic cells on the roof will generate electricity, and solar panels will produce hot water. The building will also feature a ground-source heat pump, which draws air from underground to help cool offices in summer and heat the checkout area during winter.'* (www.upstreamstrategies.co.uk/index.asp?id=146, accessed August 2008)

REFERENCES

Declaration of the United Nations Conference on the Human Environment (1972), Stockholm, www.unep.org/Documents.Multilingual/Default.asp?DocumentID=97&ArticleID=1503

IPCC (Intergovernmental Panel on Climate Change) (2001) *Climate Change 2001: Working Group III: Mitigation*, UNEP and WMO, www.grida.no/climate/ipcc_tar/wg3/089.htm, accessed August 2007

Langdon, D. and Steven Winter Associates Inc (2004) *GSA LEED Cost Study: Final Report*, US General Services Administration, Washington, DC

Matthiessen, L. F. and Morris, P. (2004) *Costing Green: A Comprehensive Cost Database and Budgeting Methodology*, Davis Langdon Associates, San Francisco, CA

Vancouver Declaration on Human Settlements (Habitat I) (1976) United Nations Conference on Human Settlements, http://habitat.igc.org/vancouver/van-decl.htm.

WWF (World Wide Fund for Nature) (undated) *Building Towards Sustainability: Performance and Progress Among the UK's Leading Housebuilders*, WWF-UK, Godalming, UK

11

Private Equity: Unlocking the Sustainability Potential

Ritu Kumar

BACKGROUND AND CONTEXT

Private equity has become one of the fastest growing and dynamic asset classes, the hallmark of which is the injection of high-quality management in portfolio companies. This affords private equity investors significant opportunities to address the challenge of sustainable investing while achieving market rates of return on their investments.

The practice of taking equity holdings in privately held companies originated in the US during the 1970s, spreading later to the UK and Europe. It is now finding roots in emerging markets at a rapid pace. The industry has grown considerably over the past few years, with a loose agglomeration of 77,000 entrepreneurs worldwide and US$2 trillion assets under management globally by mid 2007 (Preqin, 2008). Although this is only 3 per cent of the US$60 trillion in capitalized stock markets, the potential for growth is enormous. Private Equity Intelligence Ltd, also known as Preqin, a provider of financial information for the private equity sector, predicts a US$5 trillion industry over the next five to seven years. The high rates of growth are driven by investment performance, value creation and the resulting investor appetite for greater allocations.

The basic tenet of private equity asset management is to draw capital into specific funds that are managed by management groups or general partners. Professional investors or limited partners invest in these funds, and enter into contractual arrangements with the management groups or general partners who advise and manage the funds for an annual fee, typically between 1.5 and 2.5 per cent of funds committed. General partners also get a share or 'carry' of 20 per cent of profits made by the fund subject to a minimum hurdle level of return. Typically, investors in private equity funds include institutional investors, sovereign wealth funds, endowments and wealthy individuals. These limited partners share in the risks and rewards of the companies in which their funds are invested, but have no day-to-day say in the management, which is the responsibility of the general partner.

Private equity funds generally have a life of ten years, and this is agreed between the investor and the general partner at the outset. The managers of the fund typically invest the capital within the first five years and hold their investments anywhere between three and five years[1] before exiting through an initial public offering (IPO) sale to another private equity firm or a strategic buyer. As such, private equity shareholders hold their investments for much longer periods than shareholders of listed stocks.

The private equity industry can be divided into three broad types of investments. First are buy outs where the private equity firm takes controlling shares or full acquisition. The equity element in the acquisition is from the fund itself, whereas the remaining financing commonly involves leverage provided through banks and the debt market. The structuring of this debt is still evolving over time depending upon the market conditions and financial innovation. The recent credit crunch in financial markets, for example, will have an impact upon deals that have a higher component of debt as opposed to equity. Recent trends show an increasing number of management buy outs in the portfolio mix of private equity investors. The second type of private equity deal is in growth capital, where investments are made in companies that are in a critical stage of expansion and the investor typically has a stake of around 20 to 30 per cent of the equity. This is typically the type of deal witnessed in most emerging markets since there is less debt involved. Venture capital, which includes start-ups or technology companies at an early stage of development, is the third category. These include a large proportion of clean tech companies and clean energy companies that have sprung up in recent years.

SUSTAINABILITY AND PRIVATE EQUITY

Sustainable private equity is defined as private equity investments that promote best practice in the areas of environment, climate change, social issues, health and safety, governance and transparency. The ownership structure of private equity and the injection of high-quality management in portfolio companies have the potential to ensure that the managers of private equity funds can make sustainability an integral element of their investment strategy.

Buyouts and growth expansion

In the case of mainstream private equity, including growth expansion and buyouts, where the general partners' stake in investee companies is large and visible, the potential to integrate sustainability factors within investment analysis and decision-making is particularly significant. Since investment managers have a close relationship with the company management, it is relatively straightforward to engage on issues relating to environmental, social and governance (ESG) factors. Very often, private equity investment managers sit on company boards, giving them direct access and influence to shape an ESG agenda. Private equity firms generally hold their investments for three to five years, a period long enough to bring about change and add value, for example, through carbon reduction programmes; energy efficiency; improved environmental standards; environmental management systems; and health and safety management systems.

The nature of private equity investments also makes it easier to integrate sustainability factors within investment analysis and decision-making, while at the same time generating sustainable returns. Three elements of such a strategy, critical for sustainable private equity to take root, relate to risk minimization, value enhancement and integrity assurance.

The first task for a responsible private equity firm must be to evaluate and minimize the market, regulatory and reputational risks for investment posed by environmental, climate change, social, ethical and governance factors. Well-defined procedures for screening all investments according to a set of social, health, safety, environmental and climate change risks should be integrated within the investment decision-making procedures. This sort of due diligence is important for identifying potential problems and action plans to reduce risks and enhance performance. The experience of firms that follow such an approach has proved that this procedure also constitutes an important tool in screening out investments that have high business integrity risks in markets where governance standards are low and political interference in business practices is rampant.

Having decided to invest in a portfolio company, the private equity firm should then develop action plans for improving the value of investments through the implementation of best-in-class ESG practices. One example here is the expanding opportunities in carbon finance. Private equity firms can actively encourage investee companies to assess the potential for reducing carbon generation through energy efficiency and other carbon reduction measures with a view to saving energy costs and taking advantage of carbon trading opportunities, such as the Clean Development Mechanism. The emerging markets private equity firm, Actis, for example, requires all of its portfolio companies to undertake energy audits, implement energy efficiency measures and explore the potential for carbon reduction in high carbon-intensive investments. In other cases, Actis is working with some of its portfolio companies to

---

BOX 11.1 CASE STUDY: ACTIS

Actis LLP is a private equity firm that invests in emerging markets in Asia, Africa and Latin America. Actis assesses the impacts of all new investments on environmental, climate change, health, safety, social and business integrity aspects as an integral part of the investment appraisal process. New investments are given a risk rating on these issues to determine the appropriate levels of management and monitoring required. Investee companies are required to sign up to an undertaking that they will comply with Actis's ESG code. A unique feature of Actis's approach is that it actively engages with portfolio companies in raising their environmental and social performance standards to meet international best practice, and in reducing their carbon footprint.

---

put in place appropriate health and safety management systems and International Organization for Standardization (ISO) standards for food safety and management.

The Actis and International Finance Corporation (IFC) examples cited in Boxes 11.1 and 11.2 underline the importance of integrating environmental and social sustainability within private equity investments in emerging markets. In many of these markets, notably the fastest-growing economies of China and India, environmental degradation, carbon emissions, pollution, natural resource constraints and social issues are already placing constraints on economic growth. In this context, and given increasing private equity activity in emerging markets, responsible investment strategies will become increasingly important for investors in these markets.

According to the Emerging Markets Private Equity Association (EMPEA), interest in emerging markets continued to increase in 2007, with 204 funds collectively raising US$59 billion in fresh capital, a 78 per cent increase from 2006 (EMPEA, 2008). Growth has also expanded to sector-specific funds, with increases in natural resources, technology, infrastructure and agriculture. This augurs well for sustainability provided the funds are managed and invested in line with procedures outlined above.

BOX 11.2 CASE STUDY: IFC

IFC, the private-sector lending arm of the World Bank, is another leading example of a private equity investor that has robust environmental and social policies in place for its fund managers and portfolio companies. IFC invests in emerging markets and sets the highest international performance standards for all of its investments. In 2005, it documented five case studies of companies exhibiting good examples of different aspects of sustainability drawn from the portfolios of private equity funds in which IFC was an investor. The sustainability themes found across the five businesses included optimizing workforce commitment; eco-efficiency and energy conservation; proactive adoption of international environmental, health and safety standards; and recycling. All companies also showed very healthy growth in revenues and earnings before interest, tax, depreciation and amortization (EBITDA) (IFC, 2005).

BOX 11.3 CASE STUDY: HUDSON CLEAN ENERGY PARTNERS

Credit Suisse–backed private equity firm Hudson Clean Energy Partners has recently announced that it will focus on investments in wind, solar and biofuels with deal sizes averaging US$100 million, although it will take a cautious approach to biofuels, given concerns about the use of food sources such as corn and other feed stocks. Other clean energy technologies, such as those focused on energy efficiency and upgrades to the electrical grid, are also on the firms' radar. The firm will focus on companies with commercialized technology, or those that are on the verge of commercialization (*Planet Ark*, 2008).

Venture capital and clean tech

Venture capital and early stage start-ups are especially suited to investments in environmental and clean technology sectors. According to New Energy Finance (NEF), by the end of 2007, venture capital/private equity (VC/PE) investments in clean energy companies was US$9.8 billion with venture capital investments reaching an all time high of US$3.5 billion. Despite the recent correction in public markets, NEF believes that the underlying fundamentals driving investments in clean energy remain strong, although deal sizes may become smaller. The narrowing of the initial public offering window will force more companies to look to VC/PE investing. In particular, NEF forecasts that energy efficiency will gain ground in early stage investments, with investors backing companies in supply- and demand-side efficiency, energy smart buildings and smart grid. This is expected to be followed by solar, power storage, biofuels and geothermal technology. Relatively less increases in the prospects for biomass, fuel cells, hydrogen and wind are expected (NEF, 2008).

BOX 11.4 CASE STUDY: HGCAPITAL

Established in 2000, HgCapital is a leading investor in the European private equity market, with US$3 billion funds under management. It has recently decided to make clean tech a sector focus by investing in a number of renewable energy projects, including start-ups. It has raised over US$2 billion in capital to support renewable power projects.

Investors and limited partners

In addition to what private equity or venture capital firms can do to become agents for sustainability, there is also a growing appetite among investors (limited partners) for mobilizing ESG analysis as a tool for managing new risks and building a better understanding of new market opportunities. For example, the two Dutch pension funds, the US$130 billion Fund for Care and Well Being (PGGM) for healthcare and social workers, and the US$310 billion Stichting

Pensioenfonds, (ABP) plan for civil servants, have jointly invested US$750 million in clean tech private equity as their latest contribution to fiduciary environmentalism (*Responsible Investor*, 2007). Similarly the California Public Employees' Retirement System (CalPERS), with assets totalling more than US$250 billion, announced that it was increasing its private equity investments as a proportion of its total portfolio from 6 to 10 per cent (Boston Consulting Group and IESE Business School, 2008). In 2004, CalPERS and the California State Teachers' Retirement System (CalSTRS) instituted a US$500 million investment in clean technology venture investing – part of the Green Wave programme – that addressed crucial environmental problems surrounding climate change. The Massachusetts Pension Reserve Investment Management (MassPRIM) has created a request for proposal system for targeted investments that combines a close review of potential financial performance with a rigorous review of economic targeting criteria around spillover community revitalization benefits.

Business ventures that combine risk-taking with an explicit mission to address issues of equity, education, public health, sanitation, etc. are also becoming the target of private equity investors. The Calvert Social Investment Fund (CSIF) focuses on companies that are providing market-based solutions to social, environmental and health problems. As a special equities component of the Calvert Social Index, all of the fund's portfolio companies must operate in a manner that is consistent with CSIF's investment principles, which are centred on governance and ethics; the workplace; the environment; product safety and impact; international operations and human rights; and indigenous peoples' rights. CSIF is currently invested in a company that works with schools, colleges and universities to provide online tutoring to colleges with fewer resources (see www.calvert.com/sri_654, accessed 12 May 2008).

THE CHALLENGE OF DISCLOSURE

The third element of a sustainability strategy – and the least currently practised – is for the private equity firm to assure the integrity of investments by transparent and accountable reporting in order to respond to rising client and societal expectations of corporate behaviour. Perhaps the biggest challenge that private equity faces at present is the demand for greater transparency and disclosure. This pressure is, in large part, the result of the recent rapid growth in private equity and the emergence of large deals and leveraged buyouts. The pressure on the private equity industry for increased transparency and disclosure has been accompanied by calls for greater regulation and a tougher taxation environment. This has been fuelled by the adverse publicity regarding huge profits that fall outside of current tax regimes. With US$2 trillion under management and large well-known companies owned by private equity houses, the industry is definitely in the public eye.

Privatization of listed companies and the consequent decline in reporting and disclosure requirements spurred the publication of the voluntary *Guidelines for Disclosure and Transparency in Private Equity* in November 2007 (Walker, 2007). The focus of the guidelines is exclusively on large UK portfolio companies and private equity firms, and on enhancement of data collection, processing and reporting on an industry-wide basis by the British Venture Capital Association. More recently, Denmark and Sweden have announced plans to prepare similar guidelines that would be applicable to portfolio companies and private equity firms of all sizes. The European Venture Capital Association has also pledged to produce voluntary guidelines by the year end.

Whereas the Walker guidelines were primarily a response to ensure accountability of huge untaxable profits, the guidelines also require large UK portfolio companies to disclose information on the company's employees, environmental matters, and social and community issues. Some clients are also requiring private equity firms to report on sustainability issues to their limited partners or investors. These are welcome initiatives and may well set the trend for better disclosure; but this is not yet a practice that is widely followed. Nor is there any obligation on private equity firms to report to the wider public.

But it is only a matter of time before this happens. According to Mark O'Hare of Preqin, the 'need for better communication with a wide constituency is accepted; the key test for the industry will be its ability to finesse this: transparency where it is needed and beneficial, whilst maintaining the ability to manage and add value to portfolio companies' (Preqin, 2008). It is important that this drive for transparency expands to include ESG factors – which would probably reveal the structural sustainability advantages of the private equity model.

NOTE

1   Real estate and infrastructure private equity funds may hold their investments for longer periods.

REFERENCES

Boston Consulting Group and IESE Business School (2008) *The Advantage of Persistence: How the Best Private Equity Firms 'Beat the Fade'*, 9 February, www.bcg.com/impact_expertise/publications/files/private_equity_feb_2008.pdf

EMPEA (Emerging Markets Private Equity Association) (2008) *Quarterly Review*, www.empea.net

IFC (International Finance Corporation) (2005) *The Promise of Private Equity, Environment, Society, and Corporate Governance: New Criteria for Success in Private Equity Investments – Case Studies from Emerging Markets*, IFC, www.ifc.org/ifcext/enviro.nsf/AttachmentsByTitle/ p_SI_PromiseofPrivateEquity/$FILE/PromiseofPrivateEquity_full.pdf

NEF (New Energy Finance) (2008) *Research Note Insight Services: VC/PE*, New Energy Finance, London, 5 March

Planet Ark (2008) 'Interview: Green private equity firm to focus on wind, solar', *Planet Ark*, 17 April

Preqin (2008) *Global Private Equity Review*, Preqin, London

Responsible Investor (2007) www.responsible-investor.com, 8 July, accessed 12 May 2008

Walker, D. (2007) *Guidelines for Disclosure and Transparency in Private Equity*, 11 November, www.altassets.com/pdfs/wwg_report_final.pdf

12

Social Businesses

Rod Schwartz[1]

INTRODUCTION

The ideals and spirit of the time we call the 'sixties' and the notion that the world can be dramatically changed for the better greatly influenced a number of individuals who had a material impact upon society in the closing decades of the second millennium. Some of these people were particularly highly motivated and exceptionally talented and chose to operate within the system to effect social change. They built organizations that have today revolutionized the way in which we think and, in particular, the way we consume. These first generation of social entrepreneurs (SEs) created businesses with a core social purpose, and often very successful ones at that. Importantly, they laid the foundations for today's generation of social entrepreneurs, whose business acumen is now matched by an intriguing array of funding and investment mechanisms.

This chapter seeks to analyse the evolution of this relatively new type of entity built by these SEs and to explore the growth in how these have (and have not) been financed since the 1970s. Our comments will largely focus on the UK marketplace. We will also discuss the future prospects for this emergent social investment sector.

THE SOCIAL BUSINESS PIONEERS

Attempts to bring a social or ethical dimension to enterprise stretch back to the co-operatives and mutual societies of the 1700s, and to the Victorian Quaker philanthropists, such as Cadbury's. In the modern era, the undoubted pioneers were Ben Cohen and Jerry Greenfield who founded Ben & Jerry's ice cream in the US and Anita and Gordon Roddick, who founded The Body Shop in the UK. They took ethical and social considerations and placed them right at the core of their product offering. Sceptics suggested that this would add unnecessary cost or turn people off; but instead the businesses thrived, enjoying rapid growth and strong financial performance. Equally, if not more importantly to the founders, these businesses changed not only the way in which people thought about ice cream or hair and beauty products, but how people thought about consumption, generally. Natural ingredients, an emphasis on recycling, interest in sourcing and fair trade, social justice and a host of other ethical and social issues were brought to the public's consciousness by these SEs via their respective social businesses. Both were also funded by the classic backers of early stage businesses, 'founders, friends, family and fools', for sums under US$20,000 in each case.

The Body Shop and Ben & Jerry's were only the first of many to come onto the scene. Inspired by similar ideals, other entrepreneurs would eventually go on to bring about lasting social change as well. A high percentage of these, particularly in the UK, were in fair trade, where producers received a much higher portion of the ultimate value of product sales. The fair trade movement, which began in the aftermath of World War II, initially concentrated on handicrafts from the developing world, and shifted into agricultural commodities and related products with a vengeance during the 1980s. Traidcraft, founded in 1979, and Twin Trading, founded in 1985, were to become leading players in this field. They assisted in founding two very successful companies in the 1990s, Café Direct and Divine Chocolate (formerly the Day Chocolate Company), focused on fair trade coffee and tea, and chocolate, respectively. This phenomenon, where one firm assists in the formation of subsequent social businesses, is a particular aspect of this sector, and moved things on from the 'friends and family' rounds of the first two businesses. Traidcraft, Twin Trading and The Body Shop, for example, all played a key role in the development of the sector by offering cash resources, mentoring and other support (see Table 12.1).

Much of this fair trade activity was originally oriented towards edible agricultural products coming from the developing world. Very recently, this has extended into clothing and other non-food agricultural commodities and even broad-based ethical online marketplaces such as the Ethical Superstore; but the sector has been concentrating on consumer-related goods since inception. In 1998, however, the Ethical Property Company was founded by Jamie Hartzell and Andy King. Its purpose was to purchase commercial property, rented to social change organizations at a discounted rate. To the best of our knowledge, this constitutes the first significant foray by an ethical business into the non-consumer sector.

At roughly the same time, progressive thinking was beginning to influence the investment world, as well. A few similarly inspired individuals founded the Socially Responsible Investing movement. UK insurer Friends Provident, with

Table 12.1 *Social business pioneers: The timeline*

Company	Founded	Activity	Founders	Backers
The Body Shop	1976	Hair and beauty products	Anita and Gordon Roddick	A local garage owner who invested US$16,000
Ben & Jerry's	1978	Ice cream	Ben Cohen and Jerry Greenfield	US$12,000 investment, of which US$4000 was borrowed
Traidcraft	1979	Fair trade products	Richard Adams	NA
Twin Trading	1985	Alternative trading and fair trade	NA	NA
Café Direct	1991	Fair trade coffee and tea	NA	Oxfam, Equal Exchange, Traidcraft and Twin Trading
Divine Chocolate	1998	Fair trade chocolate	NA	Twin Trading, The Body Shop, Christian Aid and Comic Relief
Ethical Property Company	1998	Commercial property for social change tenants	Jamie Hartzell and Andy King	The founders, who each owned a building

Source: Rod Schwartz

the launch in 1984 of its Stewardship Fund, helped bring the sector into existence. Designed to incorporate ethical principles within its investment approach, the Stewardship Fund was the UK's first ethical fund designed for retail investors. From this small beginning, the retail ethical market had grown to in excess of US$15 billion by early 2008. Bizarrely, however, it was only in rare circumstances that these funds invested in some of the emerging social businesses, such as The Body Shop. Although their ideals might be similar, it was as if the two developments took place in different worlds. The screening techniques adopted by sustainable and responsible investing (SRI) funds produced investment portfolios that were by and large identical to those of mainstream funds and did not back social businesses. This, understandably, began to frustrate social businesses, policy-makers, government officials and commentators who sense a market that is somehow 'not working'.

UNLEASHING SOCIAL INVESTMENT

To mobilize private capital for social progress, the Labour government under then Prime Minister Tony Blair and Chancellor of the Exchequer Gordon Brown established the Social Investment Task Force. Formed in 2000 under the chairmanship of venture capitalist Sir Ronald Cohen, the mission of the task force was:

> *To set out how entrepreneurial practices can be applied to obtain higher social and financial returns from social investment, to harness new talents and skills to address economic regeneration and to unleash new sources of private and institutional investment. In addition, the task force should explore innovative roles that the voluntary sector, businesses and government could play as partners in this area.*

The blue-chip task force that was co-initiated by the UK Social Investment Forum (UK SIF), the New Economics Foundation (a leading progressive think tank) and the Development Trust Association deliberated for approximately five years and announced five basic recommendations, which were to:

1   Introduce community investment tax relief.
2   Help set up community development venture capital funds.
3   Encourage disclosure by banks of their lending activities.
4   Provide greater latitude and encouragement for charitable trusts and foundations to invest in community development finance.
5   Provide support for community development finance institutions (CDFIs).

Following the task force, a number of important organizations came into existence. Many of these involve the use of tax relief to support lending to social enterprises – the community development finance institutions – which have grown since. In addition, the increased scrutiny of the major banks and their lending activities acted as a spur for greater lending in deprived communities. From our vantage point, it is doubtful that there has been much progress on the fourth point: charities and foundations by and large remain very conservative in their investment activities.

However, the focus of this chapter is investing in social businesses – in particular, equity investment – and the Social Investment Task Force played a major role in spawning a private venture capital firm called Bridges Community Ventures. This company, initially supported by US$40 million of subordinated government funding, focused on identifying and investing in businesses with an important social dimension that were also based in the UK in most deprived communities. Bridges' first fund of US$80 million has been succeeded by a second fund of over US$140 million.

At the same time, other government initiatives took shape. Venturesome, part of the Charities Aid Foundation, lends and invests in charities and social enterprises. Although utilizing a 'venture capital approach' to its work, Venturesome does not have the same financial return target as Bridges. Unltd was founded in 2002 with US$200 million of cash from the Millennium Awards

Trust, and supports social entrepreneurs. Despite its charitable status, Unltd also deploys venture capital techniques and provides support and grants, ranging from US$10,000 to US$20,000 to social entrepreneurs.

A range of privately backed 'venture philanthropy' firms, led by Impetus Trust, deploy similar techniques, although in the case of Impetus Trust the focus is on particularly 'high-impact' investments. In addition, a number of more traditional private-sector venture capital firms have been founded to operate in the field. Foursome Investments, initially backed by a wealthy German family, was founded in 1998 and currently focuses on the cleantech (renewable energy) space. Similarly, WHEB Ventures, also with the support of wealthy UK-based individuals, was founded in 1995 as a cleantech incubator and corporate finance business and has developed into a sector-focused UK-based venture capital firm. Triodos, the Dutch bank founded in 1980, opened an office in Bristol, England, in 1995. Through a range of venture capital funds, Triodos has backed social and environmental businesses as a venture capital investor in the UK and on the continent. In early 2008, Catalyst Fund Management and Research launched a venture capital fund that seeks to back social businesses with high-return objectives in education and training; health and wellness; alternative energy and the environment; and 'ethical consumerism'.

A series of 'networks' also came into existence over the last 30 years which have had a major effect on the sector. The first of these was Ashoka. Formed in 1980 by Bill Drayton, it has created over 1800 fellows; social entrepreneurs are back and are supported by Ashoka. In 1998, Klaus Schwab (founder of the World Economic Forum in Davos, Switzerland) co-founded the Schwab Foundation for Social Entrepreneurship to highlight social enterprise as a key element in addressing society's problems. Jeff Skoll, who made his billions as eBay's first president, formed the Skoll Foundation to invest in, connect and celebrate social entrepreneurs, and in the US, the Acumen Fund was founded in 2001 with very similar purposes.

A further way in which social businesses and enterprises have been encouraged is through business plan competitions. The oldest for social ventures is the Global Social Venture Competition, where five well-known business schools (Columbia, Haas, London Business School, Indian Business School and Yale), in partnership with a few others, provide mentoring, exposure and prizes to social enterprises and businesses from all over the world. Such competitions are a welcome boost to the winners and assist many of the competitors in sharpening their ideas, assisted by the free advice of a broad range of experienced judges.

TAKING STOCK

As we entered the beginning of the millennium, exciting new models were emerging. On the business side, some far-sighted idealists had brought a new form of company into existence, largely focused on consumer-related activities.

In terms of funding, initiatives have been catalysed by a few wealthy individuals or government, with only a very few private-sector entities making meaningful inroads into the area. SRI funds, though increasing in size, seem to be operating in a completely different market. But the sector's size remained microscopic in contrast with the mainstream capital markets, and substantial obstacles remained:

- Its small size places it well below the radar of the mainstream markets.
- Much of the infrastructure that serves the mainstream – lawyers, accountants, bankers and other advisers – is largely absent from the social business sector.
- Government, which has been trying to play the role of facilitator, may, in certain cases, be an obstacle. Also, its substantial size necessitates that it tread carefully in this immature sector.
- Charities and other ethically oriented investors, whom one would suspect might have a predisposition to support social businesses, are, by virtue of their innate conservatism and their somewhat bureaucratic approach to fund management, largely refraining from doing so.

The point about size is important. The US$11+ billion in SRI funds pales in comparison to the trillions of dollars managed in London. This compares with hundreds of billions raised in Europe over the past few years in private equity, and US$60+ billion invested just by UK-based firms in 2007.

Although a few advisers have begun to come into the social business space, they remain small and at a very early stage of development, which is not surprising in light of the still limited scope of commercial opportunity. In terms of information about potential investments in the sector, organizations such as Investing for Good, Catalyst, New Philanthropy Capital and Triodos all have products that begin to meet some of the needs of investors.

We will not dwell in this chapter on the issue of the tricky role that government has played; but the relative conservatism of the ethical investment community is evoking negative comment. In contrast with the US, where charities are required to invest a portion of their assets each year in 'mission-related investments' (MRIs), there is no such requirement in the UK. Charity trustee boards have thus tended to be exceptionally conservative and unimaginative in their approach, while the SRI community continues to opt for investment in large listed companies over newer social businesses.

Fortunately for the social business sector, two key trends have unfolded that have substantially changed the climate. These relate to cleantech and microfinance, both of which have entered the investment mainstream over the past few years. The case for cleantech has been obvious for years: our global economy will run out of fossil fuels and the world's natural environment is increasingly unable to cope with the consequences of continuing to burn fossil fuels, whether scarce or abundant. This has led to the rise of investment in cleantech on a massive scale, especially in the US, but even in the UK, where energy and the environment represented US$1.2 billion of new venture capital investment in 2006. Partly as a result, there are now around 60 cleantech companies listed on the main London Stock Exchange as well as the Alternative Investment Market (AIM).

In general, it has not been the historical ethical investors who have led this growth. New-style cleantech-focused fund managers, such as Impax Asset Management or Climate Change Capital, have been at the forefront. Many of the newly listed cleantech companies find that their shareholder registers are dominated not by the ethical community, but by hedge funds, high net-worth individuals and traditional 'long only' funds.

Observers argue about whether or not these new cleantech firms are truly 'social' businesses at all. 'They are just seeking profits', goes the refrain. In our view, the substantial benefit that they bring to society in enabling our economy to operate in a manner that does not destroy the atmosphere makes them perfectly suitable and highly 'social'. Moreover, the fact that they 'just' make profits makes them more sustainable and, in general, gives them the potential for faster growth and a greater ability to achieve scale and make a difference. More critically, these cleantech firms provide a badly needed link between social businesses and the investment mainstream.

Another social business sector where this has made the link to the mainstream is microfinance. Driven initially by social entrepreneurs such as the Nobel prize-winning Muhammad Yunus, more recent entrants include JPMorgan Chase, Morgan Stanley and other large investment banks. There is a certain irony to the fact that at the same time as their balance sheets are being decimated by losses on securities backed by sub-prime lending to risky mortgage borrowers in the mainly Anglo-Saxon West, developing world borrowers on very small sums are having their (higher quality!) loans pooled into vehicles that yield meaningful and growing profits for investment banks. Again, it has not been the ethical investment community that has funded this, but a newer breed of market practitioner who is putting at the disposal of social, ethical and environmental businesses significantly more substantial pools of financial capital, such as the Swiss firm Planet Finance.

More exciting to us – given their financial potential and their ability to effect social change – are some of the newer social businesses that have had an enormous impact and have enjoyed rapid growth. A number of these are still in the food-and-drink-related sector. Organix, the organic baby food company, has generated revenues in excess of US$40 million and has reportedly been sold in April 2008 for a price of over US$60 million. Abel & Cole has been a leader in home delivery of organic and locally produced foods to UK homes, and in 2007 took on private equity investment from Phoenix Equity Partners at a valuation also believed to be in excess of US$60 million. Innocent Drinks is perhaps the best-known of the brands of natural drinks manufacturers that have penetrated the market over the last few years. Such penetration has even extended into the bottled water business where Belu Water, winner of the Social Enterprise of the Year award in 2007, has enjoyed stellar sales growth since inception and a very high profile. It is largely debt and grant funded and only water-related charities may own an economic interest in its share capital. The debt capital of some these social enterprises may pay interest at rates that vary according to performance. Such debt is considered 'quasi-equity' and can be used where conventional equity is not possible.

Other consumer-related areas have also blossomed. People Tree and Adili, both ethical fashion brands, have enjoyed fast growth and recently secured funding. People Tree was backed by Dutch-based Oikocredit, while Adili raised money in December 2007 via an AIM listing. PointOV Limited, which manages the Ethical Superstore, aspires to become the Amazon of the ethical consumption world by offering online access to thousands of consumer products of an ethical or environmentally friendly nature. In April 2008, it secured its third round of venture capital funding and is aiming for more in its pursuit of a dominant position in this market. Justgiving.com, which provides an easy-to-use online portal for donors and fund-raisers to support charitable causes, has gone through several rounds of angel funding. By the spring of 2008, it was a profitable, fast-growing and valuable enterprise, reportedly worth tens of millions of UK pounds. Beyond the consumer and internet sectors, new property-based businesses have sprung up. Bio-Regional Quintain (BRQ) is a joint venture between the environmental charity Bio-regional and the mainstream property firm Quintain. BRQ is famous for its Beddington Zero Emission Development (BEDZED) community in Surrey, an iconic example of 'green building'. Ethical Property, mentioned earlier, has been funded by three rounds of sales of 'ethical shares' to private and institutional buyers, while The Hub, which offers flexible office accommodation to young firms, has relied on angel and grant funding.

These examples highlight the diversity of the new social companies coming into existence, as well as the extremely varied investment models. Each enterprise needs to find the model that best suits its capital needs, size, organizational style, profit and growth outlook, as well as the personal preferences of the controlling shareholders. The businesses will range from profit-oriented to non-profit, or even those which offer 'blended' return. For such companies, the return to shareholders will normally be sub-market, the socially oriented investors gaining 'social returns', which are a function, again, of the positive externalities generated by the business, which compensate for the lower risk-adjusted financial return. The nature of this mix will become even more varied with the launch of the Social Investment Bank, aiming to secure at least US$500 million from assets held in 'dormant' accounts. On the back of increased public and private capital, we would also expect a myriad of structured financial products to be created.

PROMISING INNOVATIONS FOR THE FUTURE

All of this is just the beginning for the sector. Although it has grown rapidly, it remains a tiny portion of the global capital markets. Several innovations and developments offer a blend of promise and excitement for the sector in the coming decade and beyond.

We mentioned above the use of 'ethical' shares in connection with the Ethical Property Company. Utilized as well by Café Direct, Traidcraft, Good Energy (a renewable energy specialist) and other companies, these shares offer investors many of the advantages of equity ownership. But the social businesses are not subject to the same onerous and costly requirements of a listing. Many of these shares trade on a matched bargain basis arranged by a stock-broking firm. The performance of these shares has been mixed over time. The lack of liquidity is something these companies are keen to address. Some are believed to be considering a listing on some of the newer-style and less expensive markets such as PLUS, used by Good Energy, while others are considering other means of increasing liquidity. One of the more ambitious ideas is to establish a Social Stock Exchange, which would seek to become the marketplace for a predefined set of social businesses to find socially minded investors. Central to all of these ideas for improving capital raising is the question of ownership. Some observers feel a business cannot be 'social' if private investors make a fortune as these firms prosper. This and other subjects evoke strong and passionate reactions from certain quarters. While this may not prevent the overall development of the social sector, it has meant that initiatives that require a clear consensus to emerge are more problematic.

Another area for further enquiry is that of social returns. The conventional wisdom in the mainstream investing business is that investors are only interested in risk-adjusted rates of return – no more and no less. The advent of SRI funds, which have performed broadly in line with traditional funds over time, means that investors receive social returns for free. The high relative growth of the sector is perhaps evidence that investors who value such returns are a meaningful and growing body. Yet, other investors are now emerging who knowingly invest in assets with returns nearly certain, or certain, to be sub-par, but sacrifice these financial returns in exchange for expected social returns. These are hard to measure, but we imagine will become an increasingly important aspect of the 'investment horizon' of investors, particularly retail or high net-worth investors over the coming years.

NOTE

1 Rod Schwartz and Catalyst Fund Management and Research Ltd, and/or its affiliates, have been professionally involved with, or are involved with, some of the companies mentioned in this chapter.

Part IV

Future Directions and Trends

13

China

Ray Cheung

OVERVIEW

With the Chinese government stepping up its efforts to improve the country's worsening ecological situation, China's environmental and renewable energy industries are poised for strong growth. As a result, 'cleantech' sectors are emerging as one of the top investment destinations with the amount of international and domestic funds going into such enterprises hitting record levels. Not only mainstream investors are seeking to profit on the Chinese green boom, but traditional socially responsible investors, who had once shunned China for its poor human rights record, as well.

The reason is simple: many of China's cleantech enterprises offer the unique opportunity to make money as well as to help the country achieve a more sustainable development path. Recent performance of some firms has proved that this win–win situation is achievable. However, before investors seek to cash in on this boom by throwing their money at these firms, they must realize that Chinese green industries face a plethora of challenges. Investors must exercise caution and learn to navigate the difficulties to meet both their financial and ethical objectives.

CHINA'S ENVIRONMENTAL SITUATION

China is facing enormous environmental and energy challenges. Nearly 700 million Chinese lack access to safe drinking water and the country is home to 16 out of the 20 most air-polluted cities in the world. In 2007, China surpassed the US as the world's largest greenhouse gas emitter nation. The degradation is having devastating consequence, with scientists estimating that more than 400,000 people die each year from the effects of air pollution. The Ministry of Environmental Protection concluded that the damage costs the Chinese economy the equivalent of 10 per cent of its annual gross domestic product (GDP), including the losses from industrial output, acid rain and desertification (Economy and Lieberthal, 2007).

Meanwhile, China's energy demand is expected to double from its 2005 level to 4 billion tonnes of coal equivalent (TCE) by 2020. Once an oil exporter, China is now the world's second largest oil consumer, with imports currently accounting for close to half of its oil supply (Credit Suisse, 2006). This growing demand and increasing foreign dependence is forcing China to aggressively develop new domestic and international energy sources.

GOVERNMENT RESPONSE

In the face of such daunting challenges, the Chinese government has launched a series of policy and administrative initiatives:

- *Eleventh Five-Year Plan (2006–2010) for Energy Development:* calls for a 10 per cent reduction of major pollutants while reducing energy intensity by 20 per cent.
- *Renewable Energy Law:* aims to increase use of renewable energy to 16 per cent by 2020 through the implementation of subsidies and tax incentives.
- *Amended Energy Conservation Law:* proposes central and local government regulatory and financial measures to improve the country's energy intensity usage.
- *Energy Law:* will consolidate four of China's pre-existing rules on coal, electricity, energy conservation and renewable energy, as well as govern the petroleum, natural gas and nuclear energy industries.
- *Bureaucratic powers of the Ministry of Environmental Protection:* these are to be strengthened.

Eleventh Five-Year Plan for Energy Development

Released in April 2007, the 11th Five-Year Plan (2006–2010) sets China's total primary energy production target for 2010 at 2.446 billion TCE, which equates to an annualized growth rate of 3.5 per cent. Under this scenario, coal, petroleum, natural gas, nuclear power, hydropower and other renewable energy sources will contribute 74.7, 11.3, 5, 1, 7.5 and 0.5 per cent, respectively. Compared to 2005, the shares of coal and petroleum are 1.8 and 1.3 percentage points lower, while those of natural gas, nuclear power, hydropower and other renewable energy sources are 1.8, 0.1, 0.8 and 0.4 percentage points higher, respectively (National Development and Reform Commission, 2007).

Table 13.1 *Renewable Energy Law energy targets*

Sector	2005	2010	2020
Hydropower	115GW	180GW	300GW
Wind power	1.3GW	5GW	30GW
Biomass power	2GW	5GW	30GW
Solar PV	0.07GW	0.3GW	1.8GW
Solar hot water	80 million m²	150 million m²	300 million m²
Ethanol	0.8 million tonnes	2 million tonnes	10 million tonnes
Biodiesel	0.05 million tonnes	0.2 million tonnes	2 million tonnes
Biomass pellets	~ 0	1 million tonnes	50 million tonnes
Biogas and biomass gasification	8 billion m³ per year	19 billion m³ per year	44 billion m³ per year
Share of total primary energy (including large hydropower)	~7.5%	10%	16%
Share of electric power capacity (excluding large hydropower)	~8%	10%	20%

Source: Renewable Energy Law, People's Republic of China

The plan states that by 2010, China will reduce its energy consumption per 10,000 renminbi (RMB) of GDP from 1.22 TCE in 2005 to approximately 0.98 TCE by 2010, a decrease of 20 per cent. Such energy savings will be achieved through the adoption of energy-efficient technologies within key industries, as well as from lower energy-consuming products made in China.

Renewable Energy Law

The Renewable Energy Law (REL), which came into effect on 1 January 2006, seeks to increase renewable energy (including large hydro) production to 16 per cent by 2020 through government support. It calls for the government to provide strategies that:

- require grid operators to purchase the electricity generated from approved renewable energy producers;
- designate research in renewable energy technologies as a funding priority; and
- provide economic incentives, such as loans, subsidies and tax incentives.

Renewable Energy Law measures already implemented

- *Rules for Renewable Energy-Generated Electrical Pricing and Cost-Sharing Management (January 2006).* Allows the government to set on-grid electricity prices according to the standard electricity price of the respective province, plus a subsidy equal to 0.25 RMB per kilowatt hour. New projects can enjoy the subsidy for the first 15 years, while wind power prices are to be determined by competitive bids for wind farm projects.

- *Provisional Measures for Administration of Special Funding for Developing Renewable Energy Resources (June 2006).* Provides a framework for grants and low-interest loans to support renewable energy projects, including biofuels for the automobile industry and solar power and geothermal fuels to heat and cool buildings.
- *Energy Rate Increase (July 2006).* Establishes a tax-exempt renewable energy surcharge (0.001 RMD per kWh) payable by end users of electricity.

Amended Energy Conservation Law

In April 2008, the Chinese government put into effect the amended Energy Conservation Law, which calls for local governments to annually submit to the state council specific energy conservation plans and to enact pollution taxes on the most energy-intensive industries, as well as to provide new financial incentives for qualified energy conservation projects (Wang, 2008).

Draft energy law

The central government is currently reviewing a draft national energy law that will consolidate four of China's pre-existing rules on coal, electricity, energy conservation and renewable energy, as well as govern the petroleum, natural gas and nuclear energy industries. To be ratified by the end of 2008, the legislation will serve as a 'constitution' for China's energy policy with specific measures to include the establishment of energy pricing systems that are mainly determined by market forces and a new ministry of energy (*Xinhua China Money*, 2006).

Ministry of Environmental Protection

The Ministry of Environmental Protection (MEP) is the main central government agency under the state council responsible for enforcing China's environmental regulations.

Long viewed as a weak bureaucracy, the MEP has been gaining more enforcement powers with new administrative standing for the passage of new regulations. In March 2008, the body was elevated from an administrative agency to a central government ministry with its regulatory jurisdiction and staff size set to expand.

The MEP's key enforcement initiatives include:

- the Environmental Impact Assessment Law – passed in 2003, the statute requires businesses to submit to the MEP, for approval, an environmental impact report of all proposed construction projects prior to ground breaking;
- the right to shut down and levy fines on polluting companies and enforce new regional permit restrictions, where the construction permits of environmentally offending firms within certain jurisdictions will be withheld until their law-breaking sites come into compliance.

With these new powers, in 2007 the MEP shut down the equivalent of 1 megawatt (MW) of small coal-fired power plants, 18.43 million tonnes of steel- and iron-processing facilities, 30 million tonnes of cement-producing facilities, and 1.7 million tonnes of paper-manufacturing factories (*Xinhua*, 2007). This follows its 2006 action of halting the construction of 56 projects, mostly energy facilities worth 218.3 billion RMB, forcing the closure of 3176 businesses for violations and ordering a halt to 82 projects, mostly steel, power and electroplating facilities, for violating the country's environmental pollution and procedure laws. Violators included four of China's largest and politically well-connected energy companies: Datang Power, Huaneng Power, Huadian Power and Guodian Power (*Economist Intelligence Unit – Business China*, 2007).

OTHER DRIVERS

Clean Development Mechanism

Another key driver is China's participation in the carbon trading scheme of the Kyoto Protocol's Clean Development Mechanism (CDM). As a developing nation signatory to the carbon emission international agreement, the country is the leading supplier of certified emission reductions (CERs) because of its ability to generate low-cost emission reductions. According to the World Bank, China accounted for 61 per cent of the international CDM carbon credit supply volume during 2006 and 50 per cent of the CDM pipeline as of the end of March 2007. The World Bank estimated that before 2010, some US$3 billion to US$5 billion of global CDM-related trade will come from China (World Bank, 2007). Many Chinese renewable energy projects are CER producers and thus receive the resultant revenues. As of the end of February 2008, China had 160 projects that were officially registered with the CDM executive board with projects estimated to achieve reductions of 5.5 million tonnes of carbon dioxide equivalent by 2012 (Office of National Coordination Committee on Climate Change, no date).

INVESTMENT TRENDS

Projections

Such conditions have led to attractive investment opportunities in the environmental and renewable energy sectors. Deutsche Bank projects that average environmental investments will grow at an annual rate of 16 per cent and will reach a cumulative US$230 billion by 2006 to 2010 (Figure 13.1). The bank predicts that investments for wastewater treatment and air purification will annually increase by a respective 25 to 30 per cent and 20 to 25 per cent in the next five years (Deutsche Bank, 2006).

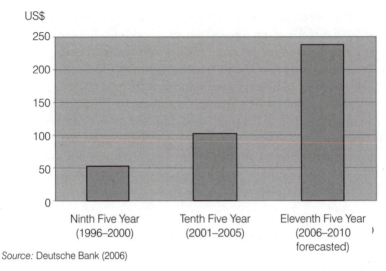

US$

Source: Deutsche Bank (2006)

Figure 13.1 *Deutsche Bank forecast of China's environmental investments*

Credit Suisse predicts that renewable energy consumption will grow at an annual rate of 7.57 per cent between 2010 and 2020 with wind, solar and biomass use to increase by a respective 19.62, 7.18 and 18.49 per cent (Credit Suisse, 2006). To achieve its renewable energy targets, New Energy Finance (NEF) estimates that China will require investments of US$174 billion over the coming 15 years (NEF, 2006).

Levels of interest

The strong outlook for growth has spurred record levels of investment into the Chinese environmental and renewable energy industries. In 2006, total investment in China's renewable energy markets reached close to US$4.5 billion, representing growth of over 100 per cent from 2005 according to New Energy Finance. The majority of the investment took the form of asset finance, which accounted for US$2.6 billion of the total (NEF, 2006).

Venture capital inflows are also booming, reaching US$420 million in 2006, a 147 per cent increase from 2005, with the average 2006 deal size US$16.2 million, according to CleanTech Network. First quarter 2007 investments exceeded US$154 million with the year end total expected to top US$580 million (Cleantech Network, 2007).

Energy generation accounted for more than 70 per cent of the overall investment in 2006 and 2007 with 13 deals worth a total US$403 million (see Table 13.2 and Figure 13.2). Wind power and biomass both accounted for two deals, which were, respectively, valued at US$22 million and US$13.2 million, while water and wastewater had six deals that totalled US$90 million (Cleantech Network, 2007).

Table 13.2 *Cleantech deal size 2006 to 2007*

Company	Technology	Date	Investor	Stage	Region	Amount (US$ million)
Jiangsu Shunda	Energy generation – solar	February 2007	Goldman Sachs	First	East	82
Solar Fun	Energy generation – solar	August 2006	CVC Good Energy	First	East	53
Jiangxi LDK	Energy generation – solar	September 2006	CDH, Netexis, JAFCO, CEF	Second	Central	48
Trina Solar	Energy generation – solar	April 2006	Merrill Lynch, Milestone	First	East	40
CEEG Nanjing PV	Energy generation – solar	May 2006	CRCI, CEF	Second	East	28
Greensaver Tech	Energy generation – battery	October 2006	SAIF	First	Central	20
Shanghai US Water	Water and wastewater	November 2006	Blue Ridge	First	Central	20

Source: Cleantech Network (2007)

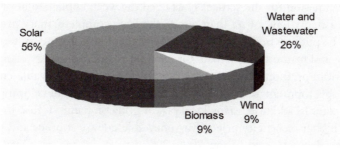

Source: Cleantech Network (2007)

Figure 13.2 *Cleantech deals by segment 2006 to 2007*

PERFORMANCE

Returns for Chinese environmental firms have been impressive, with top performers earning profit margins as high as 30 per cent. China Biodiesel in 2006 achieved a net profit margin of over 36 per cent, while solar photovoltaic maker Suntech Power earned a net profit margin of 17.30 per cent. Waste services company Shenzhen Dongjiang Environmental reported a net profit margin of over 18 per cent (based on financial data provided by Reuters).

The initial public offerings (IPOs) of Chinese environmental firms have also proved to be profitable. During the first day of its May 2007 IPO, the share price of solar maker Jiangsu Shunda closed at US$16.56, 50 per cent higher than its offer price of US$11. LDK, another solar maker which also had its IPO in May 2007, saw its first day stock price close at an 11.1 per cent gain over its offer price. For windmill-component maker China High Speed Transmission, its first-day IPO closing price in June 2007 on the Hong Kong Stock Exchange was HK$14.44, a gain of 98 per cent from its offering price of HK$7.08 (based on financial data provided by Reuters).

CHALLENGES

Despite the high returns, China's environment markets remain fraught with challenges. While total annual consumption of renewable energy (excluding traditional biomass) in 2006 grew by 1 per cent to 8 per cent of China's total primary energy consumption, the country was unable to achieve its environmental objectives. The country failed to reach its 11th Five-Year Plan goal of reducing pollution emissions by 2 per cent in 2006 while energy consumption per unit of GDP decreased only by 1.23 per cent, falling short of its 4 per cent goal. Among China's 30 provinces and regions, only Beijing city met its efficiency goal, cutting energy use per unit of output by 5.25 per cent (*Economist Intelligence Unit – Business China*, 2007).

A crucial reason for the setbacks has been the weak implementation of the Renewable Energy Law. More than ten of the law's complementary provisions have yet to be put into practice. This includes regulations for water power generation; long- and medium-term goals for national renewable energy exploitation and utilization; preferential tax provisions for the use of renewable energy in industrial development projects; and a renewable energy development and utilization plan. In addition, many local power grid companies refuse to pay the mandated higher electricity prices for renewable energy sources and provide access to the electricity grid (Wang, 2006–2007).

Meanwhile, the enforcement powers of the MEP remain severely limited. In 2006, only 70 per cent of provincial-level projects actually submitted the required environmental impact reports, with the figure dropping to only 40 per cent for city projects and 20 per cent for those in townships and counties. In addition, there were 161 major pollution incidents – the equivalent of one every two days – while public complaints reached over 600,000, a 30 per cent jump from 2005 (*Economist Intelligence Unit – Business China*, 2007).

As a result, the environmental and renewable energy markets remain fragmented, with firms only able to compete in local regions and unable expand nationally. In addition, many of the completed projects are not functioning at capacity because of a lack of local funding.

Such problems have already manifested themselves in the high-growth Chinese renewable energy industries:

* *Solar:* while Chinese domestic solar consumption continues to grow, 90 per cent of Chinese solar energy production is for export. Thus, it is extremely vulnerable to global competition and higher costs due to the shortage of

silicon supplies. Chinese firms usually pay a premium of as much as 100 per cent more than their global competitors for silicon. This increased expense often negates their lower manufacturing cost advantages (*Business Week*, 2007).

- *Wind:* Chinese wind projects are highly dependent upon the sale of carbon credits for profitability with their cost of producing electricity, on average, 1.7 to 2 times that of the cost of coal-fired power projects (*China Business Review*, 2006). In addition, the majority of Chinese wind projects are located in economically undeveloped areas of northern China and transmission to major urban areas is either technologically unfeasible or cost prohibitive.

- *Biodiesel:* distribution is fragmented, with fuel sold mostly through 25,000 privately held petrol stations in China. Sinopec and PetroChina, the country's largest oil companies, do not sell biodiesel in their collective 50,000 petrol stations across the country. Feedstock prices have skyrocketed. In 2007, oil waste prices reached over 4000 RMB per tonne, compared to the 2005 price of 1700 RMB. However, the Chinese government, which sets the price of energy, has not significantly increased the price of diesel (*Dow Jones Commodities Service*, 2006).

- *Water and wastewater:* local governments lack the sufficient financial mechanisms to collect wastewater treatment fees. As a result, most of the central government-funded urban water treatment plants are idle. In addition, polluters prefer to pay the fines rather than install wastewater treatment facilities because of the relatively minor penalties. Until February 2008, pollution fines were capped at 1 million RMB, regardless of environmental or economic impact.

The consequence is that many Chinese firms are faced with higher costs and shrinking profit margins, as well as unstable demand for their products and services. For 2007, net profit margins for some Chinese solar energy and biodiesel firms have dropped by as much 60 per cent compared to 2006.[1] The result has been significant decreases in stock values. For example, NASDAQ-listed photovoltaic maker China Sunenergy's stock price, as of May 2008, decreased by 18.4 per cent since its May 2007 IPO, while London-listed China Biodiesel's stock price, as of May 2008, dropped by 82.06 per cent since its October 2006 IPO.[2]

OPPORTUNITIES

While there are, no doubt, challenges, China's environmental investment climate will improve, albeit slowly. The government, from both the central and local levels, is actively creating new rules and financial incentives that strengthen the 11th Five-Year Plan for Energy Development and the Renewable Energy Law. New incentives include the announcement of an 23.5 billion RMB fund from

Table 13.3 *Performance of key Chinese Cleantech Investment initial public offerings*

Firm	Exchange	Date	Initial offering amount (US$ million)	Initial offer price	Current share price*	Performance
Goldwind	Shenzhen	December 2007	243	36 yen	56 yen	55.56%
ZhongDe Waste	Frankfurt	June 2007	144	26 Euros	26.98 Euros	3.77%
Jiangyin Jetion	AIM	June 2007	61	UK£151	UK£103.50	–31.46%
Yingli Green Energy	NYSE	June 2007	319	US$31	US$21.78	–29.74%
LDK Solar	NYSE	June 2007	470	US$25.45	US$33.41	31.26%
China Sunenergy	NASDAQ	May 2007	94	US$11	US$8.98	–18.36%
China Agri-Industries	HKEX	March 2007	413	HK$3.10	HK$5.52	78.06%
J. A. Solar	NASDAQ	February 2007	225	US$15	US$21.93	46.20%
Solarfun Power	NASDAQ	December 2006	150	US$19	US$13.15	–31.24%
Trina Solar	NYSE	December 2006	98	US$18.50	US$41.19	122.65%
Canadian Solar	NASDAQ	November 2006	115	US$19.76	US$27.12	37.25%
Renesola	AIM	August 2006	50	UK£13	UK£15.95	22.69%
China Biodiesel	AIM	June 2006	15	UK£85	UK£15.25	–82.06%
Suntech Power	NYSE	December 2005	455	US$15	US$43.30	188.67%
Shoto	AIM	December 2005	10	UK£136	UK£149.00	9.56%

Source: New Energy Finance (* as of 6 May 2008)

the Ministry of Finance to support energy efficiency projects. In February 2008, the Chinese legislature enacted new legislation that holds polluting enterprises to be responsible for 30 per cent of the direct economic losses of any incident they cause (*Xinhua*, 2008) Local governments are actively developing their own rules to encourage renewable energy. The municipalities of Shenzhen and Shanghai have special regulations requiring the use of solar-powered water heating systems in residential buildings, while Beijing requires the gradual phase-out of coal-burning household boilers (Energy Foundation, 2007).

As important, the country is actively using the financial markets to prevent the growth of highly energy-consuming and pollution-emitting firms. Together with the People's Bank of China, the MEP has established a 'green' credit-rating system in which the environmental compliance records of industrial borrowers are available to lenders, with poor performers to be denied bank loans (*Economist Intelligence Unit – Business China*, 2007). The initiative has so far prevented 38 companies from receiving loans from state-owned banks. The ministry also worked with the Chinese Securities and Regulatory Exchange Commission to prevent ten Chinese firms with serious environmental violations from having their IPOs in February 2008. Such mechanisms will strengthen demand for environmental products and services (*People's Daily*, 2008).

On an industry level, Chinese firms will maintain their distinct advantage as a low-cost manufacturing hub, which allows the companies to produce environmental technologies that are significantly cheaper than their global competitors. Perhaps the most powerful force for the sector's growth and profitability is that the country desperately needs to improve its ecological situation. Firms who can provide innovative products and services in the critical sectors that are cost-competitive will be in high demand.

STRATEGIES FOR SUCCESS

To successfully profit in China's environmental and renewable energy markets, investors must identify opportunities that leverage the inherent difficulties to their advantage. Sound investment objectives should:

- *Capture the value chain within the industry.* Almost all of China's environmentally related industries are projected to experience high growth. However, growth does not equate to profitability. The key is to identify the value chain within a certain sector in the industry, which will be in demand regardless of whether the industry, as a whole, is profitable. This could include component and resource suppliers, before and after market services, and financial products.
- *Identify businesses and projects that provide economic benefits as well as environmental benefits.* With China's enterprises driven principally by lower costs, environmental enterprises that also provide economic benefits will be in high demand. Firms and projects whose business models are solely dependent upon government expenditures and regulatory enforcement will face difficulties in securing the necessary revenue streams for profitability.
- *Seek out firms whose products and services can be scalable for the domestic and international markets.* Chinese businesses that are profitable in the domestic markets are likely to have competitive advantages that would allow the firms to enter the international marketplace, particularly in other developing nations. These enterprises could be poised to become global players if provided with the necessary financial and management capital.

SUSTAINABLE AND RESPONSIBLE INVESTING IN CHINA

For many SRI funds, China's environmental markets have become the ideal situation to profit from supporting positive change in the world's most populated nation. In fact, international investors have often been, and continue to be, some of the most aggressive and successful backers of Chinese clean energy companies. Despite these developments, SRI in China remains uncharted territory and there is much work to be done before these funds will achieve the social benefits that they promote.

In March 2008, Shanghai investment house Industrial Fund Management announced the establishment of a 100 million RMB mutual fund to specifically invest in listed Chinese companies that exhibit high standards of social responsibility. The vehicle follows the December 2007 launch of China's first social responsibility index, the Taida Environmental Index, which tracks 40 listed companies from ten environment-related industries, while the Bank of China International Investment Managers created its Sustainable Growth Equity Fund in May 2006. The fund also pledges to invest in Chinese companies listed on the domestic A-share markets that maintain high standards of environmental performance, corporate governance and social responsibility.

These new domestic SRI vehicles follow the deeds of international investors that were among the first to move into China's green markets. For example, Calvert – the largest US SRI house with over US$13 billion in assets under management – is one of the first limited partners to the China Environment Fund – a Chinese-focused cleantech venture capital firm that delivered handsome profits from its investments into Chinese solar energy firms whose IPOs became the darlings of Wall Street.

SRI investment in China's environmental markets certainly makes ethical sense given China's desperate need to clean up its environment. From the business side, it is also a smart move given the country's fast-growing capital markets and surging population of retail investors. Despite falling by more than 30 per cent since its October 2007 peak, the domestic A-share market is still trading at three times over its January 2006 levels.[3] By the end of 2007, there were 138 million individual stock accounts and 510,000 institutional investment accounts in China according to the China Securities Depository and Clearing Corp. Of the total, 59 million retail accounts and 113,000 institutional accounts were opened in 2007 alone.[4]

So just from these appearances, it looks like the drivers are in place for SRI in China to be a success. However, as with everything in China, the buyer must beware. The first and foremost challenge for Chinese SRI is that it cannot include a strong human rights component, such as upholding 'democratic values' – a core principle of many international SRI funds. It was human rights that led many SRI investors to boycott Chinese firms. For instance, it was not until December 2006 that the California Public Employees' Retirement System (CalPERS), the largest US public pension fund with over US$200 billion under assets, changed its policy on not investing in Chinese equities. Given the country's one-party political system, Chinese and international firms must be willing to make dubious compromises with authorities; for example, Google censored its local Chinese search engine, and Yahoo! turned over to police email records of a Chinese journalist, leading to his arrest. As a result, SRI in China will, for now, be narrowly focused on environmental industries – something that may violate the core principles of SRI.

Another road block is the transparency and behaviour of Chinese companies. For instance, corporate disclosure is a major problem. Many of the listed firms do not file annual proxy statements, and those that do so provide little detailed information pertaining to related party transactions, governance and compensation. The situation is even worse with regard to the firm's environmental performance, with less than half of Chinese listed firms releasing any such data at all. On the social responsibility front, most Chinese firms engage only in philanthropic donations (if any), rather than adopting measures that go above and beyond complying with the government's labour and environmental performance. From the sales side, there is doubt whether there is a market for SRI funds because Chinese investors traditionally seek out quick returns and view a firm's commitment to social responsibility as a barrier to profitability (*Economist Intelligence Unit*, 2006). Such questions lead to the bigger reality of the kind of standards that a Chinese firm must adhere to in order to be legitimately considered a responsible company, and whether these standards should be in line with international SRI norms. As of now, there are no clear benchmarks for Chinese funds, with many of the investment vehicles failing to disclose their SRI selection criteria.

On the flip side, SRI advocates argue that conditions are improving, with Chinese companies becoming more transparent and Chinese investors becoming more socially conscious. The Association for Sustainable and Responsible Investment in Asia (ASrIA), a Hong Kong-based non-governmental organization that promotes SRI in Asia, argues that as Chinese companies seek more market capital, such as through initial public offerings, they will be forced to improve their disclosure standards and corporate governance. In addition, ASrIA stated that Chinese investors are becoming more sophisticated and socially conscious: its surveys found that more than half of Hong Kong investors indicated that they were interested in SRI.

A more salient indicator of China's SRI development is the growing prominence of a nascent corporate social responsibility (CSR) industry. During the past few years, there has been a steady stream of Chinese companies releasing CSR reports, with the Chinese media engaging in CSR rankings. For example, state-owned PetroChina published its first CSR report in 2007 and the magazine *China Entrepreneur Club* launched an annual rating of the country's most environmentally friendly firms in 2008. Not surprisingly, there have also been an increasing number of Chinese CSR consulting firms.

This emergence of a Chinese CSR culture in China, coupled with the new SRI investment vehicles, should help create the infrastructure for uniform standards and monitoring, as well as the financial incentives for Chinese firms to be better corporate citizens. The result should be the foundation of a vibrant and indigenous Chinese SRI industry that expands the sector from simply cleantech to broader social realms. The question, therefore, for SRI in China is not whether if it will happen, but how, when and who will lead the way.

NOTES

1 For example, Suntech's September 2007 quarter net profit margin was 12.73 per cent, while China Biodiesel's July 2007 quarter net profit margin was 14.75 per cent.
2 Based on stock price on 15 February 2008.
3 SSE Composite Index (000001.SS) as of 25 March 2008.
4 See 'A perfect close for China's stock market 2007,' www.china.org.cn/english/business/237532.htm, accessed April 2008.

REFERENCES

Business Week (2007) 'China aims to clean up in solar power: Its environment is a world-class mess, but the mainland has ambitious plans to use and produce solar power cells and panels,' *Business Week*, 11 April
China Business Review (2006) 'Windpower pricing and tendering', *China Business Review*, July/August
Cleantech Network (2007) *China Cleantech Venture Capital Investment Report: 2006–2007*, July
Credit Suisse (2006) *China's Renewable Energy Sector*, Credit Suisse, 7 July
Deutsche Bank (2006) *China's Environmental Drive*, Deutsche Bank, Frankfurt, Germany, 3 November
Dow Jones Commodities Service (2006) 'China energy watch: Challenges await in drive to go green', *Dow Jones Commodities Service*, 12 December
Economist Intelligence Unit (2006) 'Goodwill investment: Can socially responsible investing succeed in China?', *Economist Intelligence Unit*, 17 July
Economist Intelligence Unit – Business China (2007) 'Mucked up bureaucracy: The continuing plight of the government agency charged with China's environmental upkeep', *Economist Intelligence Unit – Business China*, 26 February
Economy, E. and Lieberthal, K. (2007) 'Scorched earth: Will environmental risks in China overwhelm its opportunities?,' *Harvard Business Review*, June
Energy Foundation (2007) *China Renewable Energy Law Implementation Review and Evaluation*, China Sustainable Energy Program, May
National Development and Reform Commission (2007) *11th Five-Year Program for Energy Development*, April, www.china.org.cn/english/features/guideline/156529.htm
NEF (New Energy Finance) (2006) *Press Release: China to Beat Clean Energy Targets – At a Price*, NEF, London, 18 September
Office of National Coordination Committee on Climate Change (no date) *Clean Development Mechanism in China*, Office of National Coordination Committee on Climate Change of NDRC, http://cdm.ccchina.gov.cn/english/
People's Daily (2008) 'Environmental investigations are blocking IPOs', *People's Daily*, 26 February
Wang, M. (2006–2007) 'Issues related to the implementation of China's Energy Law: Analysis of the Energy Conservation Law and the Renewable Energy Law as examples', *Vermont Journal of Environmental Law*, vol 8e
Wang, M. (2008) 'Presentation: Efforts in moving towards a low carbon future: China's energy conservation and renewable energy laws', 13 February, details at http://pdf.wri.org/chinas_booming_energy_efficiency_industry.pdf
World Bank (2007) *State and Trends of the Carbon Market 2007*, World Bank, Washington, DC, May

Xinhua (2007) 'Energy efficiency and reduction pollution: A multidimensional policy approach for macro-economic controls', 5 December

Xinhua (2008) 'Tougher law to curb water pollution', *Xinhua*, 19 February 2008

Xinhua China Money (2006) 'China to draft Outline Energy Law next year', *Xinhua China Money*, 25 December

14

India

Dan Siddy

INTRODUCTION

Over the past five years, average gross domestic product (GDP) growth of 8.75 per cent has made India one of the world's fastest-growing economies. Domestic and foreign investors have flocked to the country's booming stock markets and have been eager subscribers to a steady stream of record-breaking initial public offerings (IPOs). This rapid growth has brought significant dividends to the population at large, as well as to emerging market investors: the poverty rate has fallen from 36 per cent in 1994 to less than 28 per cent in 2005, inflation has been contained and the current account deficit is moderate (IMF, 2008).

Despite this rapid growth – and, in some respects, because of it – India still faces profound sustainable development challenges that threaten to undermine continued economic expansion and stability. A wide array of social and environmental issues creates very tangible risks for India's publicly listed companies and significant opportunities for firms that can position themselves to provide solutions.

However, sustainable investment in India is still in its infancy compared to other advanced emerging economies such as Brazil and South Africa. According to an influential May 2007 report by the London-based environmental think tank TERI-Europe, Indian corporations and their domestic and international investors may be putting long-term value at risk if the gap is not closed (TERI-Europe, 2007).

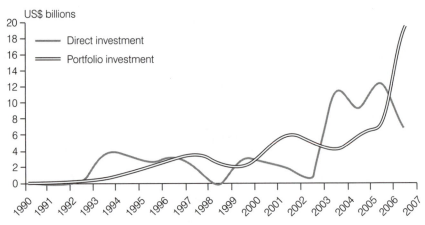

Source: Reserve Bank of India, Annual report, 2006–2007

Figure 14.1 *Foreign investment in India*

BOOMING EQUITY MARKETS IN INDIA

India's phenomenal economic performance in recent years has attracted the attention of foreign investors (see Figure 14.1). Net capital inflows into India have surged in recent years and reached US$66 billion in 2007, more than double the level in 2005 (Reserve Bank of India, 2007).

Although foreign direct investment and lending to Indian corporations have been the biggest contributors, portfolio investment by US and European equity funds has also risen rapidly. Such investors – known in India as foreign institutional investors (FIIs) – have developed large appetites for India's stock markets, which in 2007 rose by a record 47.1 per cent, the largest climb in four years. Overseas investors bought a net US$18.8 billion of stocks and bonds during January to November 2007, compared to the previous record of US$9.5 billion during the same period in 2006. At the same time, India's burgeoning middle class has contributed to record levels of domestic savings and investment.

Table 14.1 *Selected recent Indian share issues*

Name	Industry	Deal type	Date	Deal value (US$ billion)
Reliance Petroleum	Energy and power	IPO	April 2006	1.8
Cairn India	Energy and power	IPO	January 2007	1.9
DLF	Property	IPO	June 2007	2.4
Sterlite Industries	Metals	IPO	June 2007	2.0
ICICI Bank	Financials	SO	June 2007	4.7
Reliance Power	Energy and power	IPO	January 2008	3.0

Notes: IPO = initial public offering; SO = secondary offering.
Source: Ernst and Young; Bloomberg; *Financial Times*

Numerous Indian companies have established themselves as world class multinationals, and growing numbers of large firms are going public on local Indian exchanges. The market has seen several multibillion dollar IPOs and many Indian firms have also listed abroad, mainly in London, Singapore and Luxembourg, in a quest for higher valuations and visibility (see Table 14.1). Indian companies raised a record US$8.3 billion in new share issues in 2007, led mainly by the power and property sectors.

The business case for sustainable investment in India

Lower labour costs, easy access to natural resources, high demand for property and infrastructure development, and rapidly growing consumer markets are among the key drivers behind India's success story. However, these competitive advantages also involve critical environmental and social issues. Box 14.1 summarizes just some of the sustainable development fundamentals that have the potential to create or destroy long-term shareholder value in Indian companies in a major way.

On the face of it, there is a compelling case for actors in the Indian investment value chain to begin integrating environmental, social and governance (ESG) factors within corporate transparency and disclosure, advisory services, equity research, stock valuation, portfolio construction and shareholder engagement (see Box 14.2). According to TERI-Europe, the benefits arguably include:

- better differentiation of Indian stocks compared to issuers from other emerging markets in the global competition for long-term quality investors;
- more efficient allocation of capital to companies with business models and management qualities that are robust enough to succeed in the face of the ESG challenges in India and which contribute to environmentally sustainable and socially responsible development of the national economy;
- additional market-based incentives for Indian firms in growth technologies that respond to sustainable development needs such as alternative energy;
- enhanced corporate awareness of ESG risks and opportunities and more rapid transmission of global ESG know-how and business intelligence;
- additional market-based incentives for companies to comply with national ESG standards and to adopt corporate social responsibility programmes that go beyond compliance;
- increased choice for domestic retail investors through lower-risk stock-linked products that also reflect retail investors' personal values and faith-based principles;
- greater diversity, competition and innovation in fund products, sell-side research and specialized rating products;

Box 14.1 KEY DRIVERS FOR SUSTAINABLE INVESTMENT

- Major shortcomings in India's infrastructure are estimated to reduce GDP growth by 1 per cent per annum and require investment of about US$500 billion over the medium term in power and other sectors.
- Power shortages are acute and growing: the average firm reports power outages on 85 days per year and the peak deficit reached a ten-year high of 14.5 per cent in 2007.
- Coal accounts for about 60 per cent of power generation and is also the major contributor to India's greenhouse gas emissions (India is one of the world's top six largest emitters of carbon dioxide and is predicted to rank fourth in the world for total greenhouse gas emissions by 2025).
- The Indian government is currently reluctant to introduce greenhouse gas (GHG) emission reduction targets, arguing that richer industrial nations should shoulder the economic burden of the global fight against climate change.
- India is expected to be one of the first and worst affected countries to be affected by global climate change, posing major problems for human health, food production, habitat loss, population migration, infrastructure security and social stability.
- Water supplies in India are under severe stress due to shortages and pollution – the demand for water could exceed all sources of supply by 2020 unless action is taken now.
- Rapid growth has reduced poverty but inequality has risen, especially between rural and urban populations (more than 70 per cent of the population is still dependent upon India's failing agricultural economy).
- More than one quarter of India's most highly polluting companies fail to comply with applicable national environmental standards.
- Small- and medium-sized enterprises (SMEs) account for about 40 per cent of industrial production in India, but are estimated to generate 70 per cent of the total industrial pollution load nationwide.
- Many Indian companies are engaged in corporate philanthropy, but very few are integrating sustainability within the DNA of their core business strategies.
- Corporate disclosure of non-financial performance issues is limited and fewer than half a dozen Indian companies publish annual sustainability reports based on Global Reporting Initiative (GRI) guidelines.
- Corporate governance is improving but remains a concern.

- the creation of professional capacity, asset pools and consumer interest for the further development of high development-impact financial products, such as micro-insurance, micro-pensions, community investing, weather risk insurance and environmental finance.

INTERNATIONAL INVESTORS: POSITIVE INTEREST

Currently, there are very few 'global' investment funds specializing in sustainable investment in emerging market equities. However, several sustainability funds in North America and Europe have made small allocations to the emerging markets in their strategic portfolio mix.

Up-to-date data are extremely limited; but a 2003 report by the International Finance Corporation (IFC) found that around 120 or so emerging market stocks

---

**BOX 14.2 INDIAN STOCKS TYPICALLY HELD BY
'SUSTAINABLE' INVESTMENT FUNDS**

* Bajaj;
* Cipla;
* Dr Reddy's Laboratories;
* HDFC Bank;
* ICICI Bank;

* Infosys;
* Mahanagar Telephone;
* Suzlon Energy;
* Tata Motors.

Source: TERI-Europe (2007)

---

were held by a sample of developed market SRI mutual funds (Enterprising Solutions Global/International Finance Corporation, 2003). Nearly 40 per cent were South African companies. Only four were Indian companies.

Additional research undertaken in 2007 on behalf of TERI-Europe revealed several other Indian firms in the portfolios of developed market sustainability funds (see Box 14.2).

These findings suggest that, compared to other emerging markets and taking into account India's market capitalization and strong stock-market performance, Indian companies receive relatively little positive attention from international sustainable investment funds.

NEGATIVE ATTENTION

Indian firms do, however, appear to attract constructive criticism and even negative attention from some international investors as a result of social, environmental or ethical issues.

The US pension fund California Public Employees' Retirement System (CalPERS), for example, has an emerging-market portfolio of approximately US$5.2 billion split between three fund managers. CalPERS has long been an influential advocate for high standards of corporate governance, environmental sustainability and social responsibility.

CalPERS's emerging market funds are subject to negative ESG screening. Table 14.2 shows the results of this screening for one of its managers, Dimensional, as of May 2007. A relatively high proportion of Indian companies fail or risk failing CalPERS's sustainability test (see Box 14.3). The ESG issues that arise in relation to these Indian companies are wide-ranging and include:

* business relationships in Burma and Sudan;
* potential involvement in irregularities in the United Nations Oil for Food programme in Iraq;
* deaths at public protests against the construction of new steel plants;
* infringement of indigenous peoples' rights;

BOX 14.3 ESG SCREENING OF INDIAN STOCKS ON BEHALF OF CalPERS

Fail:

- ABB Ltd (India);
- Hindustan Lever;

- Mangalore Refinery and Petrochemicals Ltd.

Borderline:

- Ashok Leyland;
- Essar Steel Ltd;
- Godrej Consumer Products;
- Great Eastern Shipping;
- Hindalco Industries;
- Hindustan Construction;
- Hindustan Zinc;
- Indian Petrochemical;
- Jaiprakash Associates;
- JSW Steel Ltd;
- Larsen & Toubro;

- Nestle India;
- Petronet LNG;
- Ranbaxy Laboratories;
- Reliance Communications;
- Reliance Industries;
- Sesa Goa;
- Siemens India Ltd;
- Sterlite Industries;
- Sun Pharmaceutical;
- Tata Steel Ltd;
- United Phosphorus Ltd.

Source: TERI-Europe (2007)

- public health effects of sudden chlorine gas leaks from petrochemical plants;
- habitat loss and disturbance to endangered species arising from port construction;
- use of child labour;
- disputes over water rights;
- discrimination against members of the dalit caste;
- deviations from good manufacturing practice in the pharmaceutical industry.

Similarly, in December 2007, Norway's Government Pension Fund sold its US$13.2 million stake in Vedanta Resources Plc, a FTSE100 India-based mining multinational, due to 'systematic' environmental and human rights failures at four Indian subsidiaries. The ethics council of the fund – the world's second-largest sovereign wealth fund – found that charges raised against Vedanta's subsidiaries, including the 'forced relocation' of indigenous tribes, were 'well founded' and indicated 'a pattern in the company's behaviour where such violations are an accepted and established part of its activities'.

Table 14.2 *Sustainability screening of emerging market companies on behalf of CalPERS*

		Number of companies	
	Pass	*Fail?*	*Fail*
Brazil	22	10	–
Chile	24	5	–
Czech Republic	5	1	–
Hungary	5	–	–
India	72	22	3
Indonesia	13	2	–
Israel	17	–	–
Korea	24	20	4
Malaysia	40	5	4
Mexico	25	6	3
Philippines	8	1	–
Poland	10	1	1
South Africa	36	1	6
Taiwan	113	7	4
Thailand	17	14	2
Turkey	13	1	–
Total	**444**	**96**	**27**

Source: Dimensional (2007)

APPARENT INDIFFERENCE?

Notwithstanding the example of sustainable investment leaders such as CalPERS and Norway's government pension fund (both founding signatories to the United Nations Principles for Responsible Investment), the vast majority of foreign investors in Indian equities appear to be largely indifferent to long-term sustainability considerations despite the compelling *prima facie* business case.

For example, one of the Vedanta subsidiaries that so concerned Norway's pension fund was India's largest copper producer, Sterlite Industries, which made its IPO debut on the New York Stock Exchange in June 2007.

Sterlite and its parent had been the subject of allegations of flagrant human rights and environmental violations since at least 2005, and indeed Sterlite's prospectus disclosed that it was 'involved in a variety of litigation matters, including matters relating to alleged violations of environmental and tax laws and alleged price manipulation of our equity shares on the Indian Stock Exchanges'.

Nevertheless, the IPO raised US$2 billion and was oversubscribed fivefold, and over the following months Sterlite's share price doubled.

In November 2007, however, India's Supreme Court refused to grant permission to the Vedanta Group for open-cast bauxite mines essential to Sterlite's flagship project, a US$1 billion, 1 million tonne alumina refinery in Orissa. This controversial scheme in the east of the country involves significant environmental and social problems, ranging from involuntary resettlement and

---

Box 14.4 ABN AMRO Sustainability Fund

The ABN AMRO Sustainable Development Fund is a three-year closed-end equity scheme and was launched in March 2007. The fund invests in a universe of large, medium and small cap Indian companies from the S&P CNX 500 Index. These stocks are filtered by CRISIL, one of the country's leading research and rating firms, using an ESG template based on public disclosures made by these companies. The positively screened investment universe is then to be subject to 'traditional' financial analysis, blending company and sector views with macro-economic analysis. Extensive back-testing against past records indicates that, at its launch, the 245 companies in the fund's 'SRI universe' consistently outperformed traditional indices such as the BSE Sensex and Nifty.

Source: ABN AMRO India

---

disruption of local livelihoods to the loss of sacred tribal lands and remote forest habitats. Sterlite's stock fell sharply on the news and, as of February 2008, stands at just US$19 compared to the IPO price of US$15.

Sterlite is not an isolated example of foreign investors' bullish appetite for Indian stocks whose long-term value is likely to be obscured by a lack of attention to critical social and environmental drivers of performance. The investment prospectus for the US$2.4 billion IPO of construction giant DLF disclosed 42 pages on outstanding litigation and material developments related to its residential, commercial and industrial projects, much of it linked to the eviction of traditional occupiers of land and failure to obtain necessary environmental approvals prior to starting construction.

Very little analyst-friendly information was provided in the prospectus or by DLF itself on the company's management systems for handling social and environmental problems. There is virtually no information on how issues such as climate change, water scarcity and energy shortages will affect DLF's huge land bank and its long-term business strategy and growth objectives.

Institutional buyers oversubscribed to the IPO fivefold; 90 per cent of these bids for DLF came from foreign investors.

Domestic investors

This apparent indifference is also evident in the domestic investment market. Net assets managed by Indian mutual funds increased by over 40 per cent between 2006 and 2007 to reach the equivalent of US$80 billion – and competition is fierce. But at the time of writing, only one sustainability-themed investment fund – the ABN AMRO Sustainable Development Fund – is currently available in India (see Box 14.4).

This compares poorly with other advanced emerging economies such as Brazil and South Africa, where retail investors can now choose from dozens of such investment products, many of them with very respectable multi-year track records.

To date, ABN AMRO's India fund has raised the equivalent of US$60 million, well below the asset manager's initial expectations and a very small amount compared to the amount of capital raised by other new funds, including a large number of infrastructure funds now marketed to Indian retail investors.

Public environmental awareness and social values may be one reason for the limited penetration of sustainable investment products into the Indian retail investor market. Unfortunately, there appears to be limited information on consumer attitude surveys in this regard.

S&P ESG INDIA INDEX

A key barrier to sustainable investment in India and other emerging markets is the limited availability of good-quality ESG research by both mainstream sell-side analysts and specialist sustainable investment research firms. In addition, ESG-inclusive indices have been found to be a valuable tool for global investors (UN, 2007).

The IFC, the private-sector arm of the World Bank Group, has played a key role during recent years in trying to close this gap in information and research infrastructure. In 2006, the IFC ran an international competition offering grant funding of US$0.5 million for innovative solutions to the information inefficiencies encountered by sustainable investors in emerging markets. The result is one of the most promising initiatives for promoting sustainable investment in India: S&P ESG India Index.

The IFC-sponsored index was launched in January 2008 and was developed by a consortium of S&P, CRISIL and KLD. It provides investors with exposure to a liquid and tradable index of 50 of the best performing stocks in the Indian market as measured by ESG parameters.

Index constituents are derived from the top 500 Indian companies by total market capitalization that are listed on the National Stock Exchange (NSE). All 500 companies in the universe are subjected to a screening process that incorporates ESG indicators against which the company's disclosure practices are evaluated. Two screens are used in this 'transparency and disclosure' methodology (see Table 14.3): the social and environmental screens are based on output obtained by mapping indicators from the Global Reporting Initiative (GRI), Global Compact and Millennium Development Goals (MDGs), while the governance screen is based on S&P's existing corporate governance methodology, adapted to suit India's markets.

The screening process ultimately yields a score, or an evaluation, for each of the companies in the universe. The evaluation process seeks information relating to companies' disclosure of the ESG screen indicators available in the public domain, such as a company's annual report, website, bulletins and/or the disclo-

Table 14.3 *S&P ESG India Index: Transparency and disclosure template for assessing ESG conduct of Indian companies*

Corporate governance	Employees	Customers/ product	Environment	Community
Ownership structure and shareholder rights Financial and operational information Board and management structure and process Business ethics and corporate responsibility	Labour rights Employee health and safety Equal opportunities Employee relations/job creation	Product safety Anti-trust Customer outreach and product quality	Environmental pollution Natural resource use Management policy and performance indicators	Human rights Community investment

Source: S&P

Table 14.4 *S&P ESG India Index: Top ten companies by weight*

Company	Total market cap (US$ million)	Sector
Infosys Technology Ltd	28,922.90	Information technology
ITC Ltd	14,427.50	Consumer staples
Aditya Biria Nuvo Ltd	2535.72	Industrials
Dr Reddy's Laboratories Ltd	3102.21	Healthcare
Wipro Ltd	20,478.70	Information technology
Jubilant Organosys Ltd	946.96	Materials
Axis Bank	9616.71	Financials
GTL Ltd	333.81	Information technology
Reliance Industries Ltd	48,446.63	Energy
Hindustan Unilever	11,890.97	Consumer staples

Source: S&P; CRISIL; KLD

sure made on the stock exchanges. The final aim is to determine whether a company has made transparent disclosure, in such documents, on any of the indicators that are part of the ESG screening system.

The index's constituents include some of India's most well-known corporate names (see Table 14.4). Back-testing of historical performance shows the ESG index compares well with its benchmark, the S&P CNX Nifty.

OUTLOOK

It is too soon to tell what impact the S&P ESG India Index will have on the market. However, based on the experience of Brazil – where the São Paulo Stock Exchange launched a similar sustainability index in 2005 (again, with the support of the IFC) – the expectation is that the Indian index will:

- drive better ESG disclosure by corporates by making it easier to identify laggards and leaders;
- encourage further innovation of sustainable investment products on the domestic market (the index methodology and data already form the backbone of the ABN AMRO Sustainability Fund mentioned earlier in this chapter);
- raise awareness among international investors and provide new capacity to supply them with customized research.

In the meantime, though, TERI-Europe, for one, believes that sustainable investment in India lags far behind where it should be in relation to:

- India's future competitive edge over other emerging markets, principally China, and its share of the ever-increasing global sustainable investment market;
- the size, maturity, portfolio diversification needs and 'do good' aspirations of the sustainable investment sector in the US and other developed markets;
- India's market capitalization, high-tech/high-skill industrialization, ability to deliver outperforming returns, and strategic importance to the rest of the global economy;
- the potential undervaluation of the many Indian companies that demonstrate excellence (or have the potential for excellence) in management quality, corporate governance, social responsibility, environmental technology and environmental stewardship;
- the potential overvaluation of some other Indian companies (and some companies in other emerging markets) that have poor track records in relation to ESG issues and offer lower long-term shareholder value as a result;
- the sheer scale and strategic importance of the sustainable development challenges faced by India, and the crucial role that private enterprise and private investment play in making progress (or not) towards solving these challenges.

Further progress will probably depend largely upon a change in the overall investment climate. India has been a bull market for several years and both domestic and international investors are, arguably, paying very high multiples for Indian equities based simply on market momentum rather than fundamental analysis. Sooner or later, the economy will cycle into a more bearish market and investors will become more discerning.

Over more or less the same timeframe, ESG best practice concepts will have continued to rise up the agenda of an increasingly large cross-section of investors, especially foreign institutional investors. In addition, ESG and sustainable development issues in India generally are likely to become pronounced and will gain a higher profile in public, media, non-governmental organization (NGO) and government circles. ESG problems related to Indian, Chinese and other emerging-market companies are likely to become more frequent, more acute, more visible and more frequently associated with shareholder value destruction.

A confluence of the trends is likely to bring sustainable investment in India into sharp focus and could well lead to a tipping point. Ultimately, the big question is: who are the investors, companies and market makers that anticipate this change today and who is best positioned to become long-term winners and losers?

REFERENCES

Enterprising Solutions Global/International Finance Corporation (2003) *Towards Sustainable and Responsible Investment in Emerging Markets*, October

Dimensional (2007) *CalPERS Emerging Markets Company Report*, May

IMF (International Monetary Fund) *IMF Country Report No 08/51*, IMF, February

Reserve Bank of India (2007) *Annual Report 2006–07*, August

TERI-Europe (2007) *Sustainable Investment in India*, May

UN (2007) *Who Cares Wins: New Frontiers in Emerging Market Investment*, UN Global Compact Conference Report, July

15

Civil Society and Capital Markets

Steve Waygood

A decade after the World Business Council for Sustainable Development (WBCSD) made its first hesitant foray into the investment arena, its president, Björn Stigson, was in no doubt that 'financial markets are key in the pursuit of sustainable development because they hold the scorecard, allocate and price capital, and provide risk coverage and price risks'. Yet, Stigson added that 'if financial markets do not understand and reward sustainable behaviour, progress [in developing more sustainable business practices] will be slow' (Stigson, 2003, p6). The clear implication is that capital markets can be both a constraint and a facilitator of improved sustainability.

For an expanding body of institutions representing civil society – notably environmental and development groups and human rights organizations – capital markets are seen not just as an instrumental mechanism for changing corporate practices, but also as a target for systemic change because their current structure undermines long-term sustainable development goals. In some cases, these campaigners have influenced the target company's cost of capital, tarnished its reputation and mobilized significant shareholder votes against management. In a few extreme cases, campaigners have also motivated company brokers to reject clients and stock markets in order to bar listings. The rapid growth in capital market campaigning has created new risks for companies and their investors and has not gone unnoticed. Indeed, the *Financial Times* listed 'growing pressures from international NGOs, armed with unprecedented resources, credibility, access to company data and global communications capabilities' (Kiernan, 2005) as one of the five socio-economic mega-trends affecting the security and earning power of long-term retirement savings.

This chapter seeks to shed some light on why non-governmental organizations (NGOs) are targeting capital markets, what they can contribute, where campaigns have been effective so far and where they might go in the future.[1]

THE GROWTH OF CAPITAL MARKET CAMPAIGNING

Capital market campaigns can be traced back to the 19th century. For example, in 1888, the social reformer Dr Annie Besant (1847–1933) successfully drew attention to the low wages paid to the Bryant and May match girls by shaming shareholding clergymen. But modern 'professionalized' attempts to use the capital market did not fully emerge until the 1970s, when the anti-apartheid movement used annual general meetings (AGMs) as a mechanism to publicly embarrass companies that had operations in South Africa.

Since 1970, there has been dramatic growth in NGO use of the capital markets. Well over 30 NGOs in the UK alone have used the capital market as part of their company campaigning. Examples of such campaigning include Surfers against Sewage questioning the board at South West Water's AGM about its policy in relation to marine dumping of sewage; Campaign against the Arms Trade 'naming and shaming' local authority pension funds with holdings in defence companies such as British Aerospace (BAE); Friends of the Earth and the Royal Society for the Protection of Birds (RSPB) attempting to stop Fisons from extracting peat from sites of special scientific interest; Greenpeace, Amnesty International and World Wide Fund for Nature-UK (WWF-UK) campaigning for Shell to publish a corporate responsibility report to shareholders as a result of the Nigerian government executing Ken Saro-Wiwa, who had been campaigning against the devastation of the Niger Delta by Shell and others; The Corner House campaigning against Balfour Beatty's involvement in the Ilisu Dam in Turkey; Christian Aid targeting British Petroleum (BP) and other institutional investors in PetroChina, due to the latter's involvement in Sudan where an oil-funded civil war was under way; the Trades Union Congress benchmarking institutional investor-voting practices; and the Burma Campaign lobbying for the withdrawal of, for example, BAT and Standard Chartered from Burma due to these companies' provision of finances to a military dictatorship involved in human rights abuses.

Tactically, civil society organizations have deployed two often complementary techniques: first, pressuring investors to invest capital in one company or sector rather than another; and, second, using the rights and influence associated with share ownership to voice concerns directly with company directors and senior management. While the majority of early interventions were antagonistic, focusing on disrupting AGMs, NGOs have steadily become much more sophisticated. Recent years have seen NGOs use a broad range of different interventions, including the production of investment analysis in support of their campaign issues; direct attempts to move capital into certain investment projects and out of others; ongoing programmes of communication with investors in relation to specific issues of corporate social responsibility (CSR); and, in some cases, formal programmes of collaboration between investors and NGOs.

More strategically, some NGOs have also engaged in public policy advocacy on the rules that govern the capital market, arguing that its current structure acts as a constraint on sustainable development for two main reasons: short-termism and market failure.

The short-termism argument rests on the capital market being too nearsighted in the way in which it evaluates companies. As many sustainable development issues are inherently long term, short-termism is a particular problem for NGOs since it results in the systematic erosion of incentives for company directors to initiate performance improvements. One root cause of this is the reality that asset managers are evaluated by their clients – for example, pension funds – based on short-term criteria. This problem is increasingly acknowledged within the investment world, with the UK's Universities Superannuation Scheme arguing that:

> *There appear to be resistors to responsible investing which relate to deeply rooted characteristics of the investment decision-making system, including the mandates that pension funds and their investment consultants set; the systems for measuring and rewarding performance (which focus on peer comparison and beating benchmarks rather than on fulfilling the long-term liabilities of pension funds); and the competencies of service providers (e.g. sell-side analysts). The effect of this resulting short-termism is that less attention is paid to responsible investment matters than is appropriate – these issues are too long term in nature to affect the day-to-day behaviour of fund managers.*
> (USS, 2003)

Civil society organizations are also increasingly aware of the implications of capital market failures for sustainable development. The specific market failure argument for capital markets is that governments have failed to sufficiently internalize companies' environmental and social costs such that the consequent economic development is fully sustainable. As a result of government's failure to internalize these costs on company balance sheets, the capital market does not incorporate companies' full social and environmental costs. Indeed, until these market failures are corrected, it would be irrational for investors to incorporate companies' full social and environmental costs as they do not appear on the balance sheet and, therefore, do not affect companies' profitability or earnings per share over the investment time horizon. The key sustainable development problem is that in the very long term, future generations will not be able to enjoy such high standards of living because the stock of natural capital will have been irreparably depleted.

THE CIVIL REGULATION OF CAPITAL MARKETS

Many companies and investors on the receiving end of capital market campaigns would perhaps understandably resent these interventions. But the active engagement of civil society in market governance is, in fact, a healthy and necessary activity. Simon Zadek, for example, argues that one emerging role of civil society is to regulate corporate behaviour, deeming such activity 'civil regulation' – with the capital markets being just one arena within which this takes place (Zadek, 1998).

More broadly, there are three main contributions that NGOs can make:

1   *Enhance welfare.* When acting as civil regulators, NGO campaigns can be an effective method of achieving welfare-enhancing social and/or environmental goals. Davis et al (2006) argue that NGOs have a specific role in creating a more sustainable economy: 'In a civil society, political parties, an independent judiciary, a free press, impartial law and civic bodies are the core sustainers of democracy. Parallel institutions of a civil economy can be understood as engaged shareowners, independent monitors, credible standards and civil-society organizations participating in the marketplace.' The clear implication is that civil society organizations are an important and legitimate lever to ensure that financial institutions advocate socially responsible management to the companies in which they invest.
2   *Enhance investment analysis.* By enhancing information flows on corporate performance in social, ethical and environmental issues that may be material to share price, NGOs can improve investment analysis. One practical reason why NGOs may be a useful source of relevant investment information is that they tend to spend time analysing and lobbying for changes to public policy. Consequently, NGOs may be a useful indicator of future public policy that could be material to company evaluation. Where NGO capital market intervention contributes to enhanced investment analysis, that intervention is legitimate because it helps to improve investment decisions and market efficiency.
3   *Enhance market trust.* While NGO capital market intervention may serve to improve investment analysis, there are circumstances in which it has been detrimental to a company's share price. Although campaigns may represent a short-term financial burden for a company, this alone is not sufficient reason to render the activity illegitimate. This is because companies benefit from the existence of the capital market, and the existence of any market depends, in part, upon society's trust in order to maintain its own legitimacy. As David Korten (1995, pp 89–98) argues: 'an economic system can remain viable only so long as society has mechanisms to counter the abuses of either state or market power'. His preferred system is democratic pluralism, which combines 'the forces of the market, government and civil society'. Healthy involvement of civil society is not only legitimate, but also *necessary* for the long-term viability of capital markets.

THE IMPACT OF CAPITAL MARKET CAMPAIGNING

According to Russell Sparkes (2002, p24), 'the real beginnings of UK shareholder activism on SRI issues can be precisely dated to 14 May 1997'. This was the date of the 1997 annual general meeting of the Shell Transport and Trading Company. Shell had already received negative publicity during 1995 to 1996 over its planned disposal of the Brent Spar oil platform, and concern over human rights abuses in Nigeria culminating in the execution of Ken Saro-Wiwa. In 1997, a coalition of Greenpeace, Amnesty International and WWF-UK, along with Pensions and Investment Research Consultants (PIRC), was able to assemble enough support from local authority pension funds and church investors led by the Ecumenical Centre for Corporate Responsibility (ECCR) to file a shareholder resolution (see Box 15.1).

What is also noteworthy about this intervention was its effectiveness. Shell recommended voting against the resolution. Ultimately, however, 17 per cent of the investors who voted withheld their support from the board.[2] While this represented a formal failure of the resolution, *The Times'* city editor summed up the significance of the lack of support in the following way:

> *The fact that 11 per cent of Shell's shareholders were persuaded to vote against the company's board was a huge blow to the company and carries a strong blow to industry generally … for the opposition to have reached that level means that some substantial funds voted for change. The grey men who run the institutional funds joined with small shareholders to deliver a drastic condemnation of the company. (The Times, 1997)*

BOX 15.1 TEXT OF 1997 SHELL ANNUAL GENERAL MEETING SHAREHOLDER RESOLUTION

… in recognition of the importance of environmental and corporate responsibility policies (including those policies relating to human rights), to the company's operations, corporate profile and performance, the directors are requested to:

- *Designate responsibility for the implementation of environmental and corporate responsibility policies to a named member of the Committee of Managing Directors.*
- *Establish effective internal procedures for the implementation and monitoring of such policies.*
- *Establish an independent external review and audit procedure for such policies.*
- *Report to shareholders regularly on the implementation of such policies.*
- *Publish a report to shareholders on the implementation of such policies in relation to the company's operations in Nigeria by the end of 1997.*

Perhaps as a consequence of this scale of apparent support for the resolution, over the course of the next 18 months Shell was to take actions that substantively met the five requests contained in the resolution. PIRC was later to state that 'we consider that Shell has, in a relatively short period of time, moved as requested by the resolution "to the head of the movement for corporate responsibility"'. PIRC also stated that it believed the resolution, and the work around it, were catalytic in Shell's making these changes:

> *PIRC considers that the programme of research, meetings and discussion with the company, followed by the resolution, have had a constructive and significant impact upon the company. We welcome Shell's progress since the resolution and consider it a tribute to the ability of the directors, executives and other staff to respond positively to pressure for change both within the company and from shareholders and other groups in recent years.* (PIRC, 1998)

Knight and Pretty (2001, pp24–25) identify a value reaction in Shell's share price of almost –10 per cent from this Greenpeace campaign against Shell. In this context, this research is particularly important because it clearly demonstrates that an NGO can have a significant impact upon a company's share price (and, therefore, its cost of capital).

As a mechanism for changing corporate practices, there are rare examples where a target company has confirmed that it was influenced by the NGO campaign. This is a strong, albeit inconclusive, indicator of effectiveness. One such example was GlaxoSmithKline (GSK), when its chief executive confirmed that he was responding to concerns raised by investors and campaigners when he decided to increase affordable access to its medication in developing countries following a campaign by Oxfam.

This 'Cut the Cost' capital market campaign by Oxfam focused on the difficulties of access to medicines in developing countries. The campaign was intended to encourage 'the world's pharmaceutical companies to do more to improve access to medicines in poor countries'. Oxfam published a briefing paper that targeted investors and called on them to use their influence to encourage GSK (in particular) to develop a policy setting out how it would meet its commitment to 'maximizing affordable access … within the first three months of the company's existence' (Oxfam, 2001). This paper was launched at a briefing for City investors on 14 February 2001 with the intention of mobilizing the support of large institutional investors for its campaign.

While Oxfam was more concerned with the humanitarian consequences of pricing drugs out of the reach of people in developing countries, at the City briefing it highlighted the risks to reputation arising from GSK's position and its involvement with the South African Pharmaceutical Manufacturers Association in a case brought against the South African government, which sought the right to import cheaper medicines. Oxfam also criticized GSK for appearing to defend patents on AIDS drugs in Ghana and Uganda.

Following the campaign's launch, Jean-Pierre Garnier, chief executive of GSK, reportedly undertook to 'make the issue a priority' and subsequently published a policy on access to drugs that was cautiously welcomed by Oxfam. Similarly, the South African Pharmaceutical Manufacturers Association abandoned its case against the South African government. For GSK, according to the *Financial Times*, this was a 'significant event … amount[ing] to a recognition that their legal battle in South Africa was a public relations disaster' (*Financial Times*, 2001).

GSK's subsequent corporate social responsibility report highlighted 'increased shipments of Combivir to the developing world from 2.2 million tablets in 2001 to nearly 6 million tablets in 2002' (GSK, 2003, p3).[3] This increase approximately equates to an additional 2 million daily doses, which means that a further 5500 people per annum, approximately, have access to 'affordable' Combivir. This confirms that access to medication increased. While this increase is significant, in view of the fact that 29.4 million people were thought to be suffering from AIDS in sub-Saharan Africa alone, this increase in access is clearly sufficient to make only a small difference to the overall problem of AIDS. Nevertheless, as mentioned, the capital market intervention appears to have contributed to 5500 more people in developing countries having greater access to antiretroviral medication in 2002 – with further increases expected in subsequent years. The previous annual cost of a course of Combivir in Africa was around US$20,000. Consequently, a proxy for the value of the increase in access can be calculated and is in the order of US$110 million. Since cost price is about 10 per cent of the original cost, this means that the campaign benefit was some US$100 million.

Such NGO success with capital market campaigning has created something of a self-reinforcing circle as campaigners have promoted the benefits of capital market campaigns to each other. In the US, for example, Friends of the Earth produced *Confronting Companies Using Shareholder Power: A Hand-book for Socially Orientated Shareholder Activism* (see Chan-Fishel, 1999). In the UK, The Corner House produced *The Campaigners' Guide to the Financial Markets: Effective Lobbying of Companies and Financial Institutions* (see Hildyard and Mansley, 2001). Similarly, in The Netherlands, SOMO (the Centre for Research on Multinational Corporations) produced a wide-ranging review, *Critical Issues in the Financial Sector* (see Vander Stichele, 2004), focusing on the sector's impact upon sustainable development and its contribution to environmental destruction, and is intended as a reference for NGOs working on these issues.

Civil society views on the role of financial institutions have also begun to coalesce globally, most notably in the *Collevecchio Declaration*, named after the Italian town where it was written. This declaration is one of the most important collective contemporary statements of the changes that social and environmental campaigners would like to see, having been endorsed by more than 100 NGOs worldwide, including Greenpeace Italy; WWF national offices in Italy and the

Box 15.2 Collevecchio Declaration on Financial Institutions and Sustainability: The role and responsibility of financial institutions, June 2003

Financial institutions (FIs) such as banks and asset managers can and must play a positive role in advancing environmental and social sustainability. This declaration calls on FIs to embrace six main principles which reflect civil society's expectations of the role and responsibilities of the financial services sector in fostering sustainability.

The role and responsibility of financial institutions

The financial sector's role of facilitating and managing capital is important; and finance, like communications or technology, is not inherently at odds with sustainability. However, in the current context of globalization, financial institutions play key roles in channelling financial flows, creating financial markets and influencing international policies in ways that are too often unaccountable to citizens, and harmful to the environment, human rights and social equity.

Although the most well-known cases of resource misallocation in the financial sector have been associated with the high tech and telecom bubbles, FIs have played a role in irresponsibly channelling money to unethical companies, corrupt governments and egregious projects. In the Global South, FIs' increasing role in development finance has meant that FIs bear significant responsibility for international financial crises, and the crushing burden of developing country debt. However, most FIs do not accept responsibility for the environmental and social harm that may be created by their transactions, even though they may be eager to take credit for the economic development and benefits derived from their services. And relatively few FIs, in their role as creditors, analysts, underwriters, advisers or investors effectively use their power to deliberately channel finance into sustainable enterprises or encourage their clients to embrace sustainability.

Similarly, the vast majority of FIs do not play a proactive role in creating financial markets that value communities and the environment. As companies FIs concentrate on maximizing shareholder value, while as financiers they seek to maximize profit; this dual role means that FIs have played a key role in creating financial markets that predominantly value short-term returns. These brief time horizons provide strong incentives for companies to put short-term profits before longer-term sustainability goals, such as social stability and ecological health.

As a result, civil society is increasingly questioning FIs' accountability and responsibility, and challenging FIs' social licence to operate. As major actors in the global economy, FIs should embrace a commitment to sustainability that reflects best practice from the corporate social responsibility movement, while recognizing that voluntary measures alone are not sufficient, and that they must support regulations that will help the sector advance sustainability.

UK; Friends of the Earth national offices in Brazil, Germany, El Salvador, Australia, Canada, the Czech Republic, Lithuania and Switzerland; and the Sierra Club in the US. The declaration contains a wide-ranging analysis of the current situation (see Box 15.2) and argues that the appropriate goal of financial institutions should be 'the advancement of environmental protection and social justice rather than solely the maximization of economic growth and/or financial return', calling on financial institutions to make six commitments:

1   *commitment to sustainability:* fully integrating environmental, social and economic factors;
2   *commitment to 'do no harm':* preventing detrimental environmental and social impacts;
3   *commitment to responsibility:* paying for their full share of social and environmental risks;
4   *commitment to accountability:* enabling stakeholders to have an influential voice;
5   *commitment to transparency:* robust, regular disclosure and responsiveness to requests;
6   *commitment to sustainable markets:* actively supporting public policy which facilitates full-cost accounting.

THE FUTURE FOR CAPITAL MARKET CAMPAIGNING?

The most significant recent development in NGO capital market campaigning is the emergence of formal partnerships with institutional investors. Examples include WWF and Insight Investment working together to benchmark the UK house-building sector's performance on sustainable homes; Flora and Fauna International working with Aviva Investors, F&C, Insight Investment, Pax World and other institutional investors on the Natural Value Initiative, which seeks to benchmark the food production, processing and distribution sectors' performance on biodiversity issues; Co-operative Insurance Society (CIS) working with Forum for the Future to identify the financial benefits of sustainable investment in their *Sustainability Pays* report; and Transparency International working with F&C on bribery and corruption issues.

Perhaps the clearest instance where it is possible to form a view on the effectiveness of these partnerships is the WWF–Insight Investment example. This is because it was based on a published benchmark of corporate practices, and comparing benchmarks over time highlights what changes to corporate practices took place over the duration of the project. The second benchmark highlights a broad range of improvements by the UK house-building sector with regard to sustainable and responsible housing. While it is not possible to be certain that the benchmark motivated all such changes, there should be little doubt that the benchmark played a significant role (see Gifford, 2008, for a detailed analysis of this case study).

Such partnerships require a change in tone from adversary to partner, but continue in the vein of using the capital market as an instrumental tool for changing corporate practices. When done successfully, the NGO receives the influence, corporate access, authority, resources and financial support of the investor. In turn, the institutional investor receives improved access to policy expertise, research resources and better on-the-ground corporate performance information.

There are a number of reasons for the growth in such partnerships. One very basic reason is that there has been an exchange of specialist staff between some fund managers and NGOs, which inevitably leads to an improved understanding of their working practices and the potential for partnerships towards mutually shared aims. There has also been an increase in client interest in responsible investment, so there can be commercial benefits to fund managers from such partnerships. Most important, however, is that there is now a better understanding among a few leading fund managers that the economic development currently financed by the capital markets has become deeply unsustainable. They recognize that maximizing long-term returns to clients will require a more sophisticated understanding of corporate externalities, as well as increased collective efforts towards promoting more sustainable business practices. Such fund managers also realize that partnerships with NGOs are one part of a logical and rational response to the sustainable development problem.

The success of these early partnerships suggests that this strategy should be more widely adopted. The key will be exploring efficient ways of publishing credible, authoritative benchmarks of corporate performance on a range of sustainability issues that are periodically repeated, and on a range of material corporate responsibility issues. By highlighting leaders and laggards, such benchmarks should improve corporate practices and help to maximize the delivery of sustainable returns to shareholders over the long term.

In addition to partnerships between NGOs and investors, another interesting development is that some investment research providers – Ethical Investment Research Service (EIRIS) and Innovest, for example – have developed commercial services aimed at institutional investors that monitor NGO campaigning activity. These services highlight any alleged corporate breaches of international norms and codes of conducts by companies to their owners. Investors can find the information useful in guiding their company engagement and deepening their understanding of the quality of management – as well as in helping them to protect their own brand.

Given the growth of these partnerships, might the nature of the campaigns fundamentally shift in the future? To date, capital market campaigning has mainly targeted investors as a way of influencing corporations rather than attempting to change the structure of the capital market itself. In spite of initiatives such as the *Collevecchio Declaration*, there are very few examples of campaigns to change government policy on capital markets (notable exceptions include the New Economics Foundation and Centre for Tomorrow's Company). In view of the criticism by some NGOs of 'capitalism', this absence remains somewhat surprising. Looking ahead, we may see more attempts to generate structural reforms, including increased calls for government to reduce short-termism, an increased focus on the chain of incentives that motivate companies and investors, and more focused attempts to correct the long-term market failures arising from the capital market's promotion of unsustainable patterns of growth.

Civil society and investors may be unusual partners, but they both have a mutual interest in building capital markets that can help to deliver a more sustainable future.

NOTES

1   This chapter is updated from Waygood (2006). This book contains an analysis of a series of case studies that demonstrate the scale and nature of the historical impacts that NGOs can have had upon companies. It also provides a framework for companies and their investors to analyse, plan for and respond to various capital market campaign strategies.
2   A total of 39.9 million shares were voted in favour of the resolution, representing 10.5 per cent of votes cast, and 24.9 million shares were voted as an abstention, representing 6.5 per cent of votes cast.
3   An antiretroviral drug used in the treatment of patients with AIDS.

REFERENCES

Chan-Fishel, M. (1999) *Confronting Companies Using Shareholder Power: A Hand-book for Socially Orientated Shareholder Activism*, Friends of the Earth, Washington, DC

Davis, S., Lukomnik, J. and Pitt-Watson, D. (2006) *The Civil Economy*, Harvard Business School Press, Cambridge, MA

Financial Times (2001) Editorial, 20 April, p19

Gifford, E. J. M. (2008) *The Effectiveness of Shareholder Engagement in Improving Corporate ESG Performance*, PhD thesis, University of Sydney, Sydney, Australia

GSK (GlaxoSmithKline) (2003) *The Impact of Medicines: Corporate and Social Responsibility Report 2002*, GSK, London

Hildyard, N. and Mansley, M. (2001) *The Campaigners' Guide to the Financial Markets: Effective Lobbying of Companies and Financial Institutions*, The Corner House, London, May

Kiernan, M. (2005) 'Trustees of the world, unite!', *Financial Times*, 8 August

Knight, R. and Pretty, D. (2001) *Reputation and Value: The Case of Corporate Catastrophes*, Oxford Metrica, Oxford

Korten, D. (1995) *When Corporations Rule the World*, Earthscan, London

Mercer (2007) *PRI: Report on Progress*, PRI, Geneva

Oxfam (2001) 'Dare to lead: Public health and company wealth', briefing paper on GlaxoSmithKline, February, pp1–2

PIRC (1998) 'Environmental and corporate responsibility at Shell: The shareholder role in promoting change', November, p32

Sparkes, R. (2002) *Socially Responsible Investment: A Global Revolution*, John Wiley & Sons, Hoboken, NJ

Stigson, B. (2003) 'Future trends in global sustainability', Paper presented to the International Leadership Council Meeting, Hot Springs, 31 March

The Times (1997) 'Business ethics don't travel well', 15 May, p23

USS (Universities Superannuation Scheme) (2003) *Quarter 1 Report*, USS, London

Vander Stichele, M. (2004) *Critical Issues in the Financial Sector*, SOMO Financial Sector Report, Amsterdam, March

Waygood, S. (2006) *Capital Market Campaigning: The Impact of NGOs on Companies, Shareholder Value and Reputational Risk*, Risk Books, London

Willetts, P. (1997) 'Political globalisation and the impact of NGOs upon transnational companies', in J. Mitchell (ed) *Companies in a World of Conflict*, Royal Institute of International Affairs, Earthscan, London

Zadek, S. (1998) *The Civil Corporation*, Earthscan, London

16

Fiduciary Duty

Stephen Viederman

Since the beginning of the Industrial Revolution at the end of the 18th century, human impact upon the environment has increased exponentially. Scientists observe that since then 'Earth has endured changes sufficient to leave a global stratigraphic signature distinct from that of the Holocene or of previous Pleistocene interglacial phases, encompassing novel biotic, sedimentary and geochemical change' (*GSA Today*, 2008). *Anthropocene* is the word they created to delineate this new epoch.

It has not been until the last few decades that economics and finance began to recognize the relationship between the physical and social world, on the one hand, and the economic world, on the other. What had been identified as *externalities* by the economists, and *intangibles* and *extra-financial factors* by investors, have recently begun to be seen as material and, as a result, are becoming more integrated within financial decision-making. Mainstream mega-firms, such as Goldman Sachs, Deutsche Bank, State Street Global, Société Générale and others have recently started using social and environmental factors in their financial analysis in *some* of their specialized investment offerings. They see a market and they are offering products. A few even speak of the climate imperative as a driving force financially and politically (John Larkin, Deutsche Bank, pers comm, 24 April 2008). But the process has not yet become the norm.

This chapter offers a redefinition of fiduciary duty for the *Anthropocene*, the era of climate change, and discusses the role of sustainable investing in meeting the challenge.

FIDUCIARY DUTY

Pension funds, foundations, endowments and religious institutions, among others, are, by definition, long-term investors. To meet their fiduciary obligations, they have a legal responsibility to exercise reasonable care, skill, caution and loyalty to the purposes of the trust. For public pension funds in the US, this is interpreted as maximizing financial returns on investment for their beneficiaries. For foundations and endowments, the same standards apply with greater flexibility, but are also usually framed in terms of maximization of profit.

There is, however, legal opinion that these institutions are not constrained with regard to the use of environmental, social and governance (ESG) factors. 'In our view', the 2005 report by leading international law firm Freshfields Bruckhaus Deringer, sponsored by the United Nations Environment Programme's Finance Initiative (UNEP FI), states: 'decision-makers are required to have regard (at some level) to ESG considerations in every decision they make'. In 1997, William McKeown, a lawyer at a leading New York firm, concluded: 'In order to fulfil their responsibility to see that the corporation [foundations and non-profit organizations] meets it charitable purposes, they may have a duty to consider whether their investment decisions will further those charitable purposes, or at least not run counter to them.' But in the absence of case law, and in the presence of inertia, maximization of financial return remains the goal (UNEP FI, 2005; see also Solomon and Coe, 1997, and McKeowen, 1997).

The largest global investors have not rushed to embrace these approaches, at least not in the US. Finance committees have generally been very slow in their approach to investing in new funds that have social *and* financial goals. Data on performance has been difficult to compare and benchmarks are not readily available because there is no standard approach to sustainable investing. This wariness contrasts with committee embrace of newly developed purely financial investments that 'promise' high rates of return in the short term. In the testosterone-driven world of institutional investing, maximizing returns is still the gold standard (Hotz, 2008), and is presumed to be the standard necessary to meet obligations of fiduciary duty.

Research has shown that US financial institution executives 'are willing to sacrifice economic value in order to meet a short-run earnings target. The preference for smooth earnings is so strong that 78 per cent of the surveyed executives would give up economic value for smooth earnings.' In addition, the authors found 'that 55 per cent of managers would avoid initiating a very positive net project value if it meant falling short of the current quarter's consensus earnings' (Graham et al, 2004).

ExxonMobil represents a paradigmatic case of the conflict between short-term and long-term profit generation. The world's largest corporation by market capitalization is an old-fashioned oil and gas company that identifies itself now as 'taking on the world's toughest energy problems'. In November 2007, Rex Tillerson, chairman and chief executive officer (CEO), publicly stated for the first time: 'it is increasingly clear that climate change poses risks to society and ecosystems that are serious enough to warrant action – by individuals, by businesses and by governments' (Tillerson, 2007). ExxonMobil has, however, refused to respond to a shareowner proxy resolution asking the company to 'adopt a policy on renewable energy research, development and sourcing'.[1] Given the long lead time to develop alternatives and renewables, and the approach of 'peak oil', renewable energy investment would contribute to their profitability in the next decades. Similarly, with their greenhouse gas (GHG) emissions increasing, they have refused the request of shareowners to set goals for reducing their GHG emissions. Although highly profitable now, are ExxonMobil's profits going to be sustainable, and is ExxonMobil in its pursuit of profit now limiting options for future generations?

Corporations also assume a fiduciary duty to their owners, although it is not necessarily solely to maximize shareowner wealth. Rather, they are required only to carry out the 'lawful directives of shareholders'. Thus, managers can engage in activities that reduce shareholder wealth as long as they 'do not engage in fraud or self-dealing and make rational, informed decisions'. But they, too, despite case law that supports this conclusion, are driven by the market to achieve the highest profit (Mackey et al, 2007).

THE CLIMATE CHALLENGE TO INVESTING AS USUAL

At this time, the beginning of the third century of the *Anthropocene*, climate change is the greatest human-induced challenge we face. The need to mitigate and adapt to the effects of climate change is likely to be the defining issue of the 21st century and must be approached urgently and seriously (IPCC, 2007; Pielke et al, 2008; Stern, 2008a, 2008b).

Although often framed as an *environmental* problem, climate change is much more. It is a *social*, *ethical* and *moral* problem. It is also truly a global problem from which no one can escape.

The question of what is a maximum rate of return comes into question, however, when we consider the risks of climate for society, with both short- and long-term ramifications. Is maximization of profit sufficient if the so-called *extra-financial* returns accelerate the consequences of climate change? Is a company operating in the best interests of its long-term shareowners if it fails to take actions now that will give greater assurance of high returns later, just so they can achieve maximum short-term financial returns?

What good is a maximum rate of return on investment if it fouls the air, poisons the water, degrades the land, changes the climate, and contributes to greater inequalities among people? Is it sufficient for some of us to reap financial return and to consume the products and services resulting from these investments, while all of us, and our children and grandchildren, face the prospect of increased morbidity and mortality, and, except for a few, a decreased quality of life? Societies including economic systems will be disrupted and that is not good for the companies themselves.

In effect, all of the world's population is a *universal owner* of the climate problem. It is the object of the world's corporate productive capacity and the externalities of that production, while only a very few of us reap the financial benefit. Investment is not only about how much you expect to earn. Investment is also about risk and about how much you can afford to lose. How much can *universal owners* afford to lose in the face of climate risk?

A REDEFINITION OF FIDUCIARY DUTY

What is, ultimately, needed is a new and more meaningful definition of fiduciary duty for the *Anthropocene*, a definition that accepts that the financial world and the social and environmental worlds are one and the same. There is no triple bottom line. There can only be a single bottom line that offers positive social and financial returns against which all business decisions must be measured. Fiduciary duty must transcend the solely financial responsibility of the company or the institutional investor to maximize profit. Fiduciaries must also consider the social and environmental consequences for the investors, the beneficiaries and society at large. We are all *universal owners*, as shareowners and stakeholders.

This redefinition must give weight to how ESG factors, more broadly understood than at present, affect both risks and opportunities, now and in the future. Let's look at some of the key words that currently define fiduciary duty.

'Profit', originally meaning to 'advance', and now defined in terms of 'benefit', must go beyond financial benefit. Maximizing financial profit, advancing it to its upper limits, provides goods, services and employment, but also diminishes social benefit in the real world. Money is necessary but not sufficient. As Robert Monks, investor and corporate governance activist, observes: 'The primary thing that workers need for their retirement [is] money, but don't workers also need a safe, clean, decent world in which to spend it. These ends are not economically exclusive' (Monks, 2000). Even the wealthiest among us cannot escape the assaults of climate change. As food riots around the world in April 2008 demonstrate, the poor can take no more as climate changes add further burdens to their lives.

'Prudent' in the 14th century meant to be far-seeing. Today the dictionary defines it as being circumspect, wise and exercising good judgement. The prudent financial person now looks through the rear-view mirror to conform to what has been done, rather than looking through the windscreen to see what must be done.

As financial transactions and investment vehicles become more specialized and complex, fiduciary duty must expand to encompass our greater knowledge and understanding of the long-term social and environmental costs, as well as benefits associated with investment decisions. Risks as well as opportunities must be assessed more prudently in the context of climate change. This includes the science and economics of climate risk, and also the political processes, nationally and globally, that will affect investment decisions. Investment committees may argue that they do not know how to do this. They use consultants to increase their comfort with exotic financial instruments; so, too, can they bring in climate and policy specialists. Lack of knowledge is not a reasonable response for inaction by fiduciaries.

Fiduciaries will need to seek out those investment managers and consultants who are already implementing investment programmes that focus on the *integration* of ESG factors with financial decision-making. This is not portfolio screening. They should explore different investment strategies that channel funds into new areas that are focused on climate solutions that will lead to long-term growth and sustainability, and will carry less risk and liability.

Fiduciaries will need to review their entire portfolios, not only individual assets or asset classes. Isolated investment decisions affect total portfolios that, in turn, have societal effects. For the larger fiduciaries – the *universal owners* – the financial and ESG bottom line is inevitably portfolio wide. Initially, a large long-term investor may benefit from a company in their portfolio externalizing costs but ultimately there will be a reduction in returns, overall, as the externalities negatively affect returns in other companies and assets. Raj Thamotheran and Helen Wildsmith (2007) suggest that because they are *universal owners*, collective action by large pension funds could improve long-term market returns (see also Hawley and Williams, 2000).

Fiduciaries must see themselves as *shareowners*, not simply as *shareholders*, and assume the responsibilities that go along with ownership. Owners are stewards of the capital that has been entrusted to them and cannot be passive. Being a responsible shareowner implies corporate engagement, minimally through the development of proxy voting guidelines and procedures for ESG factors, and voting of proxies. In addition, fiduciaries must demand greater accountability and transparency from the companies in their portfolios on climate factors, and policies and programmes to mitigate and adapt to climate change. These will reduce financial risk and social risk.

Fiduciaries are rightfully sensitive to the legal implications of their decisions. They should ask their lawyers *how* to accommodate these new responsibilities and obligations, rather than ask them *if* they can. There is now a significant body of research that an analytical approach to financial decision-making that integrates the risks and opportunities identified by social, environmental, political and cultural issues can compete with traditional investing styles, and produce social and environmental benefits as well (UNEP FI and Mercer, 2007).

Fiduciaries should also be aware of, and involved with, the formulation and execution of public policies that govern financial firms, transactions and markets, and climate risk (Viederman, 2004a; see also Viederman, 2008a, b).

The corporation as the most powerful economic institution in the world will determine the social and environmental state of the world as much as, if not more than, governments and international organizations. As the effects of climate change become more visible, it is incumbent upon institutional investors and corporations to exercise these fiduciary duties now. With climate change, as with most things, inaction is the worst action.

SUSTAINABLE INVESTING AND A REDEFINED FIDUCIARY DUTY

Sustainable and *sustainability*, as the terms are now generally used, cover a wide range of meanings.[2] The environment is the primary and sometimes exclusive focus of most sustainability discussions. 'Sustainability' came into common use during the 1980s in response to growing environmental concerns. The 'environment' is also conceptually clearer than most social areas, and data are more readily available and can be shown more convincingly to correlate with financial performance. 'Social' incorporates economic and financial factors, as well as political and cultural issues. 'Governance' is a measure of a company's ability to integrate environment and sustainability within its management structure, decision-making and action – to be prudent and far-seeing.

To be truly sustainable, equity and justice must be addressed in different ways than they are now (Viederman, 1995).

The term 'extra-financial' underlines the historical separation of finance from the real world – 'extra' referring to 'beyond what is normal'. Arguing that these factors are necessary for long-term financial returns, however, makes them 'financial' factors despite the fact that they have been disregarded for centuries. The difference now is the realization of their scale and impact.

'Full integration of ESG factors' raises significant questions concerning the limits of our understanding of what these factors are, how they interact and how they can be measured. 'Not everything that counts can be counted', Albert Einstein observed in his Nobel acceptance speech, 'and not everything that can be counted counts'. In addition, it raises issues relating to the limits of so-called corporate social responsibility, an ill-defined term that is often used as a substitute for ESG.

Is the desired outcome the achievement of 'long-term shareholder value', and/or meeting the needs of present and future generations? How are these outcomes related to each other and to financial decision-making? What are the timeframes? Clearly implied is the desire to change corporate behaviour since the impetus for sustainable investing reflects the financial systems' inability, as currently structured, to incorporate consideration of the long term and future generations. *Sustainable investing* has still to make clear how it is part of the process of sustaining society rather than just investing.

In order to be seen as more than a new name for an old process, sustainable investing will need to address more seriously than it has the application of 'environment' and 'sustainability', in particular. A product, such as tobacco, could be excluded because of its impact upon human health and the attendant social costs. But what about products relating to family planning and abortifacients that are decried by some and strongly approved by others who might otherwise agree on many other corporate activities? What about defence contractors? Critics have often chided social investors for not being serious by using exclusionary defence screens. They argued that people might not like wars, but defence is, nonetheless, necessary. Can an environmentally sensitive investment fund be considered sustainable if it does not assess other aspects of a company's performance, such as diversity in the workplace, a living wage and its impact upon the community?

Corporate social responsibility and *corporate citizenship* are buzzwords that have created a whole new industry. What are the limits on corporations that constrain the practice of sustainability? The answers to this question are essential in understanding what sustainable investing can legitimately expect from companies, and what issues are systemic and beyond their grasp and interventions. The latter will require action in other arenas – both political and conceptual.

James Gustav Speth, now dean of Yale's School of Forestry, has had a long and varied career at the intersection of the environment and policy. In a new book, he concludes:

> *After much searching and considerable reluctance ... that most environmental deterioration is a result of systemic failures of the capitalism we have today and that long-term solutions must seek transformative change in the key features of contemporary capitalism.*[3] (Speth, 2008)

He joins many others who have called for transformation of capitalism, or a totally new *ism*, calls little heeded by politicians, economists and businesses.

Systemic obstacles that corporations face under free market capitalism include:

- A commitment to full-cost accounting that must be a factor in sustainable investing. Externalization of environmental and social costs is still the norm.
- Ability to avoid the focus on returns in the short term that is seen even within the traditional social investment world. Today's returns, the next quarter's, but not the next quarter century's, are the benchmark. In practice, the future is discounted at a rate close to zero.
- A commitment to slow or no growth. Like a shark that must keep swimming to stay alive, so too must a company keep growing to survive. *Fortune Magazine* applauded Nike a number of years ago for creating a want for something no one knew they needed. Economic growth, at least in advanced economies, runs contrary to sustainability.

Solutions to the systemic issues requiring new paradigms of the economy and of finance are a long-term activity. The sustainable investing community has a role to play in the discussion and description of a transformed capitalism or a new *ism*. But this must also engage the intellectuals – economists and others – who are the keepers of the capitalism kingdom, and representatives of the broader population to ensure that their voices are heard in the search for something that works for all concerned. This process must begin now with a long-term commitment.

Companies are capable of more effectively addressing a number of issues that are possible within the limits of the capitalist free market economic system:

- They can make greater commitments to communities by listening better to the people most affected and acting on what they hear.
- They can make greater commitment to the environment, to human rights, to equal opportunity, to providing a living wage with pension and health benefits to their workers, and to their global supply chains with particular attention to issues such as child labour, wages and overtime.

Shareowners working together have demonstrated that they can play a significant role in encouraging corporations to be more responsive to environmental and social concerns. The obligation to exercise ownership rights must be an integral part of sustainable investing.

On a more practical level, sustainable investing also requires greater data depth, breadth and quality than are now available. This need not be a constraint to begin with, but should be a part of a near-future agenda. Currently, much of the data used is retrospective and historical.

Conceptualizations of criteria in general use are often spotty. For example:

- Corporate citizenship and corporate philanthropy are both oxymorons but are often used as stand-ins for 'community'.[4]
- Labour practice indicators are virtually non-existent, especially when the supply chain is long, reaching down to smaller producers in less developed countries.
- Social and environmental reporting not audited by outsiders has to be approached with caution. Corporate responsibility officers are constrained by lawyers from telling the whole truth for fear of litigation. The important work of the Carbon Disclosure Project (CDP) provides baselines for shareowners and governments to request setting limits on GHGs, but does not provide suasion for companies, such as ExxonMobil, to set goals. Owners must do that.

Leaders in sustainable investing will need to analyse the barriers to adopting this investment process and seek answers to the questions raised. This must be done within national contexts. As a Mercer study recently showed, there is considerable difference in the way in which institutions in different countries respond to the idea of sustainable investing. The key decision-makers and gatekeepers in institutions will need to be identified and data gathered to create understanding of the process and desired outcomes. The cultures of finance committees immersed in the ways of financial investing must be considered and changed. Knowledgeable and skilled consultants able to guide institutions in their deliberations and direct them into sustainable investment vehicles are now in short supply. Change will not come about by itself. The sustainable investing community will have to give as much attention to the process of institutionalizing sustainable investing as to the substantive issues outlined above (Viederman, 2004b).

In order to become mainstream, sustainable investing, given its long-term horizon and the short timeframe of the market, will need to demonstrate both financial and social returns. We know that ESG factors are material and useful indicators of good financial performance. But the bottom line, an indicator of successful sustainable investing, will be that it can also facilitate, over time, movement towards a new economy that leaves options open for our children and grandchildren to live in a humane world. This should not be done apologetically. Sustainable investing is no more or no less a science and an art than mainstream investing despite the latter's claims to science. Sustainable investing's claim is that it will help to bridge the chasm between the economic and human condition.

Sustainable investing must play an important role in helping societies and individuals to mitigate and adapt to climate change, reversing the consequences of conventional investing. Advancing social, environmental *and* financial benefits is the new fiduciary duty.

NOTES

1   I filed this resolution in my personal capacity as the owner of a small number of shares. ExxonMobil had recommended that shareowners vote against the resolution on the grounds that it was 'unwarrented'. At ExxonMobil annual meeting on 28 May 2008 the resolution received 27 per cent of the vote, 20 per cent more than in 2007. In many companies that would be sufficient to generate discussion between the filer and the board, but not at ExxonMobil.

2   I do not include *sustainable development* because it is a particularly troubling concept. The adjective describes a process that has been anything but sustainable (John Ehrenfeld, pers comm, May 2007).

3   Speth has been chair of the US Council of Environmental Advisers, founder and president of the World Resources Institute and administrator of the United Nations Development Programme (UNDP).

4   See Weeden (1998). A US Community Investing Index offered by Neuberger Berman/Lehman Bros in mid 2008, initiated by the Heron Foundation and constructed by Innovest Strategic Value Advisers, represents a breakthrough on community criteria.

REFERENCES

Graham, J. R., Harvey, C. R. and Rajgopal, S. (2004) *The Economic Implications of Corporate Financial Reporting*, NBER Working Paper 10550, June

GSA Today (2008) *GSA Today*, vol 18, no 2, February, pp4–8

Hawley, J. and Williams, A. (2000) *The Rise of Fiduciary Capitalism: How Institutional Investors Can Make Corporate America More Democratic*, University of Pennsylvania Press, PA

Hotz, R. L. (2008) 'Science journal: Testosterone may fuel stock-market success, or make traders tipsy', *Wall Street Journal*, 18 April, pB1

IPCC (Intergovernmental Panel on Climate Change) (2007) *Climate Change 2007: Synthesis Report*, Contribution of Working Groups I, II and III to the Fourth Assessment Report of the Intergovernmental Panel on Climate Change (Core writing team: Pachauri, R. K. and Reisinger, A., eds), IPCC, Geneva, Switzerland

Mackey, A., Mackey, T. B. and Barney, J. B. (2007) 'Corporate social responsibility', *Management Review*, vol 32, no 3, pp817–835, note 1

McKeowen, W. (1997) 'Being true to your mission: Social investments for endowments', *Journal of Investing*, winter, pp71–78

Monks, R. (2000) *The Right Response to Seattle's Warning*, The Corporate Library, 10 April, www.ragm.com/speeches/speeches_00.html, accessed May 2008

Pielke, R. Jr, Wigley, T. and Green, C. (2008) 'Dangerous assumptions', *Nature*, vol 452, 3 April, pp531–532

Solomon, L. D. and Coe, K. C. (1997) 'Social investments by nonprofit corporations and charitable trusts: A legal and business primer for foundation managers and other nonprofit fiduciaries', University of Missouri-Kansas City, *Law Review*, winter, vol 66, no 2, pp213–250

Speth, J. G. (2008) *Bridge at the Edge of the World: Capitalism, the Environment, and the Crossing from Crisis to Sustainability*, Yale University Press, Yale, as excerpted in *Yale Alumni Magazine* (2008) March/April, pp28–29

Stern, N. (2008a) *Stern Review: The Economics of Climate Change*, Cambridge University Press, Cambridge

Stern, N. (2008b) *Key Elements of a Global Deal on Climate Change*, London School of Economics and Political Science, London, UK, 30 April

Thamotheran, R. and Wildsmith, H. (2007) 'Increasing long-term market returns: Realizing the potential of collective pension fund action', *Corporate Governance: An International Review*, vol 15, no 3, May

Tillerson, R. (2007) Speech to the World Energy Assembly, Rome, Italy, 12 November

UNEP FI (United Nations Environment Programme's Finance Initiative) (2005) *A Legal Framework for the Integration of Environmental, Social and Governance Issues into Institutional Investment*, UNEP FI, Paris, October

UNEP FI and Mercer (2007) *Demystifying Response Investment Performance: A Review of Key Academic and Broker Research on ESG Factors*, UNEP FI, Paris

Viederman, S. (1995) 'Knowledge for sustainable development: What do we need to know?', in T. Trzyna (ed) *A Sustainable World: Defining and Measuring Sustainable Development*, California Institute of Public Affairs and Earthscan for IUCN, Sacramento and London

Viederman, S. (2004a) 'New directions in fiduciary responsibility', *Journal of Practical Estate Planning*, January, pp31–34

Viederman, S. (2004b) 'Addressing obstacles to social investing', *Journal of Practical Estate Planning*, April–May, pp53–56

Viederman, S. (2008a) 'Get off your assets for climate', *Green Giving*, no 2, May, CCPAN (Climate Change Philanthropy Action Network)

Viederman, S. (2008b) 'How grant makers can curb global warming', *Chronicle of Philanthropy*, 7 February

Weeden, C. (1998) *Corporate Social Investing: A Breakthrough Strategy For Giving and Getting Corporate Contributions*, Berret-Kohler, San Francisco, CA

17

The Global Agenda

Tessa Tennant

In whatever shape or form, sustainable and responsible investing (SRI) is emerging as an international phenomenon. This was not the case two decades ago in 1989, when the *Financial Times* first recognized in a leader column that 'like it or not, the days when financial decisions can be taken in a total moral vacuum are numbered'.

The real issue is how investors will respond to the challenges ahead over the next 20 years. What we face is the prospect of hundreds of millions more people entering the world of consumerism, expecting the superficially peaceful and prosperous-looking way of life that the majority take for granted in the West. On top of this social revolution, add the Earth-shatteringly destructive impacts of climate change and resource constraints, alongside religious and racial intolerance and the widening wealth gap and you have a recipe for altered nations and norms.

One possible future for SRI would simply be more of the same. SRI is a form of consumerism, which resonates with global common values that anywhere from 5 to 20 per cent of every nation cares about. Some people talk about sustainable investing being 'mainstreamed' to the extent that it disappears as an asset class. If this happened, it would be the culmination of the quietest revolution in market behaviour ever witnessed. Sadly, I doubt this will occur. Until large investment houses can fully prove that sustainability is their core and continuing mantra, not just a sound bite from a CEO, there will always be scope for social entrepreneurs to stay ahead in terms of financial innovation. Sustainable investing will continue its healthy tension between insiders and outsiders. New funds will be launched, especially in emerging markets. Contrary to many predictions that SRI funds would not take off in Asian markets, the number keeps growing, and 2007 was notable for new funds in South Korea and for Shari'ah funds in several countries. With more practitioners in all corners of the world, there is a greater chance that the sustainable investment industry develops coherence as a global force, especially in multilateral gatherings such as the World Trade Organization (WTO) and the United Nations Framework Convention on Climate Change (UNFCCC), where its voice needs to be heard.

Is this sufficient for SRI to live up to its promise? If the promise is to be the investment industry's contribution to making human activity sustainable on this one precious planet, then the answer is definitely no. Another way to understand the challenge is to realize that under current systems of production and consumption, we need at least three, possibly five, planets' worth of resources to ensure that everyone in the world can live as we do in Organisation for Economic Co-operation and Development (OECD) countries. As the great Professor Rustum Roy says: 'If the value of enoughness is not adopted, then we don't have a prayer.'

We have only one planet and the mission of SRI must surely be to drive investment towards the technology, infrastructure, cultural and corporate shifts required to achieve One Planet Living. Idealistic this may sound; but it is actually less so than 20 years ago. In fact, One Planet Investing is the modern capital market's only plausible offering as a survival strategy.

Therefore my wish list over these next five to ten years is as follows:

1   For pension funds, the largest and fastest-growing pool of capital in most markets of the world, to develop benchmarks, performance metrics and investment strategies aligned with the requirements of One Planet Investing. Is it not ridiculous that these large pools of capital have such weak and meagre guidance systems about what is happening in the real world? Reading Alan Greenspan's autobiography, I was struck by the manner of his early meteoric rise. He explains that he made his name by examining industrial output figures in ways never done before. So, where are the new analysts who lead us not into a sub-prime mortgage crisis but, instead, provide ever-improving ecological data streams and make sense of them for prudent investors and corporate decision-makers?

2   For governments to put in place the fiscal incentives and long-term policy goals that enable sustainable consumption and responsible investment. At the moment, governments seem to reward those hell-bent on raping the Earth, rather than protecting it. If a Joe Average citizen was able to show that all his investments were focused on environmental and social sustainability, then shouldn't he or she have a credit when filing tax returns? During the early 1990s, The Netherlands took a step in this direction. All countries need to follow suit. Even more critically, governments need to agree on, for example, emission reduction targets for a sustained period so that markets can move forward with confidence.

3   For the international financial institutions to scale up sustainable investment strategies for the built environment, including energy, housing, transport and water. Look to the advocacy of most leaders now – almost all have betted on technological innovation to get us out of the climate and wider sustainability fix. But it is not just about technology: new forms of social and environmental infrastructure are essential to make these technologies effective and accessible. Here is a huge investment opportunity, one that offers the potential of low-risk, long-term, bond-style investments for the world's pension funds.

4   For emerging market investors to take a leadership position. Great strides have been made in the past ten years in the dialogue between investors in Western 'developed' economies and the companies they own, in both domestic and emerging economies. You could call this d2d or d2e. The challenge for this next decade is for investors in the emerging world to develop a meaningful sustainability dialogue with their owned companies. You could call this e2e. As an example, the Bank of China could have a far more constructive influence on the activities in the Sudan via its investment in PetroChina than any amount of campaigning by Western investors. With trade flows between emerging economies growing exponentially, the e2e phenomenon must gain an ecological and humanitarian perspective too.

5   For the United Nations family to be at the forefront of SRI strategies, making it congruent with its overall mission. The UN has done much over the years to promote SRI. But it remains odd that the fund managers and trustees of these multilateral pension funds have been so resistant to sustainable investment. Nothing undermines their stated missions more. There is no excuse for inaction: the arguments about the ethics of one nation being different to another do not hold when such a wide range of UN resolutions has been universally adopted. There is now the precedent of Sweden's state pension funds adopting UN norms on environmental and labour issues as their guiding principles.

6   For the world's stock exchanges to make corporate disclosure on essential environmental and social metrics required by law. Companies have also made great strides in environmental, social and governance (ESG) disclosure. However, there is still a great range in the quality of disclosure and many companies are still free-riders. It is now reasonable to introduce regulations for improved disclosure in company accounts and in stock exchange listing requirements. Will we see company listings of ESG performance published on a regular basis in the next five years?

7   From this disclosure, for the investment consultants to develop fairer benchmarks, not just specialist indices, which reflect the sustainability alpha/beta of portfolios. The Financial Times Stock Exchange (FTSE), Sustainable Asset Management (SAM) and, more recently, the International Finance Corporation-sponsored work of KLD, Credit Rating and Information

Services of India Ltd (CRISIL) and Trucost are all contributing to the development of indices and ESG data availability. 'Real time' ESG data-feeds are still a long way off; but the coverage of markets will continue to improve in a lurching way. A new area to develop is the ESG analysis of commodity pricing where substantial anomalies still exist. Such analysis is likely to be financially lucrative, as well as improve our tools for planetary management.

Are these seven goals so unrealistic? I do not think so. Indeed, the SRI community has always been adept at reaching out, being bold about issues – think of South Africa during the 1970s and the emerging campaign on the Sudan and Darfur. It is also good at collaborating and creating new partnerships – think of the Valdez Principles, which led to the creation of the CERES, and to the inspirational work today of the International Interfaith Investment Group (3iG). SRI is also imaginative and smart – think of the South African and Brazilian stock exchange's initiatives on corporate accountability and Domini's coup in the US in triggering the Securities and Exchange Commission to rule in favour of disclosure on shareholder voting.

If you take these traits – reaching out, being bold, collaborating, being imaginative and being smart – there's nothing to stop a network of people getting things done. Add to this the SRI industry's increasing strength in all corners of the world and there's a real chance for change.

18

Conclusion: Sustainable Investing – The Art of Long-Term Performance

Nick Robins and Cary Krosinsky

UNCONVENTIONAL SUCCESS

During the dark days of the 20th century's Great Depression, John Maynard Keynes wrote from experience as a City trader, insurance executive and policy-maker about the odds stacked against the long-term investor. 'It is in the essence of his behaviour that he should be eccentric, unconventional and rash in the eyes of average opinion', Keynes wrote, adding that 'if he is successful, that will only confirm the general belief in his rashness; and if in the short run he is unsuc-cessful, which is very likely, he will not receive much mercy. Worldly wisdom teaches that it is better for reputation to fail conventionally than to succeed unconventionally' (Keynes, 1978).

This book has charted the 'unconventional success' of sustainable investing – a phenomenon that was unheard of in Keynes's day, but is certainly close in spirit to his pursuit of long-term value creation. Sustainable investing has certainly proved itself in terms of adding alpha. Cary Krosinsky (see Chapter 2) has shown how public equity funds that actively include environmental, social and governance (ESG) factors in investment strategy tend to outperform both their ethical and mainstream peers. From the field of property investing, Gary Pivo and Paul McNamara (see Chapter 10) reported a wealth of 'no-cost' and 'value-added' strategies that reduce social and environmental impacts, while also increasing net incomes or reducing risk premiums. From the investment analyst's perspective, Valery Lucas-Leclin and Sarbjit Nahal (see Chapter 4) demonstrated persuasively that companies with enhanced ESG performance offer materially reduced risk for investors in terms of beta, and that there is a growing convergence between sustainability and the world's best-managed companies.

Just as profoundly, sustainability factors have prompted the creation of entirely new investment sectors and financial markets, not least in the arena of climate change. Abyd Karmali (see Chapter 5) charted how climate change has become a mega-trend for investors, outlining the growth potential offered by the world's growing carbon markets. Looking ahead to 2020, New Energy Finance (NEF) forecast that the US carbon trading market could be worth US$1 trillion if federal and state policy-makers continue on their current path of introducing 'cap-and-trade' legislation (NEF, 2008). Carbon markets are perhaps best seen as transfer mechanisms that translate high carbon exposure for one participant into low-carbon opportunities for another. On the upside, Emma Hunt and Rachel Whittaker (see Chapter 7) highlighted the multidimensional role that clean energy investments will play in a long-term investor's overall investment strategy. As Ray Cheung (see Chapter 13) noted, emerging economies such as China are also beneficiaries of this powerful trend.

On the downside, tightening environmental constraints threaten existing business models, most notably in the power sector, as Matthias Kopp and Björn Tore Urdal illustrated in the case of the German utility RWE (see Chapter 6). With the external costs of carbon in some cases exceeding 100 per cent of annual earnings before interest, tax, depreciation and amortization (EBITDA), the road to a decarbonized power sector is set to be bumpy, with real risks of assets being stranded along the way (e.g. see Henderson Global Investors, 2005). While carbon risks and opportunities are primarily driven by regulatory intervention, in the case of water, as Katherine Miles Hill and Sean Gilbert explained (see Chapter 8), it is the raw facts of burgeoning demand and shrinking supply that is forcing investors to think again. Water is also the vector through which many of the physical impacts of climate change are expressed, notably in terms of increasing incidence of both drought and floods, along with sea-level rise.

Yet, if environmental markets have dominated the headlines over the past five years, this relates to only one pillar of sustainable development. Rod Schwartz (see Chapter 12) presented the new dynamic between the rising class of social entrepreneurs and the array of social investment techniques being deployed to fund their growth. In the social arena, microfinance has emerged as the equivalent of the clean tech boom, with Ivo Knoepfel and Gordon Hagart (see Chapter 9) showing how a new class of fixed-income instruments has been created in the process.

After two decades of both experimentation and delivery, the investment chain has started to shift towards a more sustainable model. Asset owners are reconsidering how they deploy capital and exercise the duties of ownership, investment consultants are incorporating ESG factors in the advice they provide, asset managers are introducing new funds and techniques, while investment banks are broadening their service to integrate the sustainable and responsible investing (SRI) dimension within their analysis. Furthermore, as Steve Waygood identified (see Chapter 15), the growth of new partnerships between investors and civil society hold out the potential for rebuilding public trust in financial markets.

THE DISTANCE STILL TO BE TRAVELLED

These achievements are certainly impressive. But set against the size of the world's capital markets and the scale of the sustainability transformation that is required, they serve to demonstrate the distance that has still to be travelled. As Ivo Knoepfel and Gordon Hagart (see Chapter 9) underline, it is important not to overstate the materiality of sustainability under prevailing investment frameworks. Most environmental costs have yet to be internalized within asset values. For example, in the race between energy security and climate change, the absolute flows of investment suggest that the low-carbon economy is still trailing behind the rapid re-carbonization of the global economy expressed via the unprecedented levels of capital investment currently under way in coal-fired power generation and unconventional oil such as tar sands.

Microfinance and social investments may be flourishing; but governments have yet to put in place the 'long, loud and legal' signals in the social arena that could mobilize capital for poverty elimination in ways equivalent to the carbon markets. As we have seen, the convergence of sustainability and financial analysis has only just started, with 'a long road ahead' to bring the two disciplines fully into line. And though there may be promising signs involving clean tech and even SRI in China, the overriding message from Dan Siddy's chapter on India is the continuing indifference of most domestic and international investors (see Chapter 14).

Sadly, the area where least progress has been made is in the extension of time horizons, although, as Ritu Kumar suggested (see Chapter 11), the growth of private equity offers the possibility of a longer-term approach than that which prevails on most stock markets. More philosophically, the relationship between socially responsible and sustainable investing continues to be both boon and bane. Many of the ethical and socially responsible investing pioneers prefigured today's agenda of integration and activism. But equally, much of the current innovation comes from new entrants, eager to demonstrate that sustainable investing stands on its own merits and, indeed, is wholly distinct from earlier waves of values-based investing. And as Stephen Viederman (see Chapter 16) observed in his review of fiduciary duty, there is still a way to go to show that sustainable investing is 'more than a new name for an old process'.

TRANSFORMING GLOBAL INVESTMENT

The next five years are likely to be among the most tumultuous to date for sustainable investment. The negotiation of a global deal on climate change in Copenhagen in late 2009 is set to provide a powerful focus for wider strategic issues of capital mobilization, market reform, performance standards, new alliances and social purpose. Importantly, the mood is one of optimism that, given the right frameworks and incentives, capital can be mobilized. For example, the latest *Energy Technology Perspectives* from the International Energy Agency calculates that an additional US$45 trillion will be required to halve global emissions of greenhouse gases by 2050. This, however, is not a loss in GDP, but a redirection, and will be accompanied by a net US$5 trillion in energy savings (IEA, 2008). On average, this means that over US$1.3 trillion needs to be allocated to clean energy investments, nine times greater than the record US$148 billion raised in 2007.

For sustainable investors, this is a moment of immense opportunity. But putting in place the self-reinforcing mechanisms within capital markets that supports this transformation will not come easily. As of this writing, old hands on Wall Street and the City of London suggest that the snowballing impacts of the credit crunch, soaring food and fuel prices and the resultant economic shocks will have put sustainability concerns onto the back-burner for investors. From this perspective, sustainable investing is seen merely as a cyclical bull market phenomenon, linked to the growth phase of the overall economy and driven by temporary outperformance of certain sectors or themes. Indeed, sustainable investing has been here before in the wake of the dot.com bubble on global equity markets, when the performance of many sustainability and clean tech funds was hit hard.

This analysis, however, is not just a misreading of history, but a strategic misinterpretation of the structural, secular nature of the sustainable investing phenomenon. The performance of leading SRI and clean tech funds was certainly hit temporarily in the early part of the decade. But beyond these surface perturbations, the strategic case for the integration of ESG factors was being made, resulting in a rapid surge in both fund performance and fund flows when markets began to recover.

This time around not only is the investor case for long-term sustainable investing much better understood and embedded among the world's leading institutions, but sustainable investing strategies are increasingly seen as essential to the recovery itself. For example, a group of leading analysts in the UK has advocated a 'Green New Deal' to counter economic slowdown, peak oil and climate change, financed through a new class of long-dated bonds matching the liability profile of major pension funds (Green New Deal Group, 2008). For the investment community, the task is to demonstrate that it can apply the skills of financial innovation to the challenge of sustainability with the same vigour – and more lasting success – that it dedicated to derivative instruments in the past decade.

One corollary of this is for sustainable investors to engage wholeheartedly in the creation of capital markets that are finally 'fit for purpose' for the social, economic and environmental realities of the 21st century. In the end, sustainable investing is concerned both with the behaviour of market *actors* as well as the structure and dynamics of financial *arenas*, such as the capital markets themselves. It is this dual focus that distinguishes sustainable investment and requires its practitioners to combine excellence at the micro-level in terms of fund management, with effective action at the macro-level to introduce the policy reforms that reward market participants for investing as if the long term really did matter. One immediate priority is the formalization of climate change disclosures as part of accounting standards and stock exchange listing rules. Voluntary initiatives can prove excellent testing grounds to drive innovation. But they need formal regulation to ensure comprehensiveness and comparability. If investors are to make fully informed choices on the road to a low-carbon economy, then the reporting of emissions and exposures has to become part of routine audited disclosures to the market. Equally, the voice of sustainable and responsible investors needs to be heard more loudly in wider policy-making on climate change, energy security and sustainable development. All too often the private-sector voices heard by policy-makers still represent an unsustainable status quo. Thus, at the critical 2007 Bali conference on climate change, there were few, if any, representatives of long-term sustainable investors actively involved in the negotiations, compared with the large delegations representing carbon-intensive business interests.

For sustainable investing to have credibility with others – business, govern-ments and citizens – it will need to have the highest standards of accountability. Clear cost-effective standards, independently implemented, are an essential way for the various branches of SRI to make the market breakthrough comparable to that achieved by organic food in recent years. The new practice of 'climate change investing', for one, would benefit from common benchmarks identifying which investment practices really do contribute to climate security. In the process, customer trust would be reinforced, and the often mischievous criti-cisms by opponents to sustainability would be easier to dispel. Alongside this, new indicators will be needed to track the full spectrum of fund performance. Thus, the McKinsey Global Institute suggests that the carbon productivity of the global economy has to improve by a factor of 10 in terms of tonnes of CO_2 per unit of GDP by 2050 – a shift 'comparable in magnitude to the labor productivity increases in the Industrial Revolution' (McKinsey Global Institute, 2008). The carbon productivity of investment portfolios will need to make a similar journey to ensure that value added is truly being created for investors, making the case for regular, public reporting of fund performance on carbon just as compelling as corporate reporting.

To realize the required structural changes in the world's capital markets, imaginative alliances will need to be made with emerging sustainable business groups, key policy-makers and civil society organizations. Beyond the environmental arena, encouraging signs of joint ventures between investors and civil society are coming from the health sector, notably the creation of the Access to Medicines Index, as well as the progress of the Pharma Futures collaboration. More broadly, the social pillar of sustainable investing has historically been the weakest – and might appear at first sight to be intrinsically at odds with the 'fear and greed' that drives financial markets. But the world's investment markets thrive on the platform for long-term savings created by the post-war national welfare states. During the 21st century, the need is to take inspiration from these founders and to reinvent the system of investor welfare for the global age and the imperatives of sustainable development. Here, there are two urgent and interconnected priorities. The first is how to mobilize pension funds and others to back a new generation of social equities and bonds to finance the improvement of education, healthcare, microfinance, public transport and social housing. The second is to extend the benefits of pension provision to the world's poor, with returns generated from investments in the type of projects and enterprises that are needed to make the Millennium Development Goals a reality (e.g. see Blackburn, 2007).

We started this book as credit crunched, and we end it as long-standing financial institutions disappear, having failed either to link reward with responsibility or to appreciate and properly manage systemic risk. The scale of the investment transformation ahead demands a new paradigm. The challenge for sustainable investing is not to become like today's mainstream but, rather, to replace it.

REFERENCES

Blackburn, R. (2007) 'A Global Pension Plan', *New Left Review*, vol 47, September–October, p71

Henderson Global Investors (2005) *The Carbon 100*, Henderson Global Investors, London

Green New Deal Group (2008) *A Green New Deal*, New Economics Foundation, London

IEA (International Energy Agency) (2008) *Energy Technology Perspectives*, IEA, Paris

Keynes, J. M. (1978) *The General Theory of employment, Interest and Money*, originally published 1936, Macmillan, London

McKinsey Global Institute (2008) *The Carbon Productivity Challenge*, MGI, New York

NEF (New Energy Finance) (2008) *Economic Researchers Predict $1 trillion US Carbon Trading Market by 2020*, NEF, London, 14 February

Glossary

Mercer[1]

Active ownership
The voting of company shares and/or the engaging of corporate managers and boards of directors in dialogue on environmental, social and corporate governance issues, as well as on business strategy issues. This is increasingly pursued in an effort to reduce risk and enhance long-term shareholder value. See also *collaborative engagement* and *shareholder engagement*.

Avoidance
See *negative screening*.

Best in class
The focusing of investments in companies that have historically performed better than their peers within a particular industry or sector on measures of environmental, social and corporate governance issues. This typically involves positive or negative screening or portfolio tilting.

Cleantech
A range of products, services and processes that either directly reduce or eliminate ecological impacts or have the potential to provide performance at least matching that of traditional alternatives, while requiring lower resource inputs or a different mix of inputs (Cleantech Venture Network, 2006). Cleantech is an investment theme rather than an industrial sector as it may include investments in agriculture, energy, manufacturing, materials, technology, transportation and water. In 2005, cleantech was North America's fifth largest venture capital investment category, attracting more than US$1.6 billion.

Climate change
A change of climate that is attributed to natural or anthropogenic activity which alters the composition of the global atmosphere and changes weather patterns

on a global scale. There is compelling evidence that rising concentrations of greenhouse gases in the atmosphere are attributable to human activity and are increasing the greenhouse effect and causing climate change.

Climate risks
The risks stemming from climate change that have the potential to affect companies, industries and whole economies. There are five key areas of business risk associated with climate change: regulatory, physical, litigation, competitiveness and reputational.

Collaborative engagement
The engagement activities conducted collaboratively by multiple parties (e.g. pension funds or fund managers) in order to gain leverage and minimize costs and risks (Higgs and Wildsmith, 2005). Collaborative engagement forms a subset of collaborative initiatives. See also *active ownership* and *shareholder engagement*.

Collaborative initiatives
The initiatives conducted collaboratively by multiple parties (e.g. pension funds and/or fund managers) in order to gain leverage and minimize costs and risks. The Principles for Responsible Investment, the Carbon Disclosure Project, and the national and regional social investment organizations are examples of collaborative initiatives.

Community investment
The capital from investors that is directed to communities underserved by traditional financial services. It provides access to credit, equity, capital and basic banking products that these communities would otherwise not have (Community Investing Program, 2005).

Corporate citizenship
See *corporate social responsibility*.

Corporate governance
The procedures and processes according to which an organization (in this context, mainly a company) is directed and controlled. The corporate governance structure specifies the distribution of rights and responsibilities among the different participants in the organization – such as the board, managers, shareholders and other stakeholders – and lays down the rules and procedures for decision-making. There are both national and international best practice standards (OECD, 2004).

Corporate social responsibility (CSR)
The approach to business which takes into account economic, social, environmental and ethical impacts for a variety of reasons, including mitigating risk, decreasing costs, and improving brand image and competitiveness. This

approach is sometimes implemented by means of a comprehensive set of policies and procedures integrated throughout a company. Often the policies and procedures encompass a wide range of practices related to all levels of business activity, including corporate governance, employee relations, supply chain relationships, customer relationships, environmental management, philanthropy and community involvement. Investors in companies, including institutional investors such as pension funds, can use their leverage (through responsible investment) to encourage companies to adopt CSR practices. CSR practices have been linked to improved financial performance.

Divestment
The selling or disposing of shares or other assets. Changes in corporate behaviour or investment policies can lead investors to reduce or eliminate investments. Investors who practice active ownership often view divestment as the last resort. Divestment gained prominence during the boycott of companies doing business in South Africa prior to the dismantling of apartheid. More recently, a campaign has begun to encourage divestment from companies doing business in Sudan.

Eco-efficiency
The ratio between goods produced or services rendered and the resources consumed or waste produced.

Economically targeted investment
An investment that aims to achieve a market rate of return while improving social conditions through, for example, investments that provide public housing or employment opportunities.

Emerging manager
See *minority and female owned and/or emerging manager*.

Engagement
See *shareholder engagement*.

Engagement overlay service
A third-party service that engages investee companies on behalf of shareholder clients. This is currently offered by a small number of investment fund managers and independent service providers.

Environmental, social and corporate governance (ESG)
The term that has emerged globally to describe the environmental, social and corporate governance issues that investors are considering in the context of corporate behaviour. No definitive list of ESG issues exists, but they typically display one or more of the following characteristics (Enhanced Analytics Initiative, 2005):

- issues that have traditionally been considered non-financial or non-material;
- a medium- or long-term time horizon;
- qualitative objectives that are not readily quantifiable in monetary terms;
- externalities (costs borne by other firms or by society at large) not well captured by market mechanisms;
- a changing regulatory or policy framework;
- patterns arising throughout a company's supply chain (and therefore susceptible to unknown risks);
- a public concern focus.

ESG integration
The active investment management processes that include an analysis of environmental, social and corporate governance risks and opportunities.

ESG research provider
A firm that provides environmental, social, corporate governance or ethical research for use in investment decisions or shareholder engagement activities. Traditional sell-side researchers are increasingly offering environmental, social and corporate governance research.

Ethical investing
The investment philosophy guided by moral values, ethical codes or religious beliefs. Investment decisions include non-economic criteria. This practice has traditionally been associated with negative screening.

Exclusionary screening
See *negative screening*.

Extra-financial factors
The factors that have the potential to have at least a long-term effect on financial performance but lie outside the usual span of variables that are integrated within investment decisions, irrespective of whether they are part of the research process. They include ESG factors (see *environmental, social and corporate governance*) but also traditional financial factors that are often ignored or underutilized, at least in terms of the alignment of investments with the interests of beneficiaries.

Fiduciary duties
The duties imposed upon a person who exercises some discretionary power in the interests of another person in circumstances that give rise to a relationship of trust and confidence. Fiduciary duties are the key source of limits on the discretion of investment decision-makers in common law jurisdictions. The most important fiduciary duties are the duty to act prudently and the duty to act in accordance with the purpose for which investment powers are granted (also known as the duty of loyalty) (Freshfields Bruckhaus Deringer, 2005). See also *prudent man rule*.

Greenhouse gases (GHGs)

The gases that contribute to the greenhouse effect and global warming. The gases are released into the atmosphere through the combustion of organic matter (including fossil fuels) and through natural processes. The Kyoto Protocol deals with the following greenhouse gases: carbon dioxide, nitrous oxide, methane, sulphur hexafluoride, hydrofluorocarbons and perfluorocarbons. GHGs are the focus of collaborative engagement initiatives such as the Carbon Disclosure Project.

Green investing

An investment philosophy that includes criteria relating to the environmental impact of the underlying investment.

Minority and female owned and/or emerging manager (MFOE)

Investment managers owned by minorities or females or have a relatively small amount of assets under management. The definition of 'minority' manager can vary but commonly includes those firms majority owned by African American, Native American, Asian American and Hispanic groups. In some cases, disabled or veteran owners also meet the definition for inclusion under an investor's policy in this area. The definition of 'emerging' also varies, but generally connotes a manager with between zero and several hundred million dollars in assets under management or that has a performance record of less than three years. A firm can be minority or female owned without being considered emerging, or vice versa. These managers would not ordinarily be included in a manager search and would benefit from an affirmative action programme.

Mission-based investing

The incorporation of an organization's mission within its investment decision-making process (Michael Jantzi Research Associates Ltd, 2003).

Negative screening

An investment approach that excludes some companies or sectors from the investment universe based on criteria relating to their policies, actions, products or services. Investments that do not meet the minimum standards of the screen are not included in the investment portfolio. Criteria may include environmental, social, corporate governance or ethical issues. Common negative screens exclude investments in tobacco, alcohol and weapons manufacturers. Other negative screens aim to exclude companies that are considered poor executers in the areas of environmental and social management or corporate governance.

Portfolio tilt

The adoption of a particular view on a sector or issue by overweighting or underweighting the portfolio relative to the benchmark.

Positive screening
An investment approach that includes non-traditional criteria relating to the policies, actions, products or services of securities issuers. Portfolios are tilted towards stocks that rate well on the nominated criteria. The criteria could include environmental, social, corporate governance or ethical issues. Common positive screens include measures of energy efficiency, environmental management or employment standards. Increasingly, these factors are deemed desirable attributes for both financial and non-financial measures. In this case, see also *ESG integration*.

Proxy voting
The delegation of voting rights from entitled voters who do not attend shareholders' meetings to delegates who vote on their behalf. Proxy voting allows shareholders to exercise their right to vote without committing the time involved in actually attending meetings.

Proxy voting policy
The written policy that articulates how proxy voting decisions are to be made and executed. Proxy voting policies can include specific guidance on environmental, social, corporate governance and ethical voting decisions.

Proxy voting advisory service provider
A third party who provides background information and advice in relation to proxy issues.

Prudent man rule
A common rule pertaining to fiduciary duty in Anglo-Saxon countries. The Organisation for Economic Co-operation and Development (OECD) states the rule in terms of the following broad principle: 'A fiduciary should discharge his or her duties with the care, skill, prudence and diligence that a prudent person acting in a like capacity would use in the conduct of an enterprise of like character and aims' (Galer, undated). Applications vary by country. In the US, the Employee Retirement Income Security Act of 1974 (ERISA) outlines minimum standards for private pension plans that have since been adopted by many public pension plans. See also *fiduciary duties*.

Responsible investment policy statement
A general (usually public) statement on responsible investment adopted by boards of trustees or directors that directs investment staff practices and decisions. This can be included within a broader investment policy statement and/or developed as a stand-alone responsible investment policy statement.

Responsible property investment
A property investment approach that includes the consideration of environmental, social and corporate governance issues. Energy and resource efficiency, both

in construction and ongoing operations, is a common consideration, as is social impact.

Restricted list
A list of securities that are not to be included in a portfolio by an investment manager. This typically facilitates the implementation of negative screening.

Screening
An investment approach that employs certain criteria (e.g. environmental, social, corporate governance or ethical considerations) in investment decision-making and portfolio construction. Only investments that meet certain criteria are included in investment portfolios. See also *negative screening* and *positive screening*.

Social, ethical and environmental (SEE)
The term and acronym that emerged in Europe to describe the social, ethical and environmental issues that responsible investors are considering in the context of corporate behaviour. No definitive list of SEE issues exists; but there is significant overlap with ESG issues.

Shareholder
An investor who holds preferred or common shares of a corporation.

Shareholder activism
A public or confrontational approach to shareholder engagement. In addition to shareholder engagement, pressure can be exerted on companies through strategic divestment or attempts to influence public opinion. See also *active ownership*.

Shareholder engagement
The practice of monitoring corporate behaviour and seeking changes, where appropriate, through dialogue with companies or through the use of share ownership rights, such as filing shareholder resolutions. Shareholder engagement is often employed in attempts to improve a company's performance on environmental, social and corporate governance issues.

Shareholder proposal
A shareholder request that the company or its board of directors takes particular action. Proposed by the shareholder, this request may be presented at a company's general shareholders' meeting and voted on by all shareholders. In some instances, shareholder proposals are withdrawn by shareholders or disallowed by regulators.

Shareholder resolution
See *shareholder proposal*.

Short-termism
The bias that some investors demonstrate for near- or immediate-term investment performance and share price appreciation instead of long-term investment

performance. This bias may put pressure on corporate managers to make decisions that boost short-term accounting measures of profitability rather than long-term economic profitability.

Sin stock
The stock of a company that provides goods or services that the investor has deemed unethical. Common examples include the stocks of companies that are involved in the production or provision of tobacco, alcohol, pornography or gaming facilities.

Social investment policy statement
A general statement on social investment adopted by a board of trustees. See also *responsible investment policy statement*.

Stakeholders
The individuals or organizations with an interest in the actions and impacts of an organization. They may be customers, suppliers, shareholders, employees, communities, members of special interest groups, non-governmental organizations or regulators.

Sustainability
See *sustainable development*.

Sustainability report
A report produced by an organization to inform stakeholders about its policies, programmes and performance regarding environmental, social and economic issues. Sustainability reports, also known as corporate citizenship reports, or CSR reports, are usually voluntary and relatively few are independently audited or integrated within financial reports. Numerous corporations are now employing sustainability reports to expand public disclosure beyond financial metrics. The Global Reporting Initiative provides a framework for sustainability reporting.

Sustainable development
The concept of meeting present needs without compromising the ability of future generations to meet their needs (WCED, 1987). It encompasses social welfare, protection of the environment, efficient use of natural resources and economic well-being.

Thematic investment
The selected investment in companies with a commitment to chosen responsible business products and/or services, such as environmental technologies (Higgs and Wildsmith, 2005). See also *cleantech* and *community investment*.

Triple bottom line
A holistic approach to measuring a company's performance on environmental, social and economic issues. The triple bottom line focuses companies not just on

the economic value that they add, but also on the environmental and social value that they add or destroy. See also *sustainability report*.

Universal owner

A large investor who holds a broad selection of investments in different public companies as well as other assets and who therefore is tied to the performance of markets or economies as a whole – not just to the performance of individual holdings. These investors have a vested interest in the long-term health of the economy, making public policy issues and cross-market ESG concerns particularly relevant.

NOTE

1   This glossary is excerpted from Mercer Investment Consulting (2007) *The Language of Responsible Investment: An Industry Guide to Key Terms and Organisations*, an online resource available at http://uk.mercer.com/summary.htm;jsessionid=ZUJStU3afSU0J0Na4tIu3A**.mercer04?siteLanguage=1008&idContent=1291560 (also available for download as a PDF from the same URL).

REFERENCES

Cleantech Venture Network (2006) *Cleantech Defined*, http://cleantech.com/index.cfm?pageSRC=CleantechDefined, accessed 23 November 2006

Community Investing Program (2005) *What Is Community Investing?*, www.communityinvest.org/overview/what.cfm, accessed 9 November 2006

Enhanced Analytics Initiative (2005) *What Are Extra-Financial Issues?*, www.enhancedanalytics.com/, accessed 10 November 2006

Freshfields Bruckhaus Deringer (2005) *A Legal Framework for the Integration of Environmental, Social and Governance Issues into Institutional Investment*, www.unepfi.org/fileadmin/documents/freshfields_legal_resp_20051123.pdf, accessed 24 October 2006

Galer, R. (undated) *'Prudent Person Rule' Standard for the Investment of Pension Fund Assets*, www.oecd.org/dataoecd/51/0/2763540.pdf, accessed 9 November 2006

Higgs, C. and Wildsmith, H. (2005) *Responsible Investment Trustee Toolkit*, www.uksif.org/cmsfiles/jp/Just%20Pensions%20Trustee%20Toolkit%20-%20Final.pdf, accessed 8 November 2006

Michael Jantzi Research Associates Ltd (2003) *Investing in Change: Mission-Based Investing for Foundations, Endowments, and NGOs*, Canadian Council for International Co-operation, Ottawa, Ontario, Canada

OECD (Organisation for Economic Co-operation and Development) (2004) *OECD Principles of Corporate Governance*, www.oecd.org/dataoecd/32/18/31557724.pdf, accessed 10 November 2006

WCED (World Commission on Environment and Development) (1987) *Our Common Future* (ed G. Bruntland), WCED, Oxford University Press, Oxford, UK

Sustainable and Responsible Investing Initiatives and Resources

GLOBAL INITIATIVES

Access to Medicine Index (www.atmindex.org)
Managed by the Access to Medicine Foundation, this index aims to score pharmaceutical companies according to their performance on a wide range of criteria. Index measurements and ratings will be published on the index website, providing companies, investors and other stakeholders with independent, impartial and reliable data.

Carbon Disclosure Project (CDP) (www.cdproject.net)
The Carbon Disclosure Project provides a coordinating secretariat for institutional investors with a combined US$57 trillion of assets under management. On their behalf it seeks information on the business risks and opportunities presented by climate change and greenhouse gas emissions data from over 3000 of the world's largest companies as of 2008. The CDP website is considered the largest repository of corporate greenhouse gas emissions data in the world.

Enhanced Analytics Initiative (EAI) (www.enhancedanalytics.com)
The Enhanced Analytics Initiative is an international collaboration between asset owners and managers aimed at encouraging better *extra-financial* investment research. The goal of the initiative is to provide and encourage access to research that will help investors to identify those sectors and companies that will most likely outperform over the long term and to attempt to avoid those that will underperform. The members of EAI view this as a way of encouraging more accurate pricing of stocks.

The Equator Principles (www.equator-principles.com)
An aspirational financial industry benchmark used in determining, assessing and managing social and environmental risk in project financing, especially useful for project financiers concerned about social and environmental issues that are both

complex and challenging, particularly with respect to projects in the emerging markets.

Global Reporting Initiative (GRI) (www.globalreporting.org)
The Global Reporting Initiative pioneered the development of the world's most widely used sustainability reporting framework and is committed to its continuous improvement and application worldwide. This framework sets out the principles and indicators that organizations can use to measure and report their economic, environmental and social performance.

International Association of Investors in the Social Economy (INAISE) (www.inaise.org)
The International Association of Investors in the Social Economy is a global network of socially and environmentally oriented financial institutions. Through INAISE, social investors from Norway to South Africa and from Costa Rica to Japan have been joining forces to exchange experience, disseminate information and demonstrate to the world that money can actually be a means of achieving positive social and environmental change.

International Finance Corporation (IFC) Sustainable Investing
(www.ifc.org/ifcext/enviro.nsf/Content/SustainableInvesting)
International Finance Corporation (IFC) Sustainable Investing works with international organizations, institutional investors and investment research houses to provide research and convening around new trends in sustainable finance. Since 2003, the IFC has taken concrete steps to increase the amount of sustainable portfolio equity and private equity investment in emerging markets. The goal has been set out to almost double the stock of sustainable capital in emerging markets from US$2.7 billion in 2003 – less than 0.1 per cent of emerging market stock market capitalization – to US$5 billion in 2008.

International Interfaith Investment Group (3iG) (www.3ignet.org)
The mission of 3iG is to contribute to a just and sustainable society through responsible investment in a spirit of genuine interfaith dialogue and cooperation. The represented faiths share with large pension funds a long-term perspective on investments unlike the short-term profit orientation of the general market. 3iG is designed to assist the represented faiths in facilitating and advancing their engagement in this area and to provide high-level research and information to enhance its development.

Marathon Club (www.marathonclub.co.uk)
The Marathon Club is a direct follow-up project to a competition run by the Universities Superannuation Scheme (USS) and Hewitt, which was entitled 'Managing pension funds as if the long-term really did matter'. The club has concluded that it is unlikely that funds can adopt a more long-term, responsible and active investing approach with current levels of performance on governance and investment strategic decision-making.

Pew Centre on Global Climate Change (www.pewclimate.org)
The Pew Centre on Global Climate Change brings together business leaders, policy-makers, scientists and other experts. The centre believes that these parties can and should work together to protect the climate while sustaining economic growth, and it does so by producing leading analysis and encouraging leaders and organizations to collaborate.

Pharma Futures (www.pharmafutures.org)
Pharma Futures is a consortium of pension funds from the Dutch government and education sector retirement fund (ABP), the Ohio Public Employees Retirement System of the US, and the USS of the UK. It holds that as long-term owners of pharmaceutical companies, pension funds have a substantial interest in the continued profitability of a sector that has historically created considerable shareholder value. At the same time, Pharma Futures concurs that significant change is inevitable for the global healthcare sector and that dialogue between the investment community and pharmaceutical executives will enhance understanding of both transition challenges and evaluation of what constitutes good change management.

Sustainable Financial Markets Network (www.sustainablefinancialmarkets.net)
The Sustainable Financial Markets Network is an international network of finance-sector professionals, academics and others who have an active interest in long-term investing. They feel that the recurring crises recently experienced in the global financial markets are not isolated incidents. Rather, they believe that this instability is evidence that the financial market system is in need of well thought-out reform so that it can better serve its core purpose of creating long-term sustainable value. The network's goal is to foster interdisciplinary collaboration on research and advocacy projects between market professionals, academics and other opinion leaders.

United Nations Environment Programme's Finance Initiative (UNEP FI)
(www.unepfi.org)
The arm of the United Nations most focused on investors, the United Nations Environment Programme's Finance Initiative facilitates leading working groups as it involves asset managers, property, insurance, climate change, reporting standards, biodiversity and water among others. UNEP FI was and continues to be the champion of the United Nations Principles for Responsible Investment, which have become something of a financial industry benchmark.

United Nations Global Compact (www.unglobalcompact.org)
The United Nations Global Compact asks its thousands of pledged companies to embrace, support and enact, within their sphere of influence, a set of core values in the areas of human rights, labour standards, the environment and anti-corruption. Over 1500 companies joined the Global Compact in 2007, but, separately, 850 were delisted for lack of compliance.

United Nations Principles for Responsible Investing (PRI) (www.unpri.org)
A benchmark of pledged best practice investment behaviour, the United Nations Principles for Responsible Investing now have over US$13 trillion in assets committed and counting. The six principles largely hold that institutional investors have a duty to act in the best long-term interests of their beneficiaries. In this fiduciary role, these investors believe that environmental, social and governance (ESG) issues can affect the performance of investment portfolios (to varying degrees across companies, sectors, regions, asset classes and through time). They also recognize that applying these principles may better align investors with broader objectives of society.

Woods Hole Research Center (www.whrc.org)
The Woods Hole Research Center conducts research, identifies policies and supports educational activities that advance the well-being of humans and of the environment. Its mission is to understand the causes and consequences of environmental change as a basis for policy solutions for a better world. Director John Holdren has become a leading communicator and adviser to the investor community in climate change.

World Business Council for Sustainable Development (WBCSD) (www.wbcsd.ch)
The World Business Council for Sustainable Development (WBCSD) is a CEO-led, global association of some 200 companies dealing exclusively with business and sustainable development. The Council provides a platform for companies to explore sustainable development, share knowledge, experiences and best practices, and to advocate business positions on these issues in a variety of forums, working with governments, non-governmental and intergovernmental organizations.

Yale's Center for Business and the Environment (http://research.yale.edu/cbey)
The Center for Business and the Environment at Yale provides a focal point for research, education and outreach to advance business solutions to global environmental problems. The Center joins the strengths of two world-renowned graduate schools ñ the and the ñ together with a network of internal and external thought leaders at the businessñenvironment interface.

NATIONAL AND REGIONAL INITIATIVES AND RESOURCES

Asia
Association for Sustainable and Responsible Investment in Asia (ASrIA)
www.asria.org

Australasia
Investor Group on Climate Change Australia/New Zealand
www.igcc.org.au

Responsible Investment Association of Australasia (RIAA)
www.eia.org.au

Belgium
Belgian Sustainable and Socially Responsible Investment Forum
www.belsif.be

Forum Ethibel
www.ethibel.org

Brazil
Centre for Sustainability Studies – Getulio Vargas Foundation
www.ces.fgvsp.br

Canada
Social Investment Organization (SIO)
www.socialinvestment.ca

Europe
Bellagio Forum for Sustainable Development
www.bfsd.org

European Social Investment Forum (EUROSIF)
www.eurosif.org

France
French Social Investment Forum (FIR)
www.frenchsif.org

Germany
Forum nachhaltige Geldanlagen
www.forum-ng.de

Italy
Forum per la Finanza Sostenibile
www.finanzasostenibile.it

Korea
Korea Sustainability Investing Forum
www.kosif.org

Latin America
Latin American Sustainable Finance Forum
www.lasff.org/en

The Netherlands
Dutch Association of Investors for Sustainable Development
www.vbdo.nl

New Zealand
Council for Socially Responsible Investment
www.csri.org.nz

South Africa
Centre for Sustainable Investment, African Institute for Corporate Citizenship
www.aiccafrica.org

Sweden
Swedish Social Investment Forum
www.swesif.org

Switzerland
Ethos Foundation
www.ethosfund.ch

UK
Ecumenical Centre for Corporate Responsibility
www.eccr.org.uk

Institutional Investors Group on Climate Change
www.iigcc.org

London Accord
www.londonaccord.org

Responsible Investor
www.responsible-investor.com

UK Social Investment Forum (UK SIF)
www.uksif.org

US
Coalition for Environmentally Responsible Economies (CERES)
www.ceres.org

Institute for Responsible Investment
www.bcccc.net/responsibleinvestment

Interfaith Center on Corporate Responsibility (ICCR)
www.iccr.org

Investor Network on Climate Risk (INCR)
www.incr.org

Responsible Property Investing Center
www.responsibleproperty.net

Social Funds
www.socialfunds.com

SRI Studies
www.sristudies.org

US Social Investment Forum (US SIF)
www.socialinvest.org

SRI ADVISORY, RESEARCH AND RATING COMPANIES

Analistas Internacionales en Sostenibildad – Spain
www.ais.com.es

Asset4 – Switzerland/Global
www.asset4.com

Avanzi – Italy
www.avanzi.org

Brooklyn Bridge & TBLI – The Netherlands
www.tbli.org

Centre for Australian Ethical Research – Australia
www.caer.org.au

Centre Info – Switzerland
www.centreinfo.ch

Dutch Sustainability Research – The Netherlands
www.dsresearch.nl

Ethical Investment Research Services (EIRIS) – UK/Global
www.eiris.org

EthiFinance – France
www.ethifinance.com

Ethix SRI Advisers – Sweden
www.ethix.se

Fundacion Ecologia y Desarrollo (EcoDes) – Spain
www.ecodes.org

GES Investment Services – Sweden
www.ges-invest.com

Good Bankers – Japan
www.goodbankers.co.jp

Innovest Strategic Value Advisers – Global
www.innovest.com

InRate – Switzerland
www.inrate.ch

Institut für Markt-Umwelt-Gesellschaft (Imug) – Germany
www.ethisches-investment.de

Kayema Investment Research and Analysis – Israel
www.kayema.com

KLD Research & Analytics – US
www.kld.com

Jantzi Research – Canada
www.jantziresearch.com

Mercer – Global
www.merceric.com

MicroRate – US
www.microrate.com

New Energy Finance (NEF) – UK
www.newenergyfinance.com

Novethic – France
www.novethic.fr

Oekom Research – Germany
www.oekomresearch.de

onValues – Switzerland
www.onvalues.ch

Pensions and Investment Research Consultants (PIRC) – UK
www.pirc.co.uk

RiskMetrics – US
www.riskmetrics.com

Scoris – Germany
www.scoris.de

Sustainable Investment Research Institute – Australia
www.siris.co.au

Sustainable Investment Research International (SiRi) – Global
www.siricompany.com

Trucost – UK/Global
www.trucost.com

Vigeo – France/Global
www.vigeo.com

Equity Returns Study Methodology – Determination of Annualized Five-Year Return for the Period 31 December 2002 to 31 December 2007

SELECTION OF FUNDS TO EXAMINE

To start, a complete review of the world's ethical, religious, social, environmental, clean energy, climate change, etc. funds was undertaken, of which there are approximately 850 at present. These funds were then further isolated to those which have existed for at least five years and had, at the time of review, US$100 million in equity under management or more. Public domain websites were reviewed to ensure that this result was 100 per cent comprehensive, and the result was a comprehensive global list of publicly facing sustainable and responsible investing (SRI) funds.

SOURCES OF RETURNS DATA

1   Where possible, we identified direct sources of returns data. We began by searching the internet by fund name or manager name. In most cases, we were able to locate websites, although the quality of (completeness) and ability to access (site navigation, language, etc.) information varied considerably.

2   Where necessary, we then examined data available through consolidated providers (e.g. TrustNet and Morningstar) and ensured consistency of methodology and returns data

3   Where points 1 and 2 failed to yield satisfactory data, we then undertook direct contact by telephone or email.

ISSUES REGARDING INFORMATION SOURCES

- In many cases, performance information was presented in factsheet form, usually a two-page PDF file. It was common, however, for the information to be presented as of 31 January 2008 or even later, which, given the significant downturn in most equity markets in 2008, significantly depressed annualized returns. In many cases, therefore, the factsheet information provided a starting point rather than a complete data set.
- It was often unclear as to whether annualized returns as stated in fund documents were as at 31 December for the fund's financial year or for annual periods ending – for example, 31 January. This necessitated cross-referencing, typically against other sources.
- In a significant number of cases, all available information, including that available from indirect sources, was in a language other than English, which we were able to navigate successfully, given varying language skills applied.
- There exist a number of standards that are applied throughout the investment industry: GIPS (Global Investment Performance Standards); UCITS (Undertakings for the Collective Investment of Transferable Securities); and MiFID (Markets in Financial Instruments Directive). These standards broadly seek to harmonize information disclosure (i.e. what is presented to investors, as opposed to how it is presented – in other words, the format). Thus, while all funds made reference to the impact that transaction charges, taxation, etc. could have upon performance, there were differences in how this was stated. Furthermore, we found no explicit reference to any of the standards (GIPS, etc.) noted above.

DETERMINING FIVE-YEAR ANNUALIZED RETURNS

Where data was available, we had to be satisfied that it met certain criteria. These were that:

- It referred to the period of 31 December 2002 to 31 December 2007.
- It included operating expenses (i.e. these had been netted out) but excluded transaction costs (i.e. those related to the purchase and sale of assets). In some cases, the fund manager had waived a significant portion of the maximum fee (occasionally retaining the right to claw these back within a certain period). Typical statements were:

> *Historical returns are gross returns compounded over the given period, assuming all growth and income have been reinvested. For example, a 10 per cent return over five years means an average of 10 per cent performance for each of the five years. The figure takes into account ongoing fees associated with a fund but ignores entry and/or exit fees.*

All performance assumes reinvestment of dividends and capital gains.

The investment performance assumes reinvestment of dividends and capital gains distributions.

The rates of return indicated take into account the changes in unit value and the reinvestment of all distributions, but not the sales, redemption, distribution or optional charges or income taxes payable by any security holder that would have reduced returns.

- As far as we could determine, it reflected the price total return performance figures calculated on a consistent basis (i.e. bid price to bid price basis – mid to mid for open-ended investment companies, or OEICs) with net income (dividends) reinvested.

CALCULATING THE ANNUALIZED FIVE-YEAR RETURN

The data extracted was in one of three original formats:

1   An annualized five-year figure: where this was available, we sought to verify the figure by sourcing annual returns and/or a total return figure.
2   A total (five-year) return figure: where this was available we sought to cross-check against annual returns and/or an annualized figure.
3   Individual annual returns.

In each, case we calculated the geometric (compounding) annualized five-year figure using the following formula:

Total return = $(1 + 2003\%) \times (1 + 2004\%) \times (1 + 2005\%) \times (1 + 2006\%) \times (1 + 2007\%)) - 1.$

Five-year annualized return = $EXP(LN(1 + \text{total return}\%))/5) - 1.$

Index